HANDBOOK OF ARTIFICIAL INTELLIGENCE AND BIG DATA APPLICATIONS IN INVESTMENTS

LARRY CAO, CFA, EDITOR

Statement of Purpose

The CFA Institute Research Foundation is a not-for-profit organization established to promote the development and dissemination of relevant research for investment practitioners worldwide.

© 2023 CFA Institute Research Foundation. All rights reserved.

Neither CFA Institute Research Foundation, CFA Institute, nor the publication's editorial staff is responsible for facts and opinions presented in this publication. This publication reflects the views of the author(s) and does not represent the official views of CFA Institute Research Foundation.

No part of this publication may be reproduced or transmitted in any form or by any means, electronic or mechanical, including photocopy, recording, or any information storage and retrieval system, without permission of the copyright holder. Requests for permission to make copies of any part of the work should be mailed to: Copyright Permissions, CFA Institute, 915 East High Street, Charlottesville, Virginia 22902. CFA® and Chartered Financial Analyst® are trademarks owned by CFA Institute. To view a list of CFA Institute trademarks and the Guide for the Use of CFA Institute Marks, please visit our website at www.cfainstitute.org.

CFA Institute does not provide investment, financial, tax, legal, or other advice. This report was prepared for informational purposes only and is not intended to provide, and should not be relied on for, investment, financial, tax, legal, or other advice. CFA Institute is not responsible for the content of websites and information resources that may be referenced in the report. Reference to these sites or resources does not constitute an endorsement by CFA Institute of the information contained therein. The inclusion of company examples does not in any way constitute an endorsement of these organizations by CFA Institute. Although we have endeavored to ensure that the information contained in this report has been obtained from reliable and up-to-date sources, the changing nature of statistics, laws, rules, and regulations may result in delays, omissions, or inaccuracies in information contained in this report.

Photo credit: yangyang / Moment / Getty Images

ISBN: 978-1-952927-33-1

DEDICATION

In memory of Frank Reilly, CFA, whose unwavering commitment to high-quality research and investment education had a profound and enduring impact on countless colleagues and students. His contribution to the CFA Institute community will always be remembered.

BIOGRAPHY

Larry Cao, CFA, is senior director of research at CFA Institute. His research interests include multi-asset strategies and fintech, such as artificial intelligence (AI), big data, and blockchain. Mr. Cao has led the development of a series of research publications on fintech and AI in investments, including "FinTech 2017: China, Asia, and Beyond"; "FinTech 2018"; "AI Pioneers in Investment Management"; and "T-Shaped Teams: Organizing to Adopt AI and Big Data at Investment Firms." His book *Multi-Asset Strategies: The Future of Investment Management* has been translated into Chinese. Mr. Cao is a frequent speaker at industry conferences on these topics.

During his time pursuing graduate studies at Harvard University and as a visiting scholar at MIT, he co-authored a paper with Nobel Laureate Franco Modigliani, published in the *Journal of Economic Literature*. Mr. Cao has over 20 years of investment industry experience. Previously, he worked at HSBC as a senior manager for the Asia-Pacific region. Mr. Cao began his career at the People's Bank of China as a US dollar fixed-income portfolio manager. Later, he worked for Munder Capital Management, managing US and international equity portfolios, and Morningstar/Ibbotson Associates, managing multi-asset investment programs for a global institutional clientele.

Mr. Cao has been interviewed by numerous business media outlets, including Bloomberg, CNN, the *Financial Times*, the *South China Morning Post*, and the *Wall Street Journal*.

Handbook of Artificial Intelligence and Big Data Applications in Investments

CONTENTS

INTRODUCTORY MATERIAL

Preamble — viii
Margaret Franklin, CFA

Foreword — ix
Aaron Low, PhD, CFA

Notes from the Reviewers — xii

About the Contributors — xiii

Introduction — xiv
Larry Cao, CFA

I. MACHINE LEARNING AND DATA SCIENCE APPLICATIONS IN INVESTMENTS

1. **On Machine Learning Applications in Investments** — 2
   Mike Chen, PhD, and Weili Zhou, CFA (Robeco)

2. **Alternative Data and AI in Investment Research** — 20
   Ingrid Tierens, PhD, CFA, and Dan Duggan, PhD (Goldman Sachs Global Investment Research)

3. **Data Science for Active and Long-Term Fundamental Investing** — 27
   Kai Cui, PhD, and Jonathan Shahrabani (Neuberger Berman)

II. NATURAL LANGUAGE UNDERSTANDING, PROCESSING, AND GENERATION: INVESTMENT APPLICATIONS

4. **Unlocking Insights and Opportunities with NLP in Asset Management** — 32
   Andrew Chin, Yuyu Fan, and Che Guan (AllianceBernstein)

5. **Advances in Natural Language Understanding for Investment Management** — 56
   Stefan Jansen, CFA (Applied AI)

6. **Extracting Text-Based ESG Insights: A Hands-On Guide** — 70
   Tal Sansani, CFA (Off-Script Systems and CultureLine.ai) and Mikhail Samonov, CFA (Two Centuries Investments and CultureLine.ai)

III. TRADING WITH MACHINE LEARNING AND BIG DATA

7. **Machine Learning and Big Data Trade Execution Support** — 92
   Erin Stanton (Virtu Financial)

8. **Machine Learning for Microstructure Data-Driven Execution Algorithms** — 100
   Peer Nagy, James Powrie, PhD, and Stefan Zohren, PhD (Man Group)

This publication qualifies for 4.75 PL credits under the guidelines of the CFA Institute Professional Learning Program.

IV. CHATBOT, KNOWLEDGE GRAPHS, AND AI INFRASTRUCTURE

9. **Intelligent Customer Service in Finance** — 108
   Xu Liang, PhD (Ping An OneConnect)

10. **Accelerated AI and Use Cases in Investment Management** — 122
    Jochen Papenbrock, Doctorate (NVIDIA)

11. **Symbolic AI: A Case Study** — 131
    Huib Vaessen (APG Asset Management)

HANDBOOK OF ARTIFICIAL INTELLIGENCE
AND BIG DATA APPLICATIONS IN
INVESTMENTS

INTRODUCTORY MATERIAL

This book can be found at cfainstitute.org/ai-and-big-data

PREAMBLE

At CFA Institute, our mission is to lead the investment profession globally by promoting the highest standards of ethics, education, and professional excellence for the ultimate benefit of society.

In particular, the closing words—"the ultimate benefit of society"—speak directly to our desire to increase the positive real-world impact of investment management by helping to lead the industry forward and staying abreast of the latest trends, which include leading-edge research into adoption practices of artificial intelligence (AI) and big data.

While many still see AI and big data as a threat, we at CFA Institute have consistently advocated "AI + HI (human intelligence)" as the winning formula for successful financial institutions in the future. Finance professionals bring an important skill set to the table, and embracing the advancement of technology and finding ways to work in harmony with the evolving fintech landscape only lead to better outcomes for our clients and more efficient ways of working. Doing so does require a reimagination of corporate culture and, indeed, the skill sets required among teams to map to this evolution.

As artificial intelligence and big data become increasingly integrated into the investment process, we see this as an opportunity to ensure that those within the industry are well equipped to evaluate and incorporate these factors properly.

Much of this work remains in early stages throughout our industry. What makes our research efforts on these subjects stand out is our dedication to providing the investment professionals' perspectives, which are so often glossed over in favor of the technical aspects of the way the technology functions. But we know the hard work comes when it is time to put these theories into practice. Early adopters' combined experiences are particularly valuable for the industry at large in the implementation of new technology.

Beyond the research we have released to guide the industry on this journey, we are creating active learning opportunities for those in the industry who are interested in mastering the skills required to guide this adoption. Our recently launched professional learning course in data science stands as a prime example in action. We also continue to evaluate and evolve the curriculum of our flagship CFA® Program to take these factors into account.

We extend our deep thanks to our collaborators throughout the industry who have dedicated time and resources to this important work, ensuring the practical nature of this handbook and the integrity of the insights included. It is our hope that this handbook will equip the industry to adopt artificial intelligence and big data practices in a meaningful way for the ultimate benefit of their clients. While the road to adoption can be challenging and complex, it is well worth the commitment. I hope you will find the same to be true on your own journey.

Margaret Franklin, CFA
President and CEO, CFA Institute

FOREWORD

Looking back to the artificial intelligence (AI) work done during the 1980s and 1990s, the new advances in AI and machine learning (ML) over the past decade must surely seem compelling and evolutionary. Breakthroughs in deep learning methodologies and pedagogies are becoming mainstream at a rate never seen before in the marketplace. Many universities have introduced courses in fintech AI (mostly in the computer science, business finance, and mathematics departments), and financial professionals have piled into fintech courses for career development. And companies are feeding this frenzy with capital and recruitment, ranging from ML DevOps to data scientists and scrum teams. While some of the enthusiasm is hype and hyperbole, new discoveries, some of which are quite startling, have made real improvements in how we operate in financial markets.

My first experience in AI was in the early 1990s using ML algorithms in the high-frequency currency markets. Chaos bifurcation, fuzzy logic, genetic algorithms, and perceptrons (early versions of the neural nets) were beginning to become popular in interpreting and trading quotes and prices as well as headline news counts during the late 1980s and early 1990s. But almost as quickly as these approaches gained popularity, markets reverted back to conventional statistical models. There is reason to believe the current wave is more sustainable than previous ones. Development and computing costs have decreased, datasets are getting larger and better defined, ML code libraries have mushroomed, and evolving tech stack architectures are formed ever so quickly to move from development to staging to production. While it can sometimes seem to be a struggle to come to terms with the maze of new wide-ranging enhancements in such a complex space, I believe it is helpful to understand the cost–benefit relationships and how investment and business operating models can benefit from this frontier.

Let us start with language. Developments in natural language processing (NLP) and deep learning are breaking boundaries that seemed difficult to breach before. Word embeddings that can infuse correlation (and thus meanings) across words in vector space have vastly improved ML's natural language understanding (NLU) and NLU capabilities, complemented by an impressive corpus of trained and labeled datasets. This development has allowed the pervasive use of sentiment analysis in handling the huge amount of news and social transmissions of views and opinions. Recent developments of transformer models (e.g., Google's LaMDA) are very close to understanding how we communicate and feel, which perhaps had a big role in considerably attenuating performance alphas for asset management. In addition, the introduction of multilayered architectures in neural networks has provided us a sense of nonlinear formulation of the data features, which has helped propagate the advent of deep learning without the mess of menial feature filtering and wrangling.

But we need to be aware of the challenges to harvesting good results. Sentiment analysis may work well in developed markets that have a free press. Producing similar outcomes in developing countries with heavy news and social media censorship and state propaganda may be difficult. It is not realistic to assume that feature loadings would work with the same effect (without proper adjustments) in such diverse cultural and regime settings.

While many of the breakthroughs are impressive, there is still a long road to reaching (if it was ever possible) the Holy Grail of investments—namely, our ability to produce accurate market forecasts. In this regard, it is useful to explore the differences between financial markets and other disciplines.

First is the importance of the time dimension. Financial analysis differs from most other sectors in the way that data obsolescence occurs, both in speed and manner. This is why we have time-series analysis, a special branch of statistics, that is almost dedicated to the behavior of financial data, as well as dataframes in Python pandas that make it possible to handle the time-dimension property of price data. Success in forecasting market prices depends heavily on time and chronological sequence of one asset vis-à-vis other assets. A consumer planning to purchase an iPhone will have little need to identify exactly when the X13 model price of $1,300 was offered. Conversely, a rational Apple investor would likely have to know the time at which Apple stock traded at, say, $150. Specifically, the decay in the information value of asset prices over time and the conditional information set contained in each asset price data point render the time stamp (of each piece of data) an important property of that data tuple.

This fact leads us to the important work done in GRU (gated recurrent unit), RNN (recurrent neural network), LSTM (long short-term memory), and attention (transformer's encoder-decoder) models—all attempting to link period memory for each piece of data with some form of time embedding. Again, we find that the limitations of these various approaches leave the results wanting. Bayesian neural networks offer promising advantages on top of the time-sequence protocol. Possible solutions may borrow from how human brains are able to extract a distant memory by similar feature transformations rather than a hard-coded LSTM that has a limited time memory threshold or an attention encoder-decoder transformer that suffers from a missing long-term context. The practical outcome at this stage would be that these networks would be excellent in trading, market making, and arbitrage applications but have less success in long-term investment mandates.

For all the tasks attempted with AI in finance, the elephant in the room must surely be our machine's ability to forecast markets. It is as aspirational as it is frustrating. Investment professionals constantly ask whether markets are efficient, while computer scientists question whether P = NP. If we believe that these two questions are related, then perhaps we may surmise that markets are efficient if and only if P = NP. The massive growth of exchange-traded funds (ETFs) versus active funds in developed capital economies reflects the increasing efficiencies in markets with big, credible data and computational power. Counterpose this perspective against the view within the computer science fraternity that P is not equal to NP (which implies that markets likely are not efficient), and we have potentially contradicting beliefs. And if we give credit to common conjectures that markets become increasingly inefficient as the time series lengthens, then the Grossman–Stiglitz (1980) paradox—that the equilibrium level of market efficiency is driven by the market costs of skills and technology to produce alphas—makes a lot of sense.

Although the P = NP conjecture appears theoretical in nature, it has many implications for the various AI applications and solutions used in capital markets. Deep learning has rendered many non-forecast-based tasks (e.g., clustering or categorization) in finance to be in the complexity class P. But stock market prediction problems are still mostly boxed in the NP class, implying that there is a good algorithm for checking a given possible solution but that there is not necessarily a good algorithm for finding solutions. The evolution of AI and ML has given us better ways of understanding, but not inevitably solving the P versus NP problem. Although current states of AI can still fail to find a polynomial-time algorithm in a specified amount of time, this lens allows us to come closer to understanding whether markets can ever be truly efficient. And although it is possible to build an AI algorithm that searches for poly-time solutions to an NP-hard problem, it may also be that the world of predictions is of such complexity that no perfect solution exists. Notwithstanding this possibility, the practical approach for most stakeholders is to find the best available ML approach (among the prevailing sets used in markets) rather than figuring out the perfect solution.

If the current thinking is to improve AI models with new layers of intelligence embeddings, then it may also be helpful to evaluate the "efficient frontier" of competing models in terms of, say, performance versus complexity (as opposed to returns versus risk). For example, new work in metalearning seeks to design models that can learn new skills or adapt to new environments quickly with few training datasets. How do such dynamic (ever-changing common sense or comprehensive learning) demands affect how we train models?

There is no guarantee that the training set's data-generating process will be the same in the test set in financial markets. Environments and how the markets perceive new information are constantly changing in global markets. Regime changes due to regulations, political economies, policy frameworks, technology, market participants, information quality, and so on, can materially change feature impact in nonstationary ways and render training sets less effective at best and disastrous in worst-case scenarios. Even within the realm of explainable empirical solutions, there have been cases that rely too much on nonrepresentative in-sample data to drive investment decisions. The use of copulas based on stable-period in-sample estimation, which produced overly optimistic ratings of asset-backed securities prior to the Global Financial Crisis (GFC), is a case in point.

Is the data-generation process (DCP) ergodic or stationary? A roulette game is very close to ergodic; the distribution of numbers that have come up in the past is very close to the probability distribution of numbers on the next spin. But a game of blackjack when dealt from a set of cards that are not reshuffled after each hand is much less ergodic. This poses a tricky problem when the training, test, and actual data come from different DCPs. Price discovery and risk–return distributions are created from multidisciplinary viewpoints and opinions in a free marketplace, with varieties of frictions, costs, and regulatory constraints. This richness in contributing features can create nonstationarity and ergodic issues, making the DCP much more difficult to calibrate. We can attribute standard volatilities in prices to noise or lead–lag frictions in price discovery, but the continued presence of black swan events (fooling the best of machines and man) tells us that all is not perfect. Such market characteristics do suggest that current AI states are still better suited to areas of success enjoyed by human-operated models or, at least, AI models with close human supervision. This includes such examples as the higher rate of success in arbitrage trading strategies over forecast-driven approaches.

Finally, it is important to augment this discussion with the ability of AI to produce explainable results. ML projects are usually not standalone but are part of a corporate strategy. Naturally, all competing blueprints bubble up to the C-suite for sponsorship. Unknown risks commonly affiliated with unexplainable methodology can be construed as recipes for black swan–type events and derail even the most promising of programs.

For example, suppose someone offers you two investment plans. Plan A offers a 10-year success rate of 70% and is a strategy based on fundamentals that can be readily understood. Plan B is marketed as a strategy that has a 10-year success rate of 80% but is a black box or cannot be easily understood. Which plan would a typical investor choose? Most rational investors would likely prefer Plan A to Plan B. The weakness of statistical models lies in their limited ability to handle large feature sets (dimensions or variables) compared with ML algorithms. But statistical models possess an advantage that is still unmatched in AI models—that is, the presence of an underlying theory that is based on fundamentals and intrinsic valuation drivers. This reinforcement layer of empirical data verification to human conjectures has always been the hallmark of research. ML may not necessarily be a black box, but there is a tendency of users to assume it is.

Although the Financial Stability Board (2017, p. 34) has indicated that progress in AI shows significant promise, regulators continue to be concerned that the "lack of interpretability will make it even more difficult to determine potential effects beyond the firms' balance sheet, for example during a systemic shock. Notably, many AI and machine learning developed models are being 'trained' in a period of low volatility." Reasons for such caution are not hard to find. The 1987 Black Monday stock crash was attributed by many to prevalent option-based program trading at that time. And in the subprime crisis of 2007, there appears to be evidence that the asymptotic independence modeling of the Gaussian copula used to price subprime default likelihood was based on a limited time dataset (stable cycle) and ignored the conventional wisdom that credit defaults tend to cluster.

Fortunately, there is an increasing body of work that attempts to shed light under the AI hood. An example is how Shapley (1953) values or SHapley Additive exPlanation (SHAP) values for machine learning model features are providing interesting insights in much the same way that *p*-values are used for statistical models. Improving ML transparency in this way not only improves conviction in decision making, but it is also helping to build new research to further our understanding of deep learning.

To conclude, it bears mentioning that the current wave of AI does not relate only to new methodologies, big data, and computational power. The additional dimension this time is the democratization of AI, with the wide involvement of professionals, researchers, educators, and policymakers. The massive allocation of resources in this field is testimony to the belief that the benefits are real. However, to make it sustainable beyond the hype of yet another wave, we need to take stock of the promise, manage our expectations, and continue to embrace differing approaches. We are proud to be part of this effort to support and disseminate the body of knowledge through this handbook.

Aaron Low, PhD, CFA
Chair, Board of Trustees,
CFA Institute Research Foundation

References

Financial Stability Board. 2017. "Artificial Intelligence and Machine Learning in Financial Services: Market Developments and Financial Stability Implications" (1 November). www.fsb.org/wp-content/uploads/P011117.pdf.

Grossman, Sanford J., and Joseph E. Stiglitz. 1980. "On the Impossibility of Informationally Efficient Markets." *American Economic Review* 70 (3): 393–408.

Shapley, Lloyd S. 1953. "A Value for n-Person Games." *Contributions to the Theory of Games* 2 (28): 307–18.

NOTES FROM THE REVIEWERS

The integration of AI applications into the investment process is gradually becoming part of modern asset management as AI innovation happens at a rapid pace. I was delighted to recommend contributors to and review this handbook, a continuation of the work of CFA Institute in the area. Over the years, I have had the opportunity to engage with innovators, subject matter experts, and practitioners focused on the integration of AI in the investment process and participated in spirited discussions as the risks, challenges, and realities of applications and, importantly, adoption, came to light and we moved from an AI revolution to evolution.

While some think of AI and big data as a threat, there is an opportunity for AI and human intelligence to evolve together to drive better investor outcomes. This requires putting theory and potential use cases into practice. This handbook provides applications currently used by investment practitioners, who share insights, successes, and challenges. Designed and curated by Larry Cao, this handbook is an invaluable reference for investment professionals on the road to adoption as AI innovation transforms our industry.

Carole K. Crawford, CFA
Managing Director, Americas and Global Events
CFA Institute

We are in an era that is both blessed and cursed by data. The pace of our accumulating data is extraordinary, and that makes distilling insights from data harder than ever. When thinking about the investment process, I emphasize the integrity and quality of the decision-making process. However, both are difficult to achieve in real life.

Most of us are trained at school with a generalized foundation of knowledge (broad based but shallow), and then we step into the real world during a certain period of time (experience is linked to a certain period). But the investment industry advocates specialization (depth of knowledge). Take myself as an example: I am an engineer by training, and I joined the investment industry just before the GFC and have been trained as a macro strategist. This means there is a built-in bias in the way I digest information (macro, not micro) and respond to the environment (strong risk aversion). Data science is a perfect tool to help mitigate these biases. State Super has been incorporating data science to support our decision-making process in the last seven years, and the output has been value accretive.

When I was asked to review this book, I was super excited, partly because I wholeheartedly believe in the importance of topics included in this handbook and partly because we need such a publication in our industry. I hope everyone enjoys this book and makes it a companion on their data science journey in the following years.

Charles Wu, CFA
Chief Investment Officer,
State Super SAS Trustee Corporation
President, CFA Society Sydney

It was very gratifying to have been asked to review this handbook. In my current role, I have had the opportunity to interact with numerous experts in the field of AI/ML investing and analysis and have gained an informed sense of the major breakthroughs and the extensive progress that have been made across the space in recent years. Having said that, many of the methods described in this handbook are still in the early stages of development. This seems to me, however, to be a strength; the reader takes away insights from practitioners who openly share their experiences in a dynamically changing environment, where trial and error remain part of the DNA.

Through engaging and straightforward writing, each chapter provides perspectives and often state-of-the-art methodologies on a different aspect of AI/ML in investing. The content is useful both for professional practitioners who are already working in the field and for those who are wishing simply to understand more about how these applications are rapidly changing the landscape of finance and investment management.

The chapters have been carefully selected and edited by Larry Cao, who can again be congratulated on pulling together a wide breadth of pertinent topics and authors and combining them with great skill.

Susan Spinner, CFA
CEO, CFA Society Germany

ABOUT THE CONTRIBUTORS

Mike Chen, PhD, Robeco

Andrew Chin, AllianceBernstein

Kai Cui, PhD, Neuberger Berman

Dan Duggan, PhD, Goldman Sachs Global Investment Research

Yuyu Fan, AllianceBernstein

Che Guan, AllianceBernstein

Stefan Jansen, CFA, Applied AI

Peer Nagy, Man Group

Jochen Papenbrock, Doctorate, NVIDIA

James Powrie, PhD, Man Group

Mikhail Samonov, CFA, Two Centuries Investments and CultureLine.ai

Tal Sansani, CFA, Off-Script Systems and CultureLine.ai

Jonathan Shahrabani, Neuberger Berman

Erin Stanton, Virtu Financial

Ingrid Tierens, PhD, CFA, Goldman Sachs Global Investment Research

Huib Vaessen, APG Asset Management

Xu Liang, PhD, Ping An OneConnect

Weili Zhou, CFA, Robeco

Stefan Zohren, PhD, Man Group

INTRODUCTION

Larry Cao, CFA
Senior Director, Research, CFA Institute

Over the last few years, in our interactions with readers of our artificial intelligence (AI) publications and audiences for our in-person and virtual presentations around the world, we have been repeatedly asked how they should begin their journey of AI adoption. This book is our attempt at providing initial answers to their questions.

Who Should Read This Handbook?

We have produced this handbook with the following target audience and objectives in mind:

- Help C-suite executives and board members with responsibility to develop and execute their firms' AI and big data strategies to get an overview of the subject and set strategic directions.
- Help knowledge engineers leading AI and big data projects at investment firms and their teams select projects.
- Help investment and technology professionals who work on T-shaped teams understand project backgrounds and implementation details.
- Help regulators stay abreast of industry developments so as to facilitate their policy development efforts.
- Help students (and the professors who are teaching them) prepare for a career on future investment teams or at regulatory agencies.

In short, if you are embarking on the journey of AI and big data adoption in finance, this book is written for you.

The AI Adoption Journey in Finance and You

There is a well-known five-stage model of the buyers' decision process for new products (Kotler and Armstrong 1998). As we studied the benefits, hurdles, and ways to overcome these challenges of AI adoption over the last few years, we came to realize that the AI adoption journeys of financial institutions and finance professionals have largely followed patterns that mirror this five-stage process. Here is a summary of our findings, which culminated in this handbook.

The five stages are awareness, interest, evaluation, trial, and adoption (see **Exhibit 1**). It is important to note that buyers have different needs at each stage. For example, at the awareness stage, they lack information about the new product, which they seek at the interest stage. At the evaluation stage, buyers look for more specific proof that the new product makes sense, and if so, they will move to the next step, trial, where they experiment with the new product. If all goes well, they will finally reach the adoption stage and start using the new product regularly.

Awareness

From 2015 to 2017, AlphaGo went from beating a human professional player at the board game Go for the first time to beating the best human Go player. The historic events brought artificial intelligence from computer labs into the public domain, quickly becoming the subject of conversation at dinner tables, at cocktail parties, and in board rooms.

Up to that point, main street and the mainstream financial services industry had focused their attention on what we later referred to as "early-stage fintech"—that is, peer-to-peer lending, mobile payments, and robo-advice. Our investigation led us to refute that these new businesses were disrupting the financial services industry, simply because they prospered where customers were un(der)-banked and fared less well where financial services were entrenched.

I also wrote in the financial press in 2016 that we believed winners would follow the model "Fin + Tech" (Cao 2016)—that is, collaboration between powerful financial institutions and powerful tech companies. The winner-takes-all model commonly seen in the internet business will not extend quite as easily to finance.

The first publication in our series, "FinTech 2017: China, Asia, and Beyond" (CFA Institute 2017), included a contributor's

Exhibit 1. The Five Stages of the Buyers' Decision Process for New Products

article highlighting that the ABCs of fintech (artificial intelligence, big data, and cloud computing) will be the driving force for change in the financial services industry. Our audience's reception, however, was lukewarm in the spring of 2017.

Interest

Google Trends showed that worldwide searches for "artificial intelligence" continuously rose for several years through 2018. This finding is consistent with our experience. We received more media requests on AI and were quoted in an Ignites article in the summer of 2017 on our positive views regarding the collaboration between Microsoft and China Asset Management, one of the top mutual fund firms in China.

Six months later, we invited Tang Xiaodong,[1] CEO of China Asset Management; Eric Chang, vice president of Microsoft Research Institute Asia; and senior executives from other sectors in finance to speak at the AI and the Future of Financial Services Forum, a major event we organized in Beijing, which was also livestreamed to satellite venues in several other financial centers in the region. It attracted a record number of participants across the region—either joining in person in Beijing or at one of the satellite venues.

In his fascinating presentation on machine learning (ML) and neural networks, Chang highlighted what Microsoft believed was going to be the winning formula of AI adoption: "AI + HI (human intelligence)," which we readily adopted because we considered it an extension of our "Fin + Tech" philosophy in the age of AI.

Tang gave an informative talk on AI's applications in asset management. Other speakers rounded out the forum with insights from their unique vantage points. The event received the highest ratings from participants, reflecting both the audience's passion for the subject and their satisfaction with our expert speakers.

My articles on the subject, from the concepts of AI, machine learning, and deep learning (Cao 2018a) to their applications in finance (Cao 2018b), published, respectively, in February and March 2018 on the *Enterprising Investor* blog were similarly popular with readers, such that the former became the blog's top ranked article of February 2018 (McCaffrey 2018a); these two articles also ranked among the top 10, for the year (McCaffrey 2018b). These articles and more from our contributors formed the core of our "FinTech 2018" report (CFA Institute 2018).

Evaluation

In late 2018, I was invited to speak at two closed-door events, one attended by technology executives at global financial institutions and the other with researchers from leading central banks and universities around the world. My fellow speakers at both events shared one frustration: They were having a hard time distilling insights from big data!

The participant demographic at both events was certainly representative of the leaders in their respective domains, which seemed to me a clear sign that AI adoption in financial services had reached what Gartner refers to as "the trough of disillusionment" in the Hype Cycle model,[2] where "interest wanes as experiments and implementations fail to deliver." In the simpler terms of the five-stage model, our audience reached the evaluation stage and needed proof that AI works before they could move forward.

We believed the best way to provide that proof would be a collection of case studies from successful early adopters who had put AI and big data to productive use in finance. To help readers relate, we selected cases based on two criteria: geography—Americas; Asia Pacific (APAC); and Europe, Middle East, and Africa (EMEA)—and line of work—stocks, bonds, asset allocation, and hedge funds. These elements formed the basic construct of the "AI Pioneers in Investment Management" report (CFA Institute 2019).

We tested the idea while speaking at the forum of the CFA Institute Annual Conference in 2019,[3] and judging from the audience's reaction and questions, they were clearly looking for concrete examples, exactly the type that we were working on, rather than a continuation of the more generic type of information we provided in 2018.

A CFA Institute Practice Analysis survey conducted in the spring of 2019 showed that adoption rates for AI and big data techniques in the industry remained low (CFA Institute 2019, pp. 8–13). We shared our perspectives in the report on the challenges the industry faced and provided our recommendation. The report was cited in the *Financial Times* and the *Harvard Business Review* and by Reuters and researchers at Deloitte and Morningstar, among others.

Trial

The day after the report was published, I spoke at an industry conference in Toronto.[4] And then I went to Singapore, before going on to speak at more than a dozen financial

---

[1]He left China Asset Management in 2019 and now leads BlackRock's China efforts (BlackRock 2019).

[2]See the "Gartner Hype Cycle" webpage at www.gartner.com/en/research/methodologies/gartner-hype-cycle.

[3]See my comments in the video "AI and Big Data in the Future of Investment Management" at https://cfainstitute.gallery.video/annual19/detail/video/6036457979001/ai-and-big-data-in-the-future-of-investment-management.

[4]Toronto, and broadly Canada, is of course also where this latest wave of AI development started.

centers in APAC and EMEA, providing us with many additional touch points with the industry and finance professionals to get a read on their needs.

The feedback we got from our readers and audiences was overwhelmingly consistent with the model prediction: They wanted to experiment with AI and big data and asked for help on where to begin.[5] Of course, every firm and every professional are unique. Providing a one-size-fits-all answer is not only challenging but also likely to be counterproductive. That said, we believe we can provide a framework, based on our own analysis and field research into cases that were successful and, even more importantly, those that were less fortunate.

The first step in the framework is building an AI-enabling organization, or T-shaped teams. We developed the concept of a T-shaped team specifically to highlight the need for communication and strategic leadership in the context of AI adoption in financial services (CFA Institute 2021). A T-shaped team comprises three distinct functions: the traditional investment function, a technology (data science) function, and an innovation function. The background and training of finance and data science professionals are so different that it makes knowledge engineers in the innovation function who can provide both communication support and strategic leadership especially important for AI adoption to succeed.

The second step in the framework is to implement the AI strategy developed by the leadership. For this step, we believed it would be most helpful to provide both executives at financial institutions looking to embark on the AI adoption journey and professionals at these institutions a menu of options they could pick and choose from that would be most appropriate for their strategy, product lineup, and staff's level of expertise in and acceptance of AI adoption. This is where this handbook comes in.

There is a plethora of books published about machine learning for investment and finance. Yet they tend to be written for quants or programmers with prior machine learning knowledge and focus on the technical aspects of implementation. The attention tends to be 80/20 between technology and finance.

This handbook is different. We strive to provide a reference book on AI and big data applications in investments written from the finance industry perspective and offer details on solutions that are in production and effectively field-tested every day.[6]

Consistent with this objective, we have encouraged contributors to include snippets of coding where they deem appropriate. We hope the more tech-savvy readers among us will find it helpful, and that the rest of us will be motivated to catch up over time.

We have summarized from our vantage point the industry's progress on the AI adoption journey and our efforts to support it (see **Exhibit 2**). What is next? The most natural scenario is that we will support the next stage of the adoption journey in much the same way as we do in other, more established areas of investment. Do let us know what you think and how we can best be of service.

Exhibit 2. The Five Stages of AI Adoption and Accompanying Research

(future editions)

---

[5]Another popular area of interest that emerged at the time was AI ethics. For additional details, see CFA Institute (2022).

[6]Many may consider "field-tested" an aspirational goal in AI and big data applications today, probably rightly so. Our operating definition of the term is that the type of solution is in production at different firms in the process of managing significant sums of money.

How Is the Handbook Organized?

In line with our understanding of the active areas of AI and big data adoption in investments (and, more broadly, finance), we have organized the handbook along four streams, each with a few chapters written by practitioners who are active in that area. Representative of the ecosystem, most of our contributors hail from investment firms, with the remaining coming from investment banks, other financial institutions, and service vendors.

Part I provides an overview of the current state of AI and big data adoption in investments. In Chapter 1, Mike Chen and Weili Zhou share their perspectives on challenges and potential pitfalls in applying ML in finance and provide an overview of the broad areas of applications. In Chapter 2, Ingrid Tierens and Dan Duggan discuss their experiences and takeaways in working with alternative data, in addition to some use cases. Chapter 3, by Kai Cui and Jonathan Shahrabani, reviews how data science can inform long-term investment decisions of active fundamental investors.

Part II covers natural language understanding, processing, and generation. Natural language processing (NLP) is a branch of AI studies that dates to the 1950s, although the latest boom is often attributed to the introduction of ML into the field since the 1980s. Its applications in investments also go back well over a decade (see, e.g., Antweiler and Frank 2004), although significant strides have been made since then, which our contributors for Chapters 4–6 focus on.

In Chapter 4, Andrew Chin, Yuyu Fan, and Che Guan provide an overview of the broad applications of natural language processing in investments today, ranging from well-known areas, such as sentiment analysis and earnings transcript analysis, to more recent applications using corporate filings in compliance and, in sales, to gain client insights from public information. In Chapter 5, Stefan Jansen discusses from a technical perspective the evolution of natural language understanding and trends in its applications. Chapter 6, by Tal Sansani and Mikhail Samonov rounds out this stream with an aspirational discussion on applying NLP in environmental, social, and governance analysis.

Part III covers trading. This is an active area of AI and big data activities, although the percentage of trades executed with AI and big data techniques remains small. Our contributors from different parts of the ecosystem shared their perspectives. Chapter 7, by Erin Stanton, highlights a few use cases at various stages of the trading process that, in aggregate, help readers piece together a picture of ML and big data application in the trading landscape. In Chapter 8, Peer Nagy, James Powrie, and Stefan Zohren of Man Group zoom in on limit order books as the microstructure data source and explain in detail how ML models can help predict spreads, trade volume, volatility, and more to inform trading decisions.

In addition to the areas mentioned thus far, there are obviously still many more AI and big data applications that are being developed and applied in investments and finance. Part IV addresses development in three of these areas.

Customer service (call centers) is one of the most tried-and-true applications for AI that has been widely applied across industries. In Chapter 9, Xu Liang of Ping An OneConnect offers an overview of financial institutions' use of AI in customer service, providing many enlightening business applications and discussing the underlying technology, such as voice, NLP, and knowledge graphs.

The current AI boom is largely driven by progress in three areas—algorithms, big data, and computing power—where computing power's contribution is often understated. In Chapter 10, Jochen Papenbrock of NVIDIA argues, supported by a number of recent cases in investments, that there is increasingly a need for accelerated computing.

AI is a fluid term. The scope of our AI and big data efforts, including this handbook, focuses on machine learning (and its various branches)—NLP, computer vision, and unstructured data. Symbolic AI is a branch of AI research that was popular before the latest AI boom, brought on by nonsymbolic AI studies, such as machine learning. In the last chapter of this handbook, Huib Vaessen shares how an automated real estate portfolio management solution based on symbolic AI can help an investment team.

The results of a CFA Institute global survey conducted when this handbook was completed support our positioning and topic selection (see **Exhibit 3**). To the question of which talents will be in most demand, 35% of respondents answered finance/investment talents with some AI and big data training and 32% answered both finance/investment and AI/big data skills. This handbook has indeed been written to help finance/investment professionals move into those two buckets.

The picture is similar in terms of topic selection. For example, 56% of the respondents are using AI and big data in data analysis, a topic that we hope this handbook has thoroughly covered throughout, and about a quarter of the respondents are using AI and big data techniques in areas outside the core investment business, such as sales and marketing or customer service, which are also well covered in the handbook. Chapter 9 focuses entirely on customer service. Chapter 4 covers applications in sales and marketing in addition to investment applications, which is partly why we allocated more space to the chapter.

Exhibit 3. Responses to CFA Institute Global Survey Questions

A. Over the next two years, which type of talents is your organization primarily looking to hire more? (select up to two)

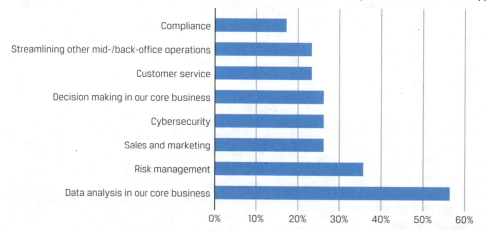

B. What business activities has your organization been routinely applying AI and big data to? (select all that apply)

As we continue our research efforts in AI and big data applications, please feel free to drop us a note and share with us your successes or needs. We will strive to serve as your knowledge engineers, building bridges between thought leaders and practitioners.

Acknowledgments

Putting together such a handbook of unique positioning for the first time was not an easy task. My gratitude goes to all who have supported our efforts.

First, I have been fortunate to work with some of the key industry practitioners putting AI and big data to work in investments and finance. Despite the tremendous demand on their time, they have all given the project much attention, often patiently working with us through multiple iterations to make sure that the chapters collectively form a coherent chorus.

My deep appreciation also goes to Aaron Low, CFA, Carole Crawford, CFA, Charles Wu, CFA, and Susan Spinner, CFA, for reading through the handbook with me from its infancy in the spring of 2022 through the final draft in the fall. Their expertise, judgment, and network have gone a long way in raising the bar for this project.

Finally, credit goes to the leadership and the project team at CFA Institute. Without their steadfast support, this handbook would have never been able to get to where it is today.

References

Antweiler, W., and M. Z. Frank. 2004. "Is All That Talk Just Noise? The Information Content of Internet Stock Message Boards." *Journal of Finance* 59: 1259–94.

Bartram, Söhnke M., Jürgen Branke, and Mehrshad Motahari. 2020. "Artificial Intelligence in Asset Management." Literature review, CFA Institute Research Foundation (28 August). www.cfainstitute.org/research/foundation/2020/rflr-artificial-intelligence-in-asset-management.

BlackRock. 2019. "BlackRock Appoints Tony Tang Head of China" (17 April). www.blackrock.com/corporate/newsroom/press-releases/article/corporate-one/press-releases/blackrock-appoints-tony-tang-head-of-china.

Cao, Larry. 2016. "FinTech and the Future of Financial Services." *Hong Kong Economic Journal* (26 May). http://startupbeat.hkej.com/?p=29681.

Cao, Larry. 2018a. "Artificial Intelligence, Machine Learning, and Deep Learning: A Primer." *Enterprising Investor* (blog; 13 February). https://blogs.cfainstitute.org/investor/2018/02/13/artificial-intelligence-machine-learning-and-deep-learning-in-investment-management-a-primer/.

Cao, Larry. 2018b. "Portfolio Managers, Artificial Intelligence Is Coming for Your Jobs." *Enterprising Investor* (blog; 9 March). https://blogs.cfainstitute.org/investor/2018/03/09/portfolio-managers-artificial-intelligence-is-coming-for-your-jobs/.

CFA Institute. 2019. "AI Pioneers in Investment Management." www.cfainstitute.org/-/media/documents/survey/AI-Pioneers-in-Investment-Management.pdf.

CFA Institute. 2022. "Ethics and Artificial Intelligence in Investment Management: A Framework for Investment Professionals." www.cfainstitute.org/-/media/documents/article/industry-research/Ethics-and-Artificial-Intelligence-in-Investment-Management_Online.pdf.

CFA Institute. 2017. "FinTech 2017: China, Asia, and Beyond" (May). https://hub.ipe.com/download?ac=72587.

CFA Institute. 2018. "FinTech 2018: The Asia Pacific Edition" (September). www.cfainstitute.org/-/media/documents/book/industry-research/fintech-booklet.pdf.

CFA Institute. 2021. "T-Shaped Teams: Organizing to Adopt AI and Big Data at Investment Firms." www.cfainstitute.org/-/media/documents/article/industry-research/t-shaped-teams.pdf.

Kotler, Philip, and Gary Armstrong. 1998. *Principles of Marketing*. Hoboken, NJ: Prentice Hall.

McCaffrey, Paul. 2018a. "Top Five Articles from February: Body Language, Data Science, Artificial Intelligence." *Enterprising Investor* (blog; 28 February). https://blogs.cfainstitute.org/investor/2018/02/28/top-five-articles-from-february-body-language-data-science-artificial-intelligence/.

McCaffrey, Paul. 2018b. "Top 10 Posts from 2018: Chart Crimes, Political Divides, AI, and the Skill Ratio." *Enterprising Investor* (blog; 27 December). https://blogs.cfainstitute.org/investor/2018/12/27/top-10-posts-from-2018-chart-crimes-political-divides-ai-and-the-skill-ratio/.

HANDBOOK OF ARTIFICIAL INTELLIGENCE AND BIG DATA APPLICATIONS IN INVESTMENTS

I. MACHINE LEARNING AND DATA SCIENCE APPLICATIONS IN INVESTMENTS

This book can be found at cfainstitute.org/ai-and-big-data

1. ON MACHINE LEARNING APPLICATIONS IN INVESTMENTS

Mike Chen, PhD
Head, Alternative Alpha Research, Robeco

Weili Zhou, CFA
Head, Quant Equity Research, Robeco

Introduction

In recent years, machine learning (ML) has been a popular technique in various domains, ranging from streaming video and online shopping recommendations to image detection and generation to autonomous driving. The attraction and desire to apply machine learning in finance are no different.

- "The global AI fintech market is predicted to grow at a CAGR of 25.3% between 2022 and 2027" (Columbus 2020).
- "A survey of IT executives in banking finds that 85% have a 'clear strategy' for adopting AI in developing new products and services" (Nadeem 2018).

Putting aside the common and widespread confusion between artificial intelligence (AI) and ML (see, e.g., Cao 2018; Nadeem 2018), the growth of ML in finance is projected to be much faster than that of the overall industry itself, as the previous quotes suggest. Faced with this outlook, practitioners may want answers to the following questions:

- What does ML bring to the table compared with traditional techniques?
- How do I make ML for finance work? Are there special considerations? What are some common pitfalls?
- What are some examples of ML applied to finance?

In this chapter, we explore how ML can be applied from a practitioner's perspective and attempt to answer many common questions, including the ones above.[1]

The first section of the chapter discusses practitioners' motivations for using ML, common challenges in implementing ML for finance, and solutions. The second section discusses several concrete examples of ML applications in finance and, in particular, equity investments.

Motivations, Challenges, and Solutions in Applying ML in Investments

In this section, we discuss reasons for applying ML, the unique challenges involved, and how to avoid common pitfalls in the process.

Motivations

The primary attraction of applying ML to equity investing, as with almost all investment-related endeavors, is the promise of higher risk-adjusted return. The hypothesis is that these techniques, explicitly designed for prediction tasks based on high-dimensional data and without any functional form specification, should excel at predicting future equity returns.

Emerging academic literature and collective practitioner experience support this hypothesis. In recent years, practitioners have successfully applied ML algorithms to predict equity returns, and ML-based return prediction algorithms have been making their way into quantitative investment models. These algorithms have been used worldwide in both developed and emerging markets, for large-cap and small-cap investment universes, and with single-country or multi-country strategies.[2] In general, practitioners have found that ML-derived alpha models outperform those generated from more traditional linear models[3] in predicting cross-sectional equity returns.

---

[1] Readers interested in the theoretical underpinnings of ML algorithms, such as random forest or neural networks, should read Hastie, Tibshirani, and Friedman (2009) and Goodfellow, Bengio, and Courville (2016).

[2] There are also numerous academic studies on using ML to predict returns. For example, ML techniques have been applied in a single-country setting by Gu, Kelly, and Xiu (2020) to the United States, by Abe and Nakayama (2018) to Japan, and by Leippold, Wang, and Zhou (2022) to China's A-share markets. Similarly, in a multi-country/regional setting, ML has been applied by Tobek and Hronec (2021) and Leung, Lohre, Mischlich, Shea, and Stroh (2021) to developed markets and by Hanauer and Kalsbach (2022) to emerging markets.

[3] For linear equity models, see, for example, Grinold and Kahn (1999).

In addition to predicting equity returns, ML has been used to predict intermediate metrics known to predict future returns. For example, practitioners have used ML to forecast corporate earnings and have found ML-derived forecasts to be significantly more accurate and informative than other commonly used earnings prediction models.[4] Another use of ML in equity investing developed by Robeco's quantitative researchers has been to predict not the entire investment universe's return but the returns of those equities that are likely to suffer a severe price drop in the near future. Investment teams at Robeco have found that ML techniques generate superior crash predictions compared with those from linear models using traditional metrics, such as leverage ratio or distance to default.[5]

What drives the outperformance of ML over other known quantitative techniques? The main conclusion from practitioners and academics is that because ML algorithms do not prespecify the functional relationship between the prediction variables (equity return, future earnings, etc.) and the predictors (metrics from financial statements, past returns, etc.), ML algorithms are not constrained to a linear format as is typical of other techniques but, rather, can uncover interaction and nonlinear relationships between the input features and the output variable(s).

Interaction and nonlinear effects

The interaction effect occurs when the prediction outputs cannot be expressed as a linear combination of the individual inputs because the effect of one input depends on the value of the other ones. Consider a stylistic example of predicting equity price based on two input features: reported earnings and an accounting red flag, where the red-flag input is binary: 0 (no cause of concern) and 1 (grave concern). The resulting ML output with these two inputs may be that when the red-flag input is 0, the output is linearly and positively related to reported earnings; in contrast, when the red-flag input is 1, the output is a 50% decrease in price regardless of the reported earnings. **Exhibit 1** illustrates this stylistic example.

ML prediction can also outperform the traditional linear model prediction due to nonlinear effects. There are many empirically observed nonlinear effects that linear models cannot model. For example, there is a nonlinear relationship between a firm's credit default swap (CDS) spread and its equity returns because equity can be framed as an embedded call option on a firm's assets, thereby introducing nonlinearity.[6] **Exhibit 2** illustrates this example. Many ML algorithms, particularly neural networks,[7] explicitly

Exhibit 1. Illustration of the Interaction Effect between Accounting Red Flags and Equity Returns

Source: Robeco.

---

[4]This conclusion was replicated and supported also by academics. For example, see Cao and You (2021).

[5]For more information on using ML for crash prediction, see Swinkels and Hoogteijling (2022).

[6]For more details, see Birge and Zhang (2018).

[7]Neural networks incorporate nonlinearity through activation functions in each neuron. Without activation functions, neural networks, regardless of their depth, reduce down to traditional linear models commonly used in finance. For more on activation functions, see Goodfellow et al. (2016).

Exhibit 2. Illustration of the Nonlinear Relationship between a CDS and Equity Returns

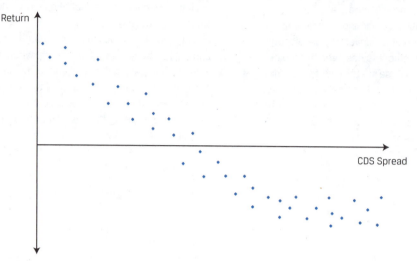

Source: Robeco.

introduce nonlinearity into the model setup, facilitating nonlinearity modeling.

Empirically, academics and practitioners have found that the interaction effect accounts for a large portion of ML techniques' outperformance, while the jury is still out on whether nonlinear effects contribute positively to the outperformance. A well-known study in the field by Gu, Kelly, and Xiu (2020, p. 2258) found that "the favorable performance of [ML algorithms] indicates a benefit to allowing for potentially complex interactions among predictors." In the study, comparing the performance of purely linear models with that of generalized linear models, the authors note that "the generalized linear model … fails to improve on the performance of purely linear methods (R^2_{OOS} of 0.19%). The fact that this method uses spline functions of individual features, but includes no interaction among features, suggests that univariate expansions provide little incremental information beyond the [purely] linear model" (Gu et al. 2020, p. 2251). However, other studies have found that both interaction and nonlinear effects contribute positively to ML models' outperformance (see, e.g., Abe and Nakayama 2018; Swinkels and Hoogteijling 2022; Choi, Jiang, and Zhang 2022).

Find relationships from the data deluge

Another attraction of applying ML to financial markets is the promise of having the algorithm discover relationships not specified or perhaps not known by academics and practitioners—that is, *data mining*, which historically has been a pejorative in quantitative finance circles.

Another term being used, perhaps with a more positive connotation, is "knowledge discovery."

With the ongoing information and computing revolution and the increased popularity of quantitative finance, the amount of financial data is growing at a rapid pace. This increased amount of data may or may not embody relevant information for investment purposes. Since many of the data types and sources are new, many investors do not have a strong prior opinion on whether and how they can be useful. Thus, ML algorithms that are designed to look for relationships have become attractive for practitioners and academics in the hope that, even without specifying a hypothesis on the economic relationship, the ML algorithm will figure out the link between inputs and outputs. Although ML algorithms have built-in mechanisms to combat overfitting or discovering spurious correlations between input features and output predictions,[8] caution must still be taken to avoid discovering nonrepeatable and nonreplicable relationships and patterns. Later in this chapter, we will address this issue further and consider other challenges practitioners face when implementing ML in live portfolios. But first, we will discuss what makes the financial market different from other domains in which ML has shown tremendous success.

Unique Challenges of Applying ML in Finance

When applying ML for investments, great care must be taken because financial markets differ from domains where

---

[8]Examples include *k*-fold cross-validation, dropout, and regularization. For deeper discussions, see Hastie et al. (2009) and Goodfellow et al. (2016).

ML has made tremendous strides. These differences can mitigate many of the specific advantages ML algorithms enjoy, making them less effective in practice when applied in real-life situations. A few of these differences follow.

Signal-to-noise ratio and system complexity

Financial data have a low signal-to-noise ratio. For a given security, any one metric is generally not a huge determinant of how that security will perform. For example, suppose Company XYZ announced great earnings this quarter. Its price can still go down after the announcement because earnings were below expectations, because central banks are hiking interest rates, or because investors are generally long the security and are looking to reduce their positions. Compare this situation with a high signal-to-noise domain—for example, streaming video recommendation systems. If a person watches many movies in a specific genre, chances are high that the person will also like other movies in that same genre. Because financial returns compress high-dimensional information and drivers (company-specific, macro, behavioral, market positioning, etc.) into one dimension, positive or negative, the signal-to-noise ratio of any particular information item is generally low.

It is fair to say that the financial market is one of the most complex man-made systems in the world. And this complexity and low signal-to-noise ratio can cause issues when ML algorithms are not applied skillfully. Although ML algorithms are adept at detecting complex relationships, the complexity of the financial market and the low signal-to-noise ratio that characterizes it can still pose a problem because they make the true relationship between drivers of security return and the outcome difficult to detect.

Small vs. big data

Another major challenge in applying ML in financial markets is the amount of available data. The amount of financial data is still relatively small compared with many domains in which ML has thrived, such as the consumer internet domain or the physical sciences. The data that quantitative investors traditionally have used are typically quarterly or monthly. And even for the United States, the market with the longest available reliable data, going back 100 years, the number of monthly data points for any security we might wish to consider is at most 1,200. Compared with other domains where the amount of data is in the billions and trillions, the quantity of financial data is minuscule. To be fair, some of the newer data sources, or "alternative data," such as social media posts or news articles, are much more abundant than traditional financial data. However, overall, the amount of financial data is still small compared with other domains.

The small amount of financial data is a challenge to ML applications because a significant driver of an ML algorithm's power is the amount of available data (see Halevy, Norvig, and Pereira 2009). Between a simple ML algorithm trained on a large set of data versus a sophisticated ML algorithm trained on a relatively smaller set of data, the simpler algorithm often outperforms in real-life testing. With a large set of data, investors applying ML can perform true cross-validation and out-of-sample testing to minimize overfitting by dividing input data into different segments. The investor can conduct proper hyperparameter tuning and robustness checks only if the amount of data is large enough. The small amount of financial data adds to the challenges of applying ML to financial markets mentioned earlier—the financial markets' high system complexity and low signal-to-noise ratio.

Stationarity vs. adaptive market, irrationality

Finally, what makes financial markets challenging for ML application in general is that markets are nonstationary. What we mean is that financial markets adapt and change over time. Many other domains where ML algorithms have shined are static systems. For example, the rules governing protein unfolding are likely to stay constant regardless of whether researchers understand them. In contrast, because of the promised rewards, financial markets "learn" as investors learn what works over time and change their behavior, thereby changing the behavior of the overall market. Furthermore, because academics have been successful over the last few decades in discovering and publishing drivers of market returns—for example, Fama and French (1993)—their research also increased knowledge of *all* market participants and such research changes market behavior, as noted by McLean and Pontiff (2016).

The adaptive nature of financial markets means not only that ML algorithms trained for investment do not have a long enough history with which to train the model and a low signal-to-noise ratio to contend with but also that the rules and dynamics that govern the outcome the models try to predict also change over time. Luckily, many ML algorithms are adaptive or can be designed to adapt to evolving systems. Still, the changing system calls into question the validity and applicability of historical data that can be used to train the algorithms—data series that were not long enough to begin with. To further complicate the issue, financial markets are man-made systems. Their results are the collective of individual human actions, and human beings often behave irrationally—for example, making decisions based on greed or fear.[9] This irrationality characteristic does not exist in many of the other domains in which ML has succeeded.

---

[9] There have been various studies on how greed and fear affect market participants' decision-making process. See, for example, Lo, Repin, and Steenbarger (2005).

How to Avoid Common Pitfalls When Applying ML in Finance

This section addresses some potential pitfalls when applying ML to financial investment.[10]

Overfitting

Because of the short sample data history, overfitting is a significant concern when applying ML techniques in finance. This concern is even stronger than when applying traditional quantitative techniques, such as linear regression, because of the high degrees of freedom inherent in ML algorithms. The result of overfitting is that one may get a fantastic backtest, but out-of-sample, the results will not live up to expectations.

There are some common techniques used in ML across all domains to combat overfitting. They include cross-validation, feature selection and removal, regularization, early stopping, ensembling, and having holdout data.[11] Because of the lower sample data availability in finance, some of these standard techniques might not be applicable or work as well in the financial domain as in others.

However, there are also advantages to working in the financial domain. The most significant advantage is human intuition and economic domain knowledge. What we mean by this is that investors and researchers applying machine learning can conduct "smell tests" to see whether the relationships found by ML algorithms between input features and output predictions make intuitive or economic sense. For example, to examine the relationship between inputs and outputs, one can look at Shapley additive explanation (SHAP) value, introduced by Lundberg and Lee (2017). SHAP value is computed from the average of the marginal contribution of the feature when predicting the targets, where the marginal contribution is computed by comparing the performance after withholding that variable from the feature set versus the feature set that includes the variable.

Exhibit 3 plots SHAP values from Robeco's work on using ML to predict equity crashes,[12] where various input features are used to predict the probability of financial distress of various stocks in the investment universe. The color of each dot indicates the sign and magnitude of a feature, where red signals a high feature value and blue denotes a low feature value. Take Feature 25, for example. As the feature value increases (as indicated by the color red), the ML algorithm predicts a higher probability of financial distress.

And as the feature value decreases (as indicated by the color blue), the ML algorithm predicts a lower probability of financial distress. With this information, experienced investors can apply their domain knowledge to see whether the relationship discovered by the ML algorithm makes sense. For example, if Feature 25, in this case, is the leverage ratio and Feature 1 is distance to default,[13] then the relationship may make sense. However, if the features are flipped (Feature 25 is distance to default and Feature 1 is the leverage ratio), then it is likely that the ML algorithm made a mistake, possibly through overfitting.

Another approach to mitigate overfitting and having ML algorithms find spurious correlations is to try to eliminate it from the start. *Ex post* explanation via SHAP values and other techniques is useful, but investors can also apply their investment domain knowledge to curate the input set to select those inputs likely to have a relationship with the prediction objective. This is called "feature engineering" in ML lingo and requires financial domain knowledge. As an example, when we are trying to predict stock crash probability, fundamental financial metrics such as profit margin and debt coverage ratio are sensible input features for the ML algorithm, but the first letter of the last name of the CEO, for example, is likely not a sensible input feature.

Replicability

There is a debate about whether there is a replicability crisis in financial research.[14] The concerns about replicability are especially relevant to results derived from applying ML because, in addition to the usual reasons for replicability difficulties (differences in universe tested, *p*-hacking, etc.), replicating ML-derived results also faces the following challenges:

- The number of tunable variables in ML algorithms is even larger than in the more traditional statistical techniques.

- ML algorithms are readily available online. Investors can often download open-sourced algorithms from the internet without knowing the algorithm's specific version used in the original result, random seed, and so on. In addition, if one is not careful, different implementations of the same algorithm can have subtle differences that result in different outcomes.

To avoid replicability challenges, we suggest ML investors first spend time building up a robust data and code

---

[10] For additional readings, see, for example, López de Prado (2018); Arnott, Harvey, and Markowitz (2019); Leung et al. (2021).
[11] See Hastie et al. (2009) and Goodfellow et al. (2016) for more discussion on these techniques.
[12] For more details, see Swinkels and Hoogteijling (2022).
[13] See Jessen and Lando (2013) for more discussion on distance to default.
[14] See Harvey, Liu, and Zhu (2016) and Hou, Xue, and Zhang (2020) for more discussion on the replicability crisis in finance.

Exhibit 3. SHAP Value between Input Features and ML Output Predicting Financial Distress

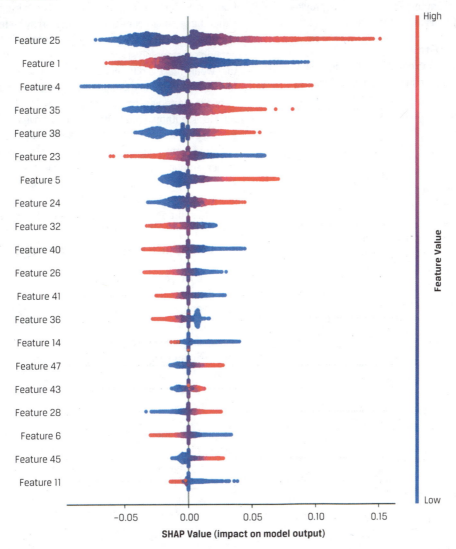

Source: Swinkels and Hoogteijling (2022).

infrastructure to conduct ML research and experiments. This includes, but is not limited to, the following:

- A robust system for code version control, a way to specify and fix all parameters used in the algorithm, including ML algorithm version number, investment universe tested, hyperparameters, feature sets used, and so on

- Documentation of all the tested iterations and hypotheses, including those that failed to show good results (in other words, showing the research graveyards)

Such documentation listed above may not be possible regarding publicly disclosed results, but it should at least be attempted when discussing and verifying results within the same organization.

Lookahead bias/data leakage

Lookahead bias is another commonly known issue for experienced quant investors that applies to ML. An example would be that if quarterly results are available only 40 days after the quarter end, the quarterly data should be used only when available historically[15] and not at the quarter end date.

---

[15]This is called "point-in-time" in the quant investment industry.

Other cases can be more subtle. For example, if one conducts research over a period that includes the tech bubble and its subsequent crash (2000–2002) and the investment universe tested does not include information technology (IT) firms, then it is incumbent upon the investor to provide a sensible reason why IT firms are not included.

Related to lookahead bias and a more general problem directly related to ML is the problem of data leakage. Data leakage occurs when data used in the training set contain information that can be used to infer the prediction, information that would otherwise not be available to the ML model in live production.

Because financial data occur in time series, they are often divided chronologically into training, validation, and testing sets. ML predictive modeling aims to predict outcomes the model has not seen before. One form of data leakage can occur if information that should be in one set ends up in another among the three sets of data (training, validation, and testing). When this occurs, the ML algorithm is evaluated on the data it has seen. In such cases, the results will be overly optimistic and true out-of-sample performance (that is, the live performance of the algorithm) will likely disappoint. This phenomenon is called "leakage in data."

Another type of data leakage is called "leakage in features." Leakage in features occurs when informative features about the prediction outcome are included but would otherwise be unavailable to ML models at production time, even if the information is not in the future. For example, suppose a company's key executive is experiencing serious health issues but the executive has not disclosed this fact to the general public. In that case, including that information in the ML feature set may generate strong backtest performance, but it would be an example of feature leakage.

Various techniques can be applied to minimize the possibility of data leakage. One of the most basic is to introduce a sufficient gap period between training and validation sets and between validation and testing. For example, instead of having validation sets begin immediately after the end of the training set, introduce a time gap of between a few months and a few quarters to ensure complete separation of data. To prevent data leakage, investors applying ML should think carefully about what is available and what is not during the model development and testing phases. In short, common sense still needs to prevail when applying ML algorithms.

Implementation gap

Another possible pitfall to watch out for when deploying ML algorithms in finance is the so-called implementation gap, defined as trading instruments in the backtest that are either impossible or infeasible to trade in live production. An example of an implementation gap is that the ML algorithm generates its outperformance in the backtest mainly from small- or micro-cap stocks. However, in live trading, either these small- or micro-cap stocks may be too costly to trade because of transaction costs or there might not be enough outstanding shares available to own in the scale that would make a difference to the strategy deploying the ML algorithm. As mentioned, implementation affects all quant strategies, not just those using ML algorithms. But ML algorithms tend to have high turnover, increasing trading cost associated with smaller market-cap securities. Similar to small- or micro-cap stocks, another example of an implementation gap is shorting securities in a long–short strategy. In practice, shorting stocks might be impossible or infeasible because of an insufficient quantity of a given stock to short or excessive short borrowing costs.[16]

Explainability and performance attribution

A main criticism of applying machine learning in finance is that the models are difficult to understand. According to Gu et al. (2020, p. 2258), "Machine learning models are often referred to as 'black boxes,' a term that is in some sense a misnomer, as the models are readily inspectable. However, they are complex, and this is the source of their power and opacity. Any exploration of the interaction effect is vexed by vast possibilities for identity and functional forms for interacting predictors."

Machine learning for other applications might not need to be fully explainable at all times; for example, if the ML algorithm suggests wrong video recommendations based on the viewers' past viewing history, the consequences are not catastrophic. However, with billions of investment dollars on the line, asset owners demand managers that use ML-based algorithms explain how the investment decisions are made and how performance can be attributed. In recent years, explainable machine learning has emerged in the financial domain as a focus topic for both practitioners and academics.[17]

The fundamental approach to recent explainable machine learning work is as follows:

1. For each input feature, f_i, in the ML algorithm, fix its value as x. Combine this fixed value for f_i with all other sample data while replacing feature f_i with the value x. Obtain the prediction output.

2. Average the resulting predictions. This is the partial prediction at point x.

---

[16]For additional readings, see, for example, Avramov, Chordia, and Goyal (2006); López de Prado (2018); Hou et al. (2020); Avramov, Cheng, and Metzker (2022).

[17]In addition to the SHAP values discussed in Lundberg and Lee (2017), recent works in the area of explainable machine learning include Li, Turkington, and Yazdani (2020); Li, Simon, and Turkington (2022); and Daul, Jaisson, and Nagy (2022).

3. Now range the fixed value *x* over feature f_i's typical range to plot out the resulting function. This is called the "partial dependence response" to feature f_i.

This response plot, an example of which is illustrated in **Exhibit 4**, can then be decomposed into linear and nonlinear components.

Similarly, one can estimate the pairwise-interaction part of the ML algorithm, computed using joint partial prediction of features f_i and f_j, by subtracting the partial prediction of each feature independently. An example of the pairwise-interaction result is shown in **Exhibit 5**.

Exhibits 3–5 allow ML investors to understand how the input features affect the output prediction. To conduct performance attribution of an ML portfolio and decompose it into the various parts (linear, interaction, and nonlinear), one can extract the partial dependence responses and form portfolios from them. With this approach, one can get return attribution, as shown in **Exhibit 6**.

Sample ML Applications in Finance

We have seen the common pitfalls when applying ML to finance and the strategies to mitigate them. Let us now look at examples of ML applied to financial investing.[18]

Predicting Cross-Sectional Stock Returns

In this section, we discuss specifically using ML to predict cross-sectional stock returns.

Investment problem

Perhaps the most obvious application of ML to financial investments is to directly use ML to predict whether each security's price is expected to rise or fall and whether to buy or sell those securities. Numerous practitioners and academics have applied ML algorithms to this prediction task.[19]

The ML algorithms used in this problem are set up to compare cross-sectional stock returns. That is, we are interested in finding the relative returns of securities in our investment universe rather than their absolute returns.[20] The ML algorithms make stock selection decisions rather than country/industry timing and allocation decisions. Stock selection is an easier problem than the timing and allocation problem, because the algorithms have more data to work with.[21]

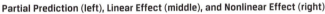

Exhibit 4. Linear and Nonlinear Decomposition of an ML Algorithm's Output to Input Feature f_i

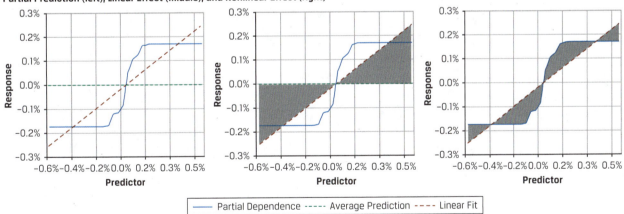

Source: Li, Turkington, and Yazdani (2020).

---

[18]For more general applications of ML to finance, see López de Prado (2019).

[19]This problem has been studied in numerous recent papers—for example, Abe and Nakayama (2018); Rasekhschaffe and Jones (2019); Gu et al. (2020); Choi, Jiang, and Zhang (2022); Hanauer and Kalsbach (2022).

[20]In addition to cross-sectional returns, Gu et al. (2020) also study the time-series problem.

[21]However, when compared with other fields, the amount of data here is still miniscule, as noted before.

Exhibit 5. Example of the Pairwise-Interaction Effect

Source: Li, Simon, and Turkington (2022).

Exhibit 6. Example ML Portfolio Return Attribution

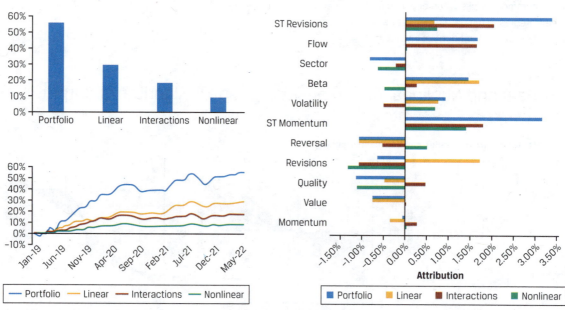

Source: Robeco.

Methodology

This problem is set up with the following three major components:

1. Investment universe: US, international, emerging market, and so on

2. ML algorithms: (boosted) trees/random forests, neural networks with *l* layers, and so on, and ensembles thereof

3. Feature set: typical financial metrics that are used in linear models, such as various price ratios (value), profitability (quality), and past returns (momentum)

Note that for Item 3, by using a very limited feature set, the ML investor is essentially applying her domain knowledge and imposing a structure on the ML algorithm to counter the limited data challenge discussed in the previous section.

Results

There are five consistent results that various practitioner and academic studies have found. First and foremost, there is a statistically significant and economically meaningful outperformance of ML algorithm prediction versus the traditional linear approach. For example, in forming a long–short decile spread portfolio from (four-layer) neural network–generated stock return prediction, a well-known study in equity return prediction (Gu et al. 2020) found that the strategy has an annualized out-of-sample Sharpe ratio of 1.35 under value weighting and 2.45 under equal weighting. For comparison, the same portfolio constructed from ordinary least squares (OLS) prediction with the same input features produced a Sharpe ratio of 0.61 and 0.83 for value weighting and equal weighting, respectively. **Exhibit 7** shows the value-weighting results.

Exhibit 7. Out-of-Sample Performance of Benchmark OLS Portfolio vs. Various ML Portfolios, Value Weighting

	OLS-3+H				PLS				PCR			
	Pred.	Avg.	Std. Dev.	Sharpe Ratio	Pred.	Avg.	Std. Dev.	Sharpe Ratio	Pred.	Avg.	Std. Dev.	Sharpe Ratio
Low (L)	−0.17	0.40	5.90	0.24	−0.83	0.29	5.31	0.19	−0.68	0.03	5.98	0.02
2	0.17	0.58	4.65	0.43	−0.21	0.55	4.96	0.38	−0.11	0.42	5.25	0.28
3	0.35	0.60	4.43	0.47	0.12	0.64	4.63	0.48	0.19	0.53	4.94	0.37
4	0.49	0.71	4.32	0.57	0.38	0.78	4.30	0.63	0.42	0.68	4.64	0.51
5	0.62	0.79	4.57	0.60	0.61	0.77	4.53	0.59	0.62	0.81	4.66	0.60
6	0.75	0.92	5.03	0.63	0.84	0.88	4.78	0.64	0.81	0.81	4.58	0.61
7	0.88	0.85	5.18	0.57	1.06	0.92	4.89	0.65	1.01	0.87	4.72	0.64
8	1.02	0.86	5.29	0.56	1.32	0.92	5.14	0.62	1.23	1.01	4.77	0.73
9	1.21	1.18	5.47	0.75	1.66	1.15	5.24	0.76	1.52	1.20	4.88	0.86
High (H)	1.51	1.34	5.88	0.79	2.25	1.30	5.85	0.77	2.02	1.25	5.60	0.77
H − L	1.67	0.94	5.33	0.61	3.09	1.02	4.88	0.72	2.70	1.22	4.82	0.88

	ENet+H				GLM+H				RF			
	Pred	Avg	Std. Dev.	Sharpe Ratio	Pred	Avg	Std. Dev.	Sharpe Ratio	Pred	Avg	Std. Dev.	Sharpe Ratio
Low (L)	−0.04	0.24	5.44	0.15	−0.47	0.08	5.65	0.05	0.29	−0.09	6.00	−0.05
2	0.27	0.56	4.84	0.40	0.01	0.49	4.80	0.35	0.44	0.38	5.02	0.27
3	0.44	0.53	4.50	0.40	0.29	0.65	4.52	0.50	0.53	0.64	4.70	0.48
4	0.59	0.72	4.11	0.61	0.50	0.72	4.59	0.55	0.60	0.60	4.56	0.46
5	0.73	0.72	4.42	0.57	0.68	0.70	4.55	0.53	0.67	0.57	4.51	0.44
6	0.87	0.85	4.60	0.64	0.84	0.84	4.53	0.65	0.73	0.64	4.54	0.49
7	1.01	0.87	4.75	0.64	1.00	0.86	4.82	0.62	0.80	0.67	4.65	0.50
8	1.16	0.88	5.20	0.59	1.18	0.87	5.18	0.58	0.87	1.00	4.91	0.71
9	1.36	0.80	5.61	0.50	1.40	1.04	5.44	0.66	0.96	1.23	5.59	0.76
High (H)	1.66	0.84	6.76	0.43	1.81	1.14	6.33	0.62	1.12	1.53	7.27	0.73
H − L	1.70	0.60	5.37	0.39	2.27	1.06	4.79	0.76	0.83	1.62	5.75	0.98

(continued)

Exhibit 7. Out-of-Sample Performance of Benchmark OLS Portfolio vs. Various ML Portfolios, Value Weighting (*continued*)

	GBRT+H				NN1				NN2			
	Pred	Avg	Std. Dev.	Sharpe Ratio	Pred	Avg	Std. Dev.	Sharpe Ratio	Pred	Avg	Std. Dev.	Sharpe Ratio
Low (L)	−0.45	0.18	5.60	0.11	−0.38	−0.29	7.02	−0.14	−0.23	−0.54	7.83	−0.24
2	−0.16	0.49	4.93	0.35	0.16	0.41	5.89	0.24	0.21	0.36	6.08	0.20
3	0.02	0.59	4.75	0.43	0.44	0.51	5.07	0.35	0.44	0.65	5.07	0.44
4	0.17	0.63	4.68	0.46	0.64	0.70	4.56	0.53	0.59	0.73	4.53	0.56
5	0.34	0.57	4.70	0.42	0.80	0.77	4.37	0.61	0.72	0.81	4.38	0.64
6	0.46	0.77	4.48	0.59	0.95	0.78	4.39	0.62	0.84	0.84	4.51	0.65
7	0.59	0.52	4.73	0.38	1.11	0.81	4.40	0.64	0.97	0.95	4.61	0.71
8	0.72	0.72	4.92	0.51	1.31	0.75	4.86	0.54	1.13	0.93	5.09	0.63
9	0.88	0.99	5.19	0.66	1.58	0.96	5.22	0.64	1.37	1.04	5.69	0.63
High (H)	1.11	1.17	5.88	0.69	2.19	1.52	6.79	0.77	1.99	1.38	6.98	0.69
H − L	1.56	0.99	4.22	0.81	2.57	1.81	5.34	1.17	2.22	1.92	5.75	1.16

	NN3				NN4				NN5			
	Pred	Avg	Std. Dev.	Sharpe Ratio	Pred	Avg	Std. Dev.	Sharpe Ratio	Pred	Avg	Std. Dev.	Sharpe Ratio
Low (L)	−0.03	−0.43	7.73	−0.19	−0.12	−0.52	7.69	−0.23	−0.23	−0.51	7.69	−0.23
2	0.34	0.30	6.38	0.16	0.30	0.33	6.16	0.19	0.23	0.31	6.10	0.17
3	0.51	0.57	5.27	0.37	0.50	0.42	5.18	0.28	0.45	0.54	5.02	0.37
4	0.63	0.66	4.69	0.49	0.62	0.60	4.51	0.46	0.60	0.67	4.47	0.52
5	0.71	0.69	4.41	0.55	0.72	0.69	4.26	0.56	0.73	0.77	4.32	0.62
6	0.79	0.76	4.46	0.59	0.81	0.84	4.46	0.65	0.85	0.86	4.35	0.68
7	0.88	0.99	4.77	0.72	0.90	0.93	4.56	0.70	0.96	0.88	4.76	0.64
8	1.00	1.09	5.47	0.69	1.03	1.08	5.13	0.73	1.11	0.94	5.17	0.63
9	1.21	1.25	5.94	0.73	1.23	1.26	5.93	0.74	1.34	1.02	6.02	0.58
High (H)	1.83	1.69	7.29	0.80	1.89	1.75	7.51	0.81	1.99	1.46	7.40	0.68
H − L	1.86	2.12	6.13	1.20	2.01	2.26	5.80	1.35	2.22	1.97	5.93	1.15

Notes: OLS-3+H is ordinary least squares that preselect size, book-to-market, and momentum using Huber loss rather than the standard l2 loss. PLS is partial least squares. PCR ENet+H, GLM+H, RF, GBRT+H, and NN1 to NN5 are neural networks with one to five hidden layers.

Source: Gu et al. (2020).

The second consistent result is that what drives the outperformance of ML-based prediction versus that of linear models is that ML algorithms not only are limited to linear combinations of feature sets but can formulate higher-order functional dependencies, such as nonlinearity and interaction. To test whether higher-order effects can contribute to security prediction, one can compare linear machine learning models (for example, LASSO and RIDGE) with models that consider nonlinear and complex interaction effects (such as trees and neural networks). Investors at Robeco have found that higher-order machine learning models outperform their simpler linear competitors. The outperformance of higher-order machine learning models was also confirmed by academics,[22] as evident from Exhibit 7.

Between nonlinearity and interactions, interactions have the greater impact on model performance. This also can be seen in Exhibit 7, where the performance of the generalized linear model with Huber loss (GLM+H) is inferior to those models that consider interaction, boosted trees, and neural networks.

Third, ML investors have found that the features that most determine prediction outcomes are remarkably consistent regardless of the specific ML algorithms used. This is somewhat of a surprise because the various ML algorithms, such as boosted trees and neural networks, use dissimilar approaches to arrive at their outcomes. However, the similar importance assigned to certain input features confirms that these are salient characteristics that drive cross-sectional stock returns. From Robeco's own experience and various published studies, the characteristics that dominate cross-sectional returns are found to be short-term reversals, stock and sector return momentum, return volatility, and firm size.

Fourth, simple ML algorithms outperform more complicated ML algorithms. This result is very likely because, since there are not much data to train on, the simpler models, due to their parsimonious nature, are less likely to overfit and thereby perform better out of sample. We confirm this observation from Exhibit 7, where the best out-of-sample Sharpe ratio is achieved by a neural network with four hidden layers.

Fifth, the more data there are, the better the ML prediction algorithm performs. This is fundamental to the nature of ML algorithms, as observed by Halevy et al. (2009) for general machine learning applications and confirmed by Choi, Jiang, and Zhang (2022) in a financial context.

Predicting Stock Crashes

In this section, we discuss the example of using ML to predict stock crashes.

Investment problem

Rather than predicting the rank order of future returns, another application for ML algorithms may simply be to predict the worst-performing stocks—that is, those most likely to crash.[23] The results of this prediction can be applied in such strategies as conservative equities,[24] where the securities most likely to crash are excluded from the investment universe. That is, win by not losing.

Methodology

A crash event for equities is defined as a significant drop in a stock's price relative to peers; thus, it is idiosyncratic rather than systematic when a group of stocks or the market crashes. The ML prediction is set up as follows:

1. Investment universe: US, international, emerging market, and so on
2. ML algorithms: logistic regression, random forest, gradient boosted tree, and ensemble of the three
3. Feature set: various financial distress indicators—such as distance to default, volatility, and market beta—in addition to traditional fundamental financial metrics

As one can see, the problem setup is very similar to that of cross-sectional stock return prediction. The main differences are the objective function of the ML algorithm (ML prediction goal) and the input feature set (feature engineering). Care should be taken in determining both components to ensure the prediction algorithm solves the stated problem and performs well out of sample.

Results

The performance of the portfolio of stocks with the highest distress probability versus that of the market is shown in **Exhibit 8**. We see that the performance of the ML algorithm is greater than that obtained using traditional approaches for both developed and emerging markets.

Looking at the sector composition of the likely distressed stocks, shown in **Exhibit 9**, we see that the ML algorithm choices are reasonable, as technology stocks dominated during the bursting of the dot-com bubble in the early 2000s and financial stocks dominated during the Global Financial Crisis of 2008. Overall, we see a wide sector dispersion for the likely distressed stocks, indicating that the prediction return is mostly from stock selection rather than sector allocation.

---

[22]For more discussion, see Choi, Jiang, and Zhang (2022) and Gu et al. (2020).

[23]This ML prediction task is studied in Swinkels and Hoogteijling (2022).

[24]Also called low-volatility equity, among other names.

Exhibit 8. Market Return vs. Return of a Portfolio Consisting of Likely Distressed Stocks, Estimated under Various Prediction Approaches

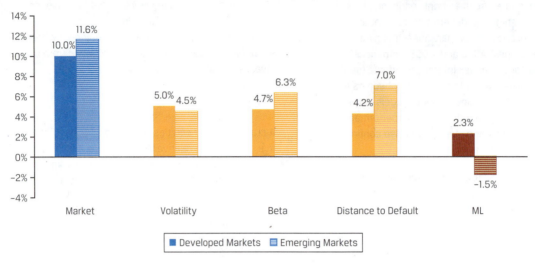

Source: Swinkels and Hoogteijling (2022).

Exhibit 9. Sector Composition of the ML-Predicted Likely Distressed Stocks

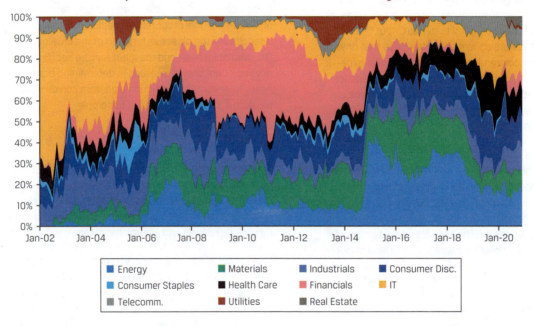

Source: Swinkels and Hoogteijling (2022).

Predicting Fundamental Variables

In this section, we discuss the example of using ML to predict company fundamentals.

Investment problem

Predicting stock returns is notoriously hard. As mentioned previously, there are potentially thousands of variables (dimensions) that can affect a stock's performance—investor sentiment, path dependency, and so on. The various factors, endogenous and exogenous, ultimately get translated into only a one-dimensional response—higher return (up) or lower return (down). An easier task may be to use ML algorithms to predict company fundamentals, such as return on assets and corporate earnings. Company fundamentals also have the additional beneficial characteristic of being more stable than stock returns, making them better suited for ML predictions. Because of these reasons, company fundamentals prediction is another popular application of ML algorithms in the financial domain. In this section, we look at the findings from a popular study[25] where ML algorithm-predicted earnings forecasts are compared with those from more traditional approaches.

Methodology

The investment universe is the US stock market, excluding the financial and utility sectors. The study was conducted over the period 1975–2019.

Six different ML models were tested: three linear ML models (OLS, LASSO, and ridge regression) and three nonlinear ML models (random forest, gradient boosting regression, and neural networks). Six traditional models were used as a benchmark to compare against ML models: random walk, autoregressive model, models from Hou, van Dijk, and Zhang (2012; HVZ) and So (2013; SO), the earnings persistence model, and the residual income model. Various ensembles of these models were also tested.

The feature set is composed of 28 major financial statement line items and their first-order differences. So, there are 56 features in total.

Results

The results are shown in **Exhibit 10**. Consistent with the results for cross-sectional stock returns, Cao and You (2021) found that machine learning models give more accurate earnings forecasts. The linear ML models are more accurate than the benchmark traditional models (by about 6%), and the nonlinear ML models are more accurate than the linear ML models (by about 1%–3% on top of the linear model). Not only are the ML models more accurate; the traditional models autoregression, HVZ, SO, earnings persistence, and residual income were not more accurate than the naive random walk model. The ensemble models, traditional or machine learned, were more accurate than the individual models alone, with the order of accuracy preserved: ML ensemble beating traditional methods, ensemble and nonlinear ML ensemble beating linear ML ensemble.

The ML models' better performance can be attributed to the following:

- They are learning economically meaningful predictors of future earnings. One can make this conclusion by examining feature importance through such tools as Shapley value.

- The nonlinearity and interaction effects are useful in further refining the accuracy of forward earnings predictions, as evidenced by the higher performance of nonlinear ML models compared with linear ML models.

The takeaway from this study is the same as in the previous two examples. That is, ML models can provide value on top of traditional models (especially due to nonlinearity and interaction components), and ensembling is one of the closest things to a free lunch in ML, much like diversification for investing.

NLP in Multiple Languages

So far, we have discussed problems where ML algorithms are used for prediction. Another major category for ML applications is textual language reading, understanding, and analysis, which is called "natural language processing" (NLP). Modern NLP techniques use neural networks to achieve the great capability improvements they have made in recent years. NLP is discussed in other chapters of this book, so we will not discuss the techniques extensively here, but we will discuss one NLP application that can be interesting for practitioners.

Investment problem

Investing is a global business, and much of the relevant information for security returns is written in the local language. In general, a global portfolio may invest in 20–30 different countries,[26] while a typical investor may understand only two or three languages, if that. This fact presents a problem, but fortunately, it is a problem that we can attempt to solve through ML algorithms.

From the perspective of Western investors, one language of interest is Chinese. The Chinese A-share market is both large and liquid. But understanding Chinese texts on A-share investing can be challenging because Chinese is not an alphabetical language and it follows very different grammatical constructs than English. In addition, since retail investors dominate the Chinese A-share market,[27] a subculture of investment slang has developed, where terms used are often not standard Chinese, thereby compounding the problem for investors without a strong local language understanding.

In a paper by Chen, Lee, and Mussalli (2020), the authors applied ML-based NLP techniques to try to understand investment slang written in Mandarin Chinese by retail investors in online stock discussion forums. We discuss the results of that paper here.

---

[25] For more details, see Cao and You (2021). The problem of ML company fundamentals prediction was also examined in Alberg and Lipton (2017).

[26] The MSCI All Country World Index (ACWI) covers stocks from 26 countries.

[27] Some studies have concluded that in the A-share market, retail trading volume can be up to 80% of the total. In recent years, institutional market trading has proportionally increased as the Chinese market matures.

Exhibit 10. Prediction Accuracy Results from Cao and You (2021)

| | Mean Absolute Forecast Errors | | | | Median Absolute Forecast Errors | | | |
| | | Comparison with RW | | | | Comparison with RW | | |
	Average	DIFF	t-Stat	%DIFF	Average	DIFF	t-Stat	%DIFF
Benchmark model								
RW	0.0764				0.0309			
Extant models								
AR	0.0755	−0.0009	−2.51	−1.15%	0.0308	−0.0001	−0.22	−0.24%
HVZ	0.0743	−0.0022	−3.63	−2.82%	0.0311	0.0002	0.64	0.76%
EP	0.0742	−0.0022	−2.79	−2.85%	0.0313	0.0004	1.02	1.42%
RI	0.0741	−0.0023	−3.15	−3.07%	0.0311	0.0002	0.66	0.74%
SO	0.0870	0.0105	5.19	13.78%	0.0347	0.0039	5.50	12.56%
Linear machine learning models								
OLS	0.0720	−0.0045	−5.04	−5.83%	0.0306	−0.0002	−0.60	−0.73%
LASSO	0.0716	−0.0048	−5.32	−6.31%	0.0304	−0.0004	−1.11	−1.43%
Ridge	0.0718	−0.0047	−5.19	−6.11%	0.0305	−0.0003	−0.87	−1.08%
Nonlinear machine learning models								
RF	0.0698	−0.0066	−6.44	−8.64%	0.0296	−0.0012	−3.10	−3.97%
GBR	0.0697	−0.0068	−6.08	−8.86%	0.0292	−0.0016	−4.23	−5.34%
ANN	0.0713	−0.0051	−5.38	−6.67%	0.0310	0.0001	0.24	0.38%
Composite models								
COMP_EXT	0.0737	−0.0027	−3.89	−3.58%	0.0311	0.0002	0.56	0.66%
COMP_LR	0.0717	−0.0047	−5.25	−6.16%	0.0305	−0.0004	−1.02	−1.33%
COMP_NL	0.0689	−0.0075	−6.99	−9.87%	0.0292	−0.0017	−3.92	−5.55%
COMP_ML	0.0693	−0.0071	−7.12	−9.35%	0.0294	−0.0015	−3.75	−4.81%

Notes: RW stands for random walk. AR is the autoregressive model. HVZ is the model from Hou et al. (2012). SO is the model from So (2013). EP is the earnings persistence model. RI is the residual income model. RF stands for random forests. GBR stands for gradient boost regression. ANN stands for artificial neural networks. COMP_EXT is an ensemble of traditional models. COMP_LR is an ensemble of linear ML models. COMP_NL is an ensemble of nonlinear ML models. COMP_ML is an ensemble of all ML models.

Source: Cao and You (2021).

Methodology

1. Download and process investment blogs actively participated in by Chinese A-share retail investors.
2. Apply embedding-based NLP techniques and train on the downloaded investment blogs.
3. Starting with standard Chinese sentiment dictionaries, look for words surrounding these standard Chinese sentiment words. By the construct of the embedding models, these surrounding words often have the same contextual meaning as the words in the standard sentiment dictionaries, whether they are standard Chinese or slang. An example of this is shown in **Exhibit 11**.

Results

Using this technique, we can detect investment words used in standard Chinese and the slang used by retail investors. In Exhibit 11, the red dot illustrates the Chinese word for "central bank." The column on the right side of Exhibit 11 shows the words closest to this word, and the closest is the word that translates to "central mother" in Chinese. This is a slang word often used by Chinese retail investors as a substitute for the word "central bank" because central banks often take actions to calm down market tantrums, much like a mother does to her children when they have tantrums.

The embedded words also exhibit the same embedded word vector arithmetic made famous by the following example (see Mikolov, Yih, and Zweig 2013): King – Man + Woman ≈ Queen. For example, **Exhibit 12** shows the following embedded Chinese word relationship: Floating red – Rise + Fall ≈ Floating green.[28]

Exhibit 11. Embedded Chinese Words from A-Share Investor Blogs Projected onto a 3-D Space

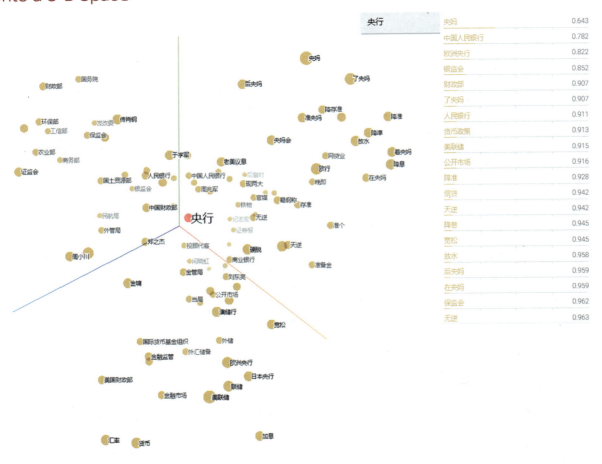

Source: Chen et al. (2020).

Exhibit 12. Chinese Word Embedding Still Preserves Vector Arithmetic

$$飘红 - 涨 + 跌 ≈ 飘绿$$

Source: Chen et al. (2020).

---

[28]In contrast to most of the world's markets, in the Chinese stock market, gains are colored red whereas losses are colored green.

This study illustrates that ML techniques not only are useful for numerical tasks of results prediction but can also be useful in other tasks, such as foreign language understanding.

Conclusion

In this chapter, we gave an overview of how ML can be applied in financial investing. Because there is a lot of excitement around the promise of ML for finance, we began the chapter with a discussion on how the financial market is different from other domains in which ML has made tremendous strides in recent years and how it would serve the financial ML practitioner to not get carried away by the hype. Applying ML to the financial market is different from applying ML in other domains in that the financial market does not have as much data, the market is nonstationary, the market can often behave irrationally because human investor emotions are often a big driver of market returns, and so on. Given these differences, we discussed several common pitfalls and potential mitigation strategies when applying machine learning to financial investing.

In the second half of the chapter, we discussed several recent studies that have applied ML techniques to investment problems. Common findings of these studies are as follows:

- ML techniques can deliver performance above and beyond traditional approaches if applied to the right problem.
- The source of ML algorithms' outperformance includes the ability to consider nonlinear and interaction effects among the input features.
- Ensembling of ML algorithms often delivers better performance than what individual ML algorithms can achieve.

We showed that in addition to predicting numerical results, ML could also help investors in other tasks, such as sentiment analysis or foreign language understanding. Of course, the applications discussed here are only a small subset of what ML can do in the financial domain. Other possible tasks include data cleaning, fraud detection, credit scoring, and trading optimization.

Machine learning is a powerful set of tools for investors, and we are just at the beginning of the journey of applying ML to the investment domain. Like all techniques, machine learning is powerful only if applied to the right problems and if practitioners know the technique's limits. Having said that, we believe one can expect to see a lot more innovation and improved results coming out of this space going forward.

References

Abe, M., and H. Nakayama. 2018. "Deep Learning for Forecasting Stock Returns in the Cross-Section." In *Advances in Knowledge Discovery and Data Mining*, edited by D. Phung, V. Tseng, G. Webb, B. Ho, M. Ganji, and L. Rashidi, 273–84. Berlin: Springer Cham.

Alberg, J., and Z. Lipton. 2017. "Improving Factor-Based Quantitative Investing by Forecasting Company Fundamentals." Cornell University, arXiv:1711.04837 (13 November). https://arxiv.org/abs/1711.04837.

Arnott, R., C. Harvey, and H. Markowitz. 2019. "A Backtesting Protocol in the Era of Machine Learning." *Journal of Financial Data Science* 1 (1): 64–74.

Avramov, D., S. Cheng, and L. Metzker. 2022. "Machine Learning vs. Economic Restrictions: Evidence from Stock Return Predictability." *Management Science* (29 June).

Avramov, D., T. Chordia, and A. Goyal. 2006. "Liquidity and Autocorrelations in Individual Stock Returns." *Journal of Finance* 61 (5): 2365–94.

Birge, J., and Y. Zhang. 2018. "Risk Factors That Explain Stock Returns: A Non-Linear Factor Pricing Model." Working paper (9 August).

Cao, K., and H. You. 2021. "Fundamental Analysis via Machine Learning." Emerging Finance and Financial Practices eJournal.

Cao, Larry. 2018. "Artificial Intelligence, Machine Learning, and Deep Learning: A Primer." *Enterprising Investor* (blog; 13 February). https://blogs.cfainstitute.org/investor/2018/02/13/artificial-intelligence-machine-learning-and-deep-learning-in-investment-management-a-primer/.

Chen, M., J. Lee, and G. Mussalli. 2020. "Teaching Machines to Understand Chinese Investment Slang." *Journal of Financial Data Science* 2 (1): 116–25.

Choi, D., W. Jiang, and C. Zhang. 2022. "Alpha Go Everywhere: Machine Learning and International Stock Returns." Working paper (29 November). Available at https://papers.ssrn.com/sol3/papers.cfm?abstract_id=3489679.

Columbus, Louis. 2020. "The State of AI Adoption In Financial Services." *Forbes* (31 October). www.forbes.com/sites/louiscolumbus/2020/10/31/the-state-of-ai-adoption-in-financial-services/?sh=1a4f7be62aac.

Daul, S., T. Jaisson, and A. Nagy. 2022. "Performance Attribution of Machine Learning Methods for Stock Returns Prediction." *Journal of Finance and Data Science* 8 (November): 86–104.

Fama, E., and K. French. 1993. "Common Risk Factors in the Returns on Stocks and Bonds." *Journal of Financial Economics* 33 (1): 3–56.

Goodfellow, I., Y. Bengio, and A. Courville. 2016. *Deep Learning*. Cambridge, MA: MIT Press.

Grinold, R., and R. Kahn. 1999. *Active Portfolio Management: A Quantitative Approach for Producing Superior Returns and Controlling Risk*. New York: McGraw Hill.

Gu, S., B. Kelly, and D. Xiu. 2020. "Empirical Asset Pricing via Machine Learning." *Review of Financial Studies* 33 (5): 2223–73.

Halevy, A., P. Norvig, and F. Pereira. 2009. "The Unreasonable Effectiveness of Data." *IEEE Intelligent Systems* 24 (2): 8–12.

Hanauer, M., and T. Kalsbach. 2022. "Machine Learning and the Cross-Section of Emerging Market Stock Returns." Working paper (5 December).

Harvey, C., Y. Liu, and H. Zhu. 2016. "... and the Cross-Section of Expected Returns." *Review of Financial Studies* 29 (1): 5-68.

Hastie, T., R. Tibshirani, and J. Friedman. 2009. *The Elements of Statistical Learning: Data Mining, Inference, and Prediction*, 2nd ed. New York: Springer.

Hou, K., M. van Dijk, and Y. Zhang. 2012. "The Implied Cost of Capital: A New Approach." *Journal of Accounting and Economics* 53 (3): 504–26.

Hou, K., C. Xue, and L. Zhang. 2020. "Replicating Anomalies." *Review of Financial Studies* 33 (5): 2019–133.

Jessen, C., and D. Lando. 2013. "Robustness of Distance-to-Default." 26th Australasian Finance and Banking Conference 2013 (16 August).

Leippold, M., Q. Wang, and W. Zhou. 2022. "Machine Learning in the Chinese Stock Market." *Journal of Financial Economics* 145 (2): 64–82.

Leung, E., H. Lohre, D. Mischlich, Y. Shea, and M. Stroh. 2021. "The Promises and Pitfalls of Machine Learning for Predicting Stock Returns." *Journal of Financial Data Science* 3 (2): 21–50.

Li, Y., Z. Simon, and D. Turkington. 2022. "Investable and Interpretable Machine Learning for Equities." *Journal of Financial Data Science* 4 (1): 54–74.

Li, Y., D. Turkington, and A. Yazdani. 2020. "Beyond the Black Box: An Intuitive Approach to Investment Prediction with Machine Learning." *Journal of Financial Data Science* 2 (1): 61–75.

Lo, A., D. Repin, and B. Steenbarger. 2005. "Greed and Fear in Financial Markets: A Clinical Study of Day-Traders." NBER Working Paper No. w11243.

López de Prado, M. 2018. "The 10 Reasons Most Machine Learning Funds Fail." *Journal of Portfolio Management* 44 (6): 120–33.

López de Prado, M. 2019. "Ten Applications of Financial Machine Learning." Working paper (22 September).

Lundberg, S., and S. Lee. 2017. "A Unified Approach to Interpreting Model Predictions." NIPS 17: Proceedings of the 31st Conference on Neural Information Processing Systems: 4768–77.

McLean, R., and J. Pontiff. 2016. "Does Academic Research Destroy Stock Return Predictability?" *Journal of Finance* 71 (1): 5–32.

Mikolov, T., W. Yih, and G. Zweig. 2013. "Linguistic Regularities in Continuous Space Word Representations." Proceedings of NAACL-HLT 2013: 746–51. www.aclweb.org/anthology/N13-1090.pdf.

Nadeem, Monisa. 2018. "Clearing the Confusion: AI vs. Machine Learning vs. Deep Learning." Global Tech Council (25 November). www.globaltechcouncil.org/artificial-intelligence/clearing-the-confusion-ai-vs-machine-learning-vs-deep-learning/.

Rasekhschaffe, K., and R. Jones. 2019. "Machine Learning for Stock Selection." *Financial Analysts Journal* 75 (3): 70-88.

So, E. 2013. "A New Approach to Predicting Analyst Forecast Errors: Do Investors Overweight Analyst Forecasts?" *Journal of Financial Economics* 108 (3): 615–40.

Swinkels, L., and T. Hoogteijling. 2022. "Forecasting Stock Crash Risk with Machine Learning." White paper, Robeco.

Tobek, O., and M. Hronec. 2021. "Does It Pay to Follow Anomalies Research? Machine Learning Approach with International Evidence." *Journal of Financial Markets* 56 (November).

2. ALTERNATIVE DATA AND AI IN INVESTMENT RESEARCH

Ingrid Tierens, PhD, CFA
Managing Director, Goldman Sachs Global Investment Research

Dan Duggan, PhD
Vice President, Goldman Sachs Global Investment Research

Artificial Intelligence (AI) and alternative data are not new concepts in investment research or finance. AI can be broadly defined as using computers to mimic human problem solving. Alternative data can be broadly defined as any data in a nonstructured format. The arrival of computers in financial firms and the arrival of nonstructured data in digital format meant that entrepreneurial finance professionals started to see opportunities to address financial use cases by leveraging these tools instead of primarily relying on the human brain, helped by pen, paper, an abacus, or a calculator. If you define investment decision making as trying to make objective sense of a wide spectrum of diverse data to allocate capital, the appeal of AI and alternative data to improve investment decisions should not come as a surprise. Although early attempts to codify human decision making may not meet today's definition of AI and alternative data, because they may have been either too ambitious or have had a marginal impact by today's standards, they paved the way for an innovation cycle that is by now well under way in the financial services industry, well past its early adoption cycle, and affecting all facets of how financial firms conduct their business. From enhancing investment insights to constructing better portfolios, optimizing trading decisions, streamlining client service, reducing operational issues, better aligning products to client needs, and extracting better business intelligence insights, AI and alternative data are leaving their fingerprints everywhere.

Embedding AI and alternative data into the day-to-day activities of an investment analyst is not mission impossible. It can be compared with executing a New Year's resolution, such as learning a new language, getting in better shape, or running your first marathon. Resolutions become reality through commitment, persistence, and resilience. The journey of Goldman Sachs Global Investment Research (GIR) over the past five-plus years illustrates that you do not need expensive "equipment" (i.e., an unlimited budget) and an army of "coaches with name recognition" (i.e., hard-to-find talent) to make a difference. Hard work by open-minded people who collectively buy into the mission, bring different components to the table, learn from each other, and collaborate to execute on the joint mission to produce leading-edge investment insights will lead to a noticeable impact. This chapter demonstrates that you can start small and that investment analysts are not bystanders but play a crucial role in making AI and alternative data part of their lexicon and research process.

Where Can AI and Alternative Data Be Additive? Investment Research Use Cases

Alternative data and AI, including machine learning (ML) and natural language processing (NLP), are not an end in and of themselves but are additional tools in the research toolkit to create differentiated investment insights. The key to their use in investment research is appreciating that alternative data and AI do not define the investment thesis but, instead, help prove or disprove it. AI and nontraditional data can be additive across the spectrum of investment strategies, as long as the AI and data efforts are aligned with a particular strategy. Comparing and contrasting systematic and fundamental investment strategies can be enlightening in this regard.

At first glance, AI and alternative data sound as if they may only provide an advantage to systematic strategies because of their quantitative nature. Within the AI and alternative data spectrum, however, there are many niche datasets and techniques that may provide added value for fundamental strategies that can successfully incorporate data and data science expertise in their investment process. Let us take a closer look at use cases for each strategy.

For a systematic strategy where breadth matters more than depth, datasets and data analysis techniques need to be applicable across many securities. Therefore, it should not come as a surprise that systematic managers focus their time and effort more on alternative datasets or techniques that can be applied to a large investment universe. Factors extracted from text have been added to many quant investment processes, because NLP analysis can be easily repeated across company filings, news articles, and other documents that are available for large sets of securities. In addition, sophisticated econometric techniques can be helpful to convert individual alphas into more solid multifactor alphas and, in turn, into more robust portfolios. But even within systematic strategies, AI and alternative data use may differ significantly, especially when the investment horizon is taken into account. For example, intraday news sentiment indicators may be helpful for high-frequency trading strategies, but relatively less value adding for an investment professional focused on an investment horizon spanning weeks or months, even if the signals can be applied to thousands of securities.

For a fundamental strategy where depth matters more than breadth, a portfolio manager or analyst will go deep into specific use cases and will put a higher premium on precision than a systematic manager dealing with a diversified portfolio and for whom each holding has less of an impact on performance. Moreover, niche datasets can be more useful for fundamental analysts or portfolio managers to complement the information set they draw from, thus providing a fuller mosaic view. For example, consumer sentiment via social media, brick-and-mortar foot traffic, and even consumer search trends around product cycles offer different angles to create a more complete picture for consumer-focused sectors. And while sectors with more digital presence—for example, retail and technology, media, and telecommunications—were early targets for AI and alternative data applications, GIR has seen many use cases in both single-stock and macro research that may not seem like obvious candidates for successful AI or alternative data use. Examples include leveraging app downloads in the medical device space and localized market share analysis for membership in managed care organizations or even quarry production.

Which Alternative Data Should I Pay Attention To? Data Sourcing in a World of Overwhelming Data Supply

Keeping up with the supply of alternative and big data is a Herculean task. There is an overabundance of providers because the barriers to entry in this space have become very low. Providers of "traditional" data tend to be established organizations that typically offer curated datasets and have many years of experience with data due diligence and support. With alternative data, the onus of due diligence has shifted from the data producer more to the data consumer. There are clear parallels with the production and consumption of news, where the due diligence and fact checking have similarly shifted from the news provider more to the news consumer.

The investment needed to bring onboard vendors, ingest data, and test the data can outweigh the benefits of a new data source, and the licensing costs can further tip the scale. Given how time consuming the due diligence process can be, the data acquisition efforts within GIR are demand driven. Research analysts as subject matter experts in their field typically have a good idea of the type of data that may be useful for the investment thesis they are pursuing. While they may not have locked in a specific data source, may not be aware of the most scalable way to obtain the data, or may not be comfortable manipulating unstructured data, working backwards from their use case and initial data ideas provides a good starting point. Ideas for nontraditional data can emerge when analysts question whether they have the full mosaic of data to assess their thesis and whether the datasets they have used so far continue to provide a comprehensive picture.

In addition, new data sources do not necessarily need to offer orthogonal information but can also be value adding if they offer legacy data in a more scalable and more timely fashion. The questions that today's analysts are trying to answer are, in essence, no different from what their predecessors tried to address, such as the following: How is a new product launch perceived by the marketplace? What do price trends and inventories look like? How do changing demographics affect the economy? What is different or alternative is that the analyst no longer needs to visit stores, run in-person surveys, or pursue other manual paths to get answers. A continually increasing amount of relevant information is now available in digital format on a much larger scale and in a timelier fashion or more frequently than was the case in the past. The qualifier "alternative" in alternative data may be a bit of a misnomer from that perspective.

Some investment managers who are very data driven have a separate, dedicated data-scouting effort, possibly an extension of the team that interacts with market data vendors and brokers to surface new and novel datasets. GIR has not gone down that path, because it has found that having the subject matter experts—the analysts—take at least co-ownership of identifying relevant data sources for their specific use cases outweighs the scalability a data scout may bring to the table. Where research analysts often need help is in how to efficiently analyze the relevant data, especially as datasets have become more complex and harder to wrangle. GIR's Data Strategy team, a dedicated team with a more focused analytical and quantitative background, collaborates with single-stock and macro research teams to help them achieve that objective through its GS Data Works initiative.

Use Cases for Alternative Data at Goldman Sachs Global Investment Research

With time and people in short supply, GIR's Data Strategy team cannot chase every data idea, so it prioritizes data that can be relevant for multiple teams or have a high probability of being used by at least one team on an ongoing basis. Data budget constraints obviously also play a role, especially in a research setting where success in execution of research ideas mostly accrues to the benefit of third parties. Fortunately, the explosion of data includes a diverse and abundant number of publicly available datasets that have proven useful for research purposes when properly combined with other data sources already being considered. **Exhibit 1** provides an overview of alternative data types used across the Goldman Sachs research division.

Exhibit 1. Types of Alternative Data Used in Goldman Sachs Research

Source: Goldman Sachs Global Investment Research.

- If the research use case has a geographic component, geospatial data may enter the equation. Datasets comprise not only dedicated geospatial measurements, such as mobile foot traffic data, satellite imagery, and government population and demographic data, but also a wide variety of information with inherent geographical importance, such as store locations or electric vehicle charging stations. GIR's understanding of brick-and-mortar retail sales is greatly enhanced by analyzing locations of retailers and their competitors. Similarly, leveraging public environmental service data (e.g., location-specific landfill capacities and lifetimes) provides a deeper understanding of the competitive pricing landscape in the environmental services industry.

- If the research use case has an online component, digital information can be additive. Datasets include app downloads, online point-of-sale information, website visits, product counts and pricing, and search trends. Example use cases include quantifying consumer interest (e.g., search intensity and active user counts) to better understand user engagement and assessing product launches or distress situations through social media sentiment, app downloads, and product-specific data.

- If the research use case can be addressed by searching through text, NLP techniques may uncover additional insights. This category is quite broad, covering a wide range of unstructured data, from earnings call transcripts and company filings to tweets and blog posts. David Kostin, the chief US equity strategist at Goldman Sachs, publishes a quarterly S&P 500 Beige Book, which leverages NLP to identify relevant themes each earnings cycle, one of the many research areas where NLP has proven to be additive.

The three categories in Exhibit 1 are prone to overlap, as many datasets span multiple dimensions. Ultimately, the combination of dimensions provides a more complete mosaic to better answer most research questions. GIR thus often uses more than one category to enhance its mosaic. For example, a company's pricing power can be derived not only from many product codes and prices (digital) but potentially also from its local market share in certain geographic regions (geospatial). In addition, commentary about the company's pricing power during earnings calls may be informative for a covering analyst (NLP).

Which Component of an AI Effort Is the Most Time Consuming? The Underappreciated Power of Doing the Data Grunt Work

Do not expect AI to provide insights if you do not understand the data you apply AI to. Data scientists will be successful only if they appreciate the nuances, strengths, and weaknesses of the data that go into their modeling efforts. Cases of algorithmic bias caused by algorithms trained on biased data have made the news in areas outside investments, but that does not mean investment applications are immune to being misguided because of data issues. This is an area where investment professionals who may not have data science skills but are subject matter experts can make a real difference. It is unrealistic to expect a data scientist to understand each investment use case, just as it is unrealistic to expect each research analyst to be a data science expert. However, if the two sides have an open mind to learn from each other and iterate, tremendous synergies and unique opportunities to expand each other's skill sets will surface.

Before making final decisions on sourcing a particular dataset, trying to identify a small test case is strongly recommended to give a good flavor of the data without time-consuming technological or due diligence hurdles. Again, this is where the subject matter expert can play a pivotal role. GIR's data strategists have witnessed more than once that a few targeted questions from an experienced analyst during a meeting with a data provider highlighted a data shortcoming, which led to shelving the data source. Even after onboarding a new data source, you need to stay alert because the data may evolve over time, especially if the provider has limited experience providing data or is unfamiliar with how the financial services industry may use its data. Goldman Sachs has dealt with situations where underlying inputs to the data were removed, added, or edited. If, in addition, the data you are sourcing are derived from underlying inputs, getting enough transparency in the algorithms used to create the derived data will add more complexity to the task of familiarizing yourself with the data. The following are a few important considerations depending on the type of data you are looking at.

- For large and complex datasets, one of the most general questions to ask is how comprehensive the data are. Certain data fields may have missing values, which can bias computational estimates such as averages and sums. Such bias has been observed in, for example, pricing data attained via web scraping, the practice of programmatically extracting publicly-available information from websites. The dataset may already have a layer of analysis to account for data problems, such as automated filling around missing data, as well as more sophisticated analysis choices, so it is important to understand the assumptions underlying that analysis layer. Another question to address is whether the data allow you to delve into the dimensions that are relevant for your investment thesis. For example, do you need style-specific breakouts in addition to aggregated counts when you lever Stock Keeping Unit (SKU) counts to assess the success of a new product launch?

- Even small datasets may be built off an analysis layer that relies on sampling, and problems can arise from techniques that either undersample or have inherent selection biases built in, such as point-of-sale, satellite imagery, or mobile foot traffic trends. Point-of-sale information that requires opt-in consumer panels may lever discounts for products in return for data use permission, which may skew demographics beyond what a simple reweighting can remedy. Similarly, parking lot car counts from satellite imagery cannot measure covered parking. Mobile foot traffic data have limited precision in malls and other multitenant structures. Whatever the dataset, the process of its construction is vital to assessing its advantages and limitations to ultimately determine its appropriateness.

- For NLP and text analysis, understanding details around the input data is also vital to interpreting results. For example, third-party aggregators of news articles may not be able to see paywall content, which may introduce subtle biases. If you search across multiple text sources, are source-specific biases and trends easy to separate and identify? Another example is sentiment analysis. Results from Instagram will likely be different from those from Twitter and Reddit. Breaking apart trends and results by source can help identify issues that could otherwise translate into misguided signals. In addition, when NLP is used for sentiment analysis to evaluate important themes, topics, or events, guarding against false positive or false negative results plays an important role and, simultaneously, provides an opportunity for a more nuanced view. For example, understanding the difference between a poor consumer product, on the one hand, and consumer frustrations at out-of-stock items or launch logistics issues, on the other hand, will not only strengthen results but also better inform investable decisions.

The bottom line is that data curation may not sound overly exciting, but it can easily determine success or failure. No matter how sophisticated the data analysis capabilities are, the AI effort will fail—or, possibly worse, create wrong outputs—if the data do not receive at least as much attention as the analysis. Again, this is not an area that GIR outsources to a different part of the organization. While there are parts of the chain that can potentially be handled by teams with more of an operational background, such as data ingestion and low-level cleaning, data curation requires the attention of the people who are familiar enough with the business use case—that is, the combination of the subject matter research experts and the data scientists. As a research division, GIR not only consumes data but also produces a substantial number of proprietary forecasts and indicators. Wearing both hats has made the Goldman Sachs research division appreciate even more how nontrivial it is to create trustworthy data.

Where Does Data Analysis Come In? Looking at the Spectrum of Analytical Approaches

Like the data landscape, the analysis landscape has expanded dramatically. For data analysis, GIR's Data Strategy team also follows a "pull" approach, as opposed to pushing a particular analytical technique in search of a problem to solve. The team works backwards from the use case at hand and collaborates with research analysts on the following questions: What are the strengths and weaknesses of approaches you have tried in the past? Are the outcomes vastly different when you make minor changes to your assumptions? Do outliers have a significant impact on the results? If any of these answers is yes, it may be time to try more sophisticated approaches that can add robustness to the research findings.

Also like the data landscape, where data fees and required effort are counterbalancing factors to simply load up on more data, explainability and required effort need to be weighed against the promises of AI. If a more straightforward approach to analyzing the data works, GIR tries to avoid adding unnecessary complexity. For example, when tracking inflation as a theme in earnings calls, GIR found that simply counting mentions of inflation was a robust proxy for a much more complex screen consisting of a combination of nearly 200 terms. But when the situation calls for more complex analysis, data scientists need to be able to provide enough intuition so that research analysts are comfortable with the outcomes.

If structured appropriately, analysis frameworks can provide a significant amount of flexibility and scalability. For example, **Exhibit 2** shows the results of an analysis of the pricing power of US environmental service companies based on local market dynamics. The different shades of color indicate different spot price ranges, a proxy of pricing power. The circles indicate landfill locations scaled to capacity. While the datasets leveraged were specific to environmental services, the techniques are not. The environmental data were combined with a more mature geospatial framework that had previously answered similar

Exhibit 2. Leveraging Geospatial Analysis Applied in One Industry to Another Industry

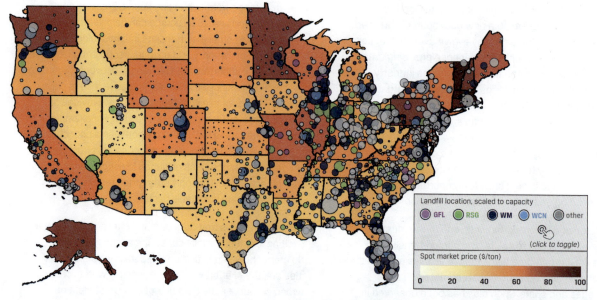

Sources: "Americas Environmental Services: Compounding Unit Profitability amid Building Local Market Share," published by lead equity analyst Jerry Revich, CFA, on 6 April 2021. Analysis by Goldman Sachs Global Investment Research based on data compiled from the *Waste Business Journal,* the New York State Department of Environmental Conservation, the California Water Boards, and other state sources.

questions for suppliers of heavy building materials, which was highlighted in the 2019 "AI Pioneers in Investment Management" report by CFA Institute.[29]

Data science techniques have made remarkable progress, from enabling self-driving cars to providing customized recommendations for a variety of services and products. Use cases for data science in financial services are expanding as well and include, for example, recommendation engines to customize dissemination of research and further advances in trading algorithms that benefit from vast amounts of high-frequency order and execution data. However, many dynamics in financial markets are inherently unstable and adaptive in nature; that is, the amount of data that can be used for modeling and running in-sample and out-of-sample analyses is limited. This reality puts some limitations on how far these techniques can be pushed from a purely investment research perspective.

The term "AI" may also suggest that humans have no role to play in the analysis phase. As mentioned before, humans can add significant value by properly curating data, a necessary input for AI. Similarly, humans will add value by continuously assessing the results of algorithms. Breakpoints in markets, such as the COVID-19 pandemic, keep illustrating that modeling efforts need to be adapted as markets change, and humans play a critical role here. For example, some of the Goldman Sachs proprietary "nowcasting" indicators went through that adaptation cycle soon after COVID-19 became a global phenomenon, and the subject matter experts realized how extreme outliers broke down statistical relationships used in the creation of the indicators.

Finally, the use of NLP techniques for investment research purposes deserves a special mention. GIR's efforts in this field have been geared more toward surfacing specific content in a scalable fashion than interpreting the meaning or sentiment of written words. Applying NLP to a use case where the accuracy of output was essential and consistently finding through human review that the NLP output flagged too many false positives and false negatives provided a good education on some of the boundaries of NLP in a research setting.

How Do I Measure Success for an AI/Alternative Data Effort? Using a Wide Lens Instead of a Narrow Lens

The initial hype around AI and alternative data may have created unrealistic expectations, which, in turn, led to demands for hard evidence that AI and alternative data add to a financial institution's bottom line, especially in cases where new data sources come with a hefty price tag and data science expertise is hard to find. It is helpful to keep a broad perspective and evaluate these efforts, traditional or nontraditional, through multiple lenses:

- Does the approach create alpha? While this is the question that most people would like to see a concrete answer to, it is unlikely that a single dataset or single analysis technique will be an alpha generator. For systematic strategies, it may be possible to backtest a strategy with or without inclusion of the AI component and measure the marginal alpha contribution. The usual caveats related to backtesting apply, but those are no different with or without AI and alternative data.

- Does the AI effort produce unique insights in a more timely or more precise fashion? For fundamental strategies, the direct alpha added by the AI effort may be hard to assess. That said, quantifying the improvement along specific dimensions can be a useful exercise. For example, GIR's nowcasting of port congestion allowed a more real-time confirmation of the shipping disruption Ukraine experienced during the early days of its invasion by Russia and as the war has continued to evolve. GIR's distance measurements of vessels laying high-voltage cable established estimates for revenue-driving business at a very granular level. GIR's market share analyses within multiple industrial businesses, analyzed via geo-clustering, provided the basis for broader statements about company pricing power. These examples also illustrate that the majority of GIR's AI and alternative data efforts are geared toward descriptive analyses that feed into the broader investment thesis, as opposed to being prescriptive analyses that directly lead to an investment recommendation. Knowing what you hope to get out of the process can help focus the effort and suitably ground expectations of success.

- Does AI create scalability that saves valuable analyst time or allows a research hypothesis to be applied across a broader set of securities and/or applied more frequently? A good example is NLP analysis of earnings transcripts, where a GIR analyst can now easily identify themes not only across the stocks in her own coverage universe but also relative to peer companies and assess these themes going back over multiple years. Conversations with GIR analysts that started as an inquiry about the use of alternative data in some cases highlighted much lower hanging fruit, where a more systematized approach could create scalability that allowed the analysts to consider various scenarios that could not have been achieved manually.

---

[29]"AI Pioneers in Investment Management" (Charlottesville, VA: CFA Institute, 2019). https://www.cfainstitute.org/-/media/documents/survey/AI-Pioneers-in-Investment-Management.pdf.

While asking for a return on the AI investment is absolutely the right thing to do, the hurdles to justify the effort seem somewhat unfair relative to how budgets for traditional data sources and traditional data analysis (for which the costs can also add up) are determined. Trying to identify appropriate key performance indicators for an AI effort has therefore started to make people question their broader data efforts, wondering whether they are extracting sufficient return on investment across the entire data spectrum. This evolution is healthy and may lead to a more level playing field for AI-focused efforts.

Where Do I Start? It Is a Marathon, Not a Sprint

If you are embarking on your AI and alternative data journey in a setting with people who already have years of investment expertise, hiring one or two key people who have a data science background, have hands-on experience digging into data, and are genuinely interested in learning about and solving investment problems is a great starting point. Teaming up those key hires with one or two analysts who are interested in leveraging and analyzing more data, have a solid use case that has staying power, and understand that you need to iterate to get to a useful result should allow you to hit the ground running. Investment analysts who have ideas for new data to incorporate into their process and appreciate that properly analyzing those data may require trial and error are great candidates to start an organization on its path to AI and alternative data adoption and success. The initial use cases ideally do not depend on a complicated dataset that may take too long to bring on board.

Having senior sponsorship from the start is important. Those senior sponsors do not need to have familiarity with AI and alternative data themselves but need to have an appreciation that these approaches can be additive to the investment process. Their role is to provide the trailblazers some room and cover to experiment and iterate, while keeping them accountable by staying on top of (especially the initial) use cases. Once there are specific, tangible outcomes, others can get their heads around what it means in practice to lever alternative data and more sophisticated techniques. At that point, momentum to expand across the organization is created and scaling up the effort across geographies, analyst teams, and asset classes becomes a realistic next step.

Another question that is raised in this context is whether the AI and alternative data effort should be centralized or embedded in each team. As the need for having a dedicated data science expert in each team was *de minimis*, GIR went for a centralized effort that can be thought of as an extension of its research teams across the globe and across asset classes. Its centralized approach has given GIR the benefit of connecting the dots across use cases coming from different research teams.

Other teams in an investment organization can provide leverage, and it is good practice to make people in engineering, legal, and compliance departments aware of the AI and alternative data effort from Day 1, even if they do not have an immediate role to play. As the use cases expand, questions about data storage, firewalls, terms and conditions, and licensing rights for use of specific data sources will increase, which will require proper attention from those experts. In addition, as your use cases become more sophisticated, you may consider building additional functionality in house as opposed to relying on a third party to do some of the processing for you (i.e., build versus buy), which may require a dedicated engineering focus. GIR's own journey has reflected that evolution, where the first years of experience with embedding AI and alternative data provided a wealth of information on what approaches do and, more importantly, do not work and how they can fit into the workflow of a research analyst. GIR's Data Strategy team had to revisit a number of initial approaches on how to best evolve its data ecosystem but is now in a much better position to partner further with colleagues in engineering to make it a reality, as opposed to having the initial enthusiasm translate into engineering effort spent on building systems that may not have been properly thought through.

Conclusion

The impact of AI and alternative data on investment research is evolutionary, not revolutionary. Goldman Sachs looks at nonstructured, alternative, and big data as other components in the spectrum of data that may be relevant to its research process. It looks at AI, ML, and NLP as other components in the spectrum of analytical tools to make sense of the data. With the lines between traditional and alternative data becoming blurred and an increasingly ambiguous definition of what AI does or does not include, GIR does not draw artificial boundaries across these spectrums and therefore does not assess the value of AI and alternative data differently from its other data and analytical efforts. It draws from the types of data and the types of analyses as needed, often mixing unstructured data with traditional data and having more sophisticated approaches live side by side with more intuitive approaches. Subject matter and data science experts team up as appropriate, while ensuring they draw the best of man plus machine to minimize algorithmic and data biases. As this space matures further and the lines blur even more, Goldman Sachs expects that this integrated, iterative, and collaborative approach will continue to bear fruit for its investment research use cases. And because it also expects that AI and alternative data will simply become part and parcel of the research process, there may be a day when the labels "big" and "alternative" are no longer relevant!

3. DATA SCIENCE FOR ACTIVE AND LONG-TERM FUNDAMENTAL INVESTING

Kai Cui, PhD
Managing Director, Head of Equity Data Science, Neuberger Berman

Jonathan Shahrabani
Managing Director, Chief Operating Officer – Global Research Strategies, Neuberger Berman

Large-scale alternative data (alt-data) and data science are improving the investment techniques in the industry. Active asset managers with a long-term orientation particularly, given their long-term mindset and the resulting lower portfolio turnover, have differentiating opportunities to innovate in data science and big data. Therefore, sustainable, long-shelf-life data insights are as important as (if not more important than) short-term insights related to potential mispricing and time-sensitive advantages.

Long-term fundamental investors in active asset management strategies started embracing alt-data and data science two or three years later than their hedge fund peers. For example, data science has been an increasingly important capability of Neuberger Berman since 2017 across sectors, geographies, and asset classes.

Alt-data allow asset managers to "bear-hug" companies by enhancing our understanding of their operations and organizations independent of and incremental to information

Data Science Integration at Neuberger Berman

At Neuberger Berman, the data science function is deeply integrated and provides significant added value in its practices managing global equity mandates for institutional, retail, and high-net-worth investors. Idea generation is the combined effort and responsibility of both fundamental industry analysts and data scientists.

Given the vast alternative data footprint that is continuously being created by companies, the teams use research templates and data science processes—including data science–integrated scalable financial models, data modeling, and analytical tools—extensively to systematically capture and synthesize this information.

The design and construction of these research templates are a collaboration between both fundamental industry analysts and data scientists. These templates capture the key performance indicators (KPIs) for a given industry and key thesis metrics and data insights for a given company that are material to its longer-term earnings power. Simultaneously, with curated long-term fundamental support, we actively construct and track a spectrum of alt-data metrics to glean a comprehensive view of the company's real-time operational metrics and/or risk toward our long-term growth targets.

Both fundamental industry analysts and data scientists review these data on at least a weekly basis and discuss any notable upward or downward movements.

If a template is not relevant for a given industry or company (or a deep dive is required), fundamental industry analysts and data scientists partner on a custom analysis. As can be expected, custom analyses require extensive collaboration between both parties. For certain industries, such as health care, the background of the fundamental industry analyst takes on increasing importance because of the vast differences between subsectors (biotechnology, pharmaceuticals, life sciences, etc.).

During year-end reviews, fundamental industry analysts and data scientists are evaluated based on their contributions from multiple perspectives, including, but not limited to, investment performance, engagement, and strategy innovations and development. These are important drivers of incentives for both parties.

gleaned from financial statements and management interactions. The depth and breadth of alternative data, if analyzed and integrated correctly, can generate invaluable insights with a longer shelf life for long-term alpha generation.

The Operating Model and Evolution of Data Science Integration

There is no single best operating model for data science integration that fits all active asset managers. Data science must be customized to fit into each firm's own unique culture, organizational structure, core value proposition, strategic prioritization, and even innovative budgeting methods.

Evolution of the Data Science Organization

In this section, we discuss the decision of whether to use a centralized or decentralized data science team and how to evaluate the return on investment of data science initiatives.

To Centralize or Not

While a highly centralized data science team may enjoy more autonomy than decentralized teams and serve well as an innovation hub or research lab, if detached from investment decision making and business opportunities, it tends to fail to drive sustainable innovation that can be integrated or provide incremental value to the core investment platform.[30] In contrast, a completely decentralized data science team can prove economically inefficient and risk duplication of effort, especially when data scientists are less experienced.

The level of data science integration among strategies varies, and we can distinguish three stages of data science integration/engagement with investment teams even within the same firm: (1) engagement to establish credibility, (2) active and deep integration for investment evaluation, and (3) data science as part of the core investment strategy.

The level of centralization depends on the stage of data science integration. Generally, the data science team is centralized in the early to intermediate stages of development. When best practices are established and experience grows, experienced data scientists can make a more direct impact as part of an investment team's decision-making

processes. The transition will happen faster as more data scientists and analysts are developed with training in both data science and fundamental investing.

Evaluating Data Science Initiatives' Return on Investment

While it is important that all data science initiatives start with illustrating incremental added value and establishing good engagement relationships with fundamental industry analysts, rapid "time to market" and the early establishment of credibility and process momentum on the road to subsequent stages are essential as well. Notably and importantly, the KPIs for team performance and return on investment (ROI) assessment could be different when planning and prioritizing engagement/integration efforts in different stages of data science and investment process integration.

For example, driving data source coverage, metrics and insights coverage, and the number of high-quality use cases are essential in the early stage to establish credibility. When coming to more active and deeper integration, data science teams need to align performance KPIs with the measurement of investment decision-making impacts and contribution to investment performance. Furthermore, if data science is part of a core investment strategy and/or is driving innovative investment solutions for investors and prospects, additional KPIs and ROI measurements on contribution to strategic development, growth in assets under management, and client engagement are also important, in addition to the contribution to investment performance. Over time, data science efforts evolve with the growing capabilities of team members and the closer partnership with fundamental industry analysts, and we continue to enable the data science team for long-term success focusing on deeper integration into both investment decision making and innovative investment solutions.

ROI assessment of data insights and data sources also needs to be customized to the investment styles of active asset managers while taking into account such factors as investment *capacity*, which is as important as investment performance for innovative data science–integrated investment solutions. For example, alt-data may have proven to generate incremental alpha in sector-focused, cross-sectional systematic strategies, but a data science platform supporting more diversified signals and types of strategies needs further development to support diversified client demands, global exposure, and thus the larger-scale investment capacity requirement needed by a large global asset manager with a long-term orientation.

---

[30]For more discussion on centralization, see CFA Institute, "T-Shaped Teams: Organizing to Adopt AI and Big Data at Investment Firms" (2021, p. 23). www.cfainstitute.org/-/media/documents/article/industry-research/t-shaped-teams.pdf.

Analysts with Training in Both Data Science and Investments

At the 1997 Worldwide Developer Conference, Steve Jobs was asked "to express in clear terms how, say, Java, in any of its incarnations, expresses the ideas embodied in OpenDoc." His answer was to start with the key business question of how to best serve customers rather than "sitting down with engineers and figuring out what awesome technologies we have and how we are going to market that."[31]

Data scientists often have similar questions for their fundamental investing counterparts, such as, Are the vast amounts of new metrics generated from new data sources and data science techniques fully understood and appreciated by fundamental investment professionals to realize their full potential? The correct answer is also similar: Data science endeavors should start with key investment questions rather than what data and metrics data scientists have already built and how to figure out use cases out of them.

A large portion of the data created daily proves of limited value to data scientists in evaluating investment opportunities. In contrast, we focus on data insights into key controversies and thesis metrics that allow us to have an informed and, often, differentiated view on a company's earnings power relative to market expectations three to five years out.

To this end, data scientists on the team (including some with a prior background as fundamental industry analysts) have been trained internally for both data science and fundamental research skills.[32] This training ensures data scientists have a strong knowledge to initiate meaningful discussions of investment use cases in multiple industries, as well as the key drivers of earnings power. Inevitably, some mistakes have been made along the way, but they created opportunities for data scientists and fundamental analysts to learn to speak the same language and strengthen their bond.

Data scientists with a background and training in fundamental investing have a better chance of cutting through conflicting and noisy data. For example, a high number of open job listings for a given company's salesforce provides a better indication of business momentum in some industries than in others. However, it can also mean employee retention is low and signal underlying issues for an organization. Understanding the nuances of each company and its peers (competitive positioning, geographic footprint, merger and acquisition strategy, etc.) is critical.

Armed with their alternative data findings, data scientists and fundamental industry analysts are able to engage company executives on a deeper level, provide additional insights into the inner workings of the company under study, and enrich our insights into an investee organization. It is our experience that analyzing data in isolation and without context can lead to erroneous conclusions.

Longer-Term Earnings Power Insights vs. Shorter-Term Operational Monitoring

Integrating alt-data into the fundamental investing framework allows investment teams to have an informed and, often, differentiated view on a portfolio company's earnings power three to five years out. At the same time, actively constructing and tracking a spectrum of short-term alt-data metrics to develop a comprehensive view of real-time operational metrics and/or risk toward our longer-term growth targets are equally important.

For example, many investment management firms have access to some form of credit card data. Indeed, there are many third-party providers in the marketplace that scrub this type of data for subscribers and provide an easily digestible format in real time. On the surface, credit card data in raw form and slightly lagged delivery provide less of a timeliness advantage. However, these data may allow data scientists working with long-term investment teams to perform in-depth proprietary research that is better aligned with their core investment disciplines.

Although many large, publicly traded companies are heavily researched and alt-data coverage is not universally and equally distributed, it is still possible, with balanced longer-term earning power insights and shorter-term operational metrics monitoring, to have a differentiated view about earnings power relative to market consensus. A few specific examples will help illustrate this point.

An Athleisure Brand

A working, fundamental thesis postulated that the operating margin of a leading athleisure brand was at an inflection point, driven by growth in the company's digital offering. Presented with this thesis, the data science team

---

[31]For a transcript and video of the remarks by Steve Jobs, see, e.g., Sebastiaan van der Lans, "Transcript: Steve Jobs at Apple's WWDC 1997," *Sebastiaan van der Lans—On WordPress, Blockchain, Timestamps & Trust* (blog, 3 January 2020). https://sebastiaans.blog/steve-jobs-wwdc-1997/.

[32]For a related discussion on the evolution of investment and data science function integrations, see CFA Institute, "T-Shaped Teams."

recommended a proprietary analysis breaking down the average selling price (ASP) between the company's digital and brick-and-mortar transactions. The fundamental industry analyst agreed with the data science team that such an analysis would be highly valuable, particularly because the management team of the company in question provided minimal disclosure regarding its digital offerings. The results of the analysis showed a significant premium for an extended period of time on digital transactions versus brick-and-mortar transactions.

Taking it one step further, the fundamental industry analyst later proposed tracking and monitoring the ASPs of the company under review versus a major competitor as further validation of the thesis. Indeed, the ASP premium achieved by the company in digital transactions over this major competitor was materially higher over a similar period of time. This analysis contributed to our portfolio management team's initiation of an investment position in the stock, supported by our increasing confidence that the operating margins of the company could expand meaningfully above consensus expectations over the medium term and long term. At the same time, because the company was one of the best covered names by alt-data sources, an array of metrics was actively monitored to glean a comprehensive view of the company's operations, including digital app engagement, consumer interests in various product lines, pricing power, and geographic new initiatives.

A Global Luxury Brand

A fundamental industry analyst began to lose conviction when recommending a well-known global luxury company because of the Chinese government's emphasis on "common prosperity." The growth of the luxury industry in recent years has been dominated by Chinese consumers. As a way to cut across the debate, given the analyst's view that the impact of a government initiative might not be easily spotted in conventional data, the data science team captured multiple operational KPIs.

Although we did see a modest dip in some short-term data metrics, such as social media momentum, we performed an extensive analysis of the company's customer base over a comprehensive period of time, which was more indicative of the company's ability to contribute to our long-term growth targets. Specifically, our analysis revealed that many months after the government's "common prosperity"

push, the company's largest cohort of customers (female midlevel wage earners) increased their spending as a percentage of disposable income at this brand. Such an approach ultimately allowed our portfolio management teams to maintain ownership in the stock based on unobvious alt-data metrics that our data science team turned into an investible insight.

A Leading Asset Manager

A fundamental working thesis held that many investors were underestimating the growth of a new retail product offered by a leading asset manager. In addition to tracking regular asset flow data provided by the company, our fundamental industry analyst colleagues and the data science team developed an alternative method for tracking and monitoring traffic in the new product on the web portal of this specific retailer. This analysis contributed to our portfolio management teams' initiation of a position in the stock, bolstered by increased confidence in its earnings power and potential for upside growth.

Later, our ongoing tracking and monitoring of the data allowed our portfolio management team to play defense when necessary. Specifically, a sharp drop-off in web portal traffic observed by our data science team ultimately led to a more cautious outlook by our fundamental industry analyst and portfolio management teams. This, in turn, resulted in our portfolio management team's reduction (and in some cases elimination) of its position in the stock.

Conclusion

Data science and alternative data can help provide insights and added value to a range of investment processes, strategies, and portfolio management teams. However, there exists no single, self-evident methodology or road map to follow. Rather—and critically—distinct investment strategies, investment horizons, and portfolio teams each require their own individual approaches to the use of data science and the range of alternative datasets they can leverage.

The winning formula, in our opinion, is a partnership-driven approach that brings together data scientists, fundamental analysts, and portfolio managers with value-added datasets specifically built to address the firm's specific investment needs.

HANDBOOK OF ARTIFICIAL INTELLIGENCE AND BIG DATA APPLICATIONS IN INVESTMENTS

II. NATURAL LANGUAGE UNDERSTANDING, PROCESSING, AND GENERATION: INVESTMENT APPLICATIONS

This book can be found at cfainstitute.org/ai-and-big-data

4. UNLOCKING INSIGHTS AND OPPORTUNITIES WITH NLP IN ASSET MANAGEMENT

Andrew Chin
Head of Quantitative Research and Chief Data Scientist, AllianceBernstein

Yuyu Fan
Senior Data Scientist, AllianceBernstein

Che Guan
Senior Data Scientist, AllianceBernstein

Introduction

A confluence of events is affecting the asset management industry, forcing industry participants to rethink their competitive positioning and evolve to survive in the new world order. Geopolitical, regulatory, technological, and social trends are upending long-held norms, and the status quo is likely an untenable option for many firms. These forces are creating a host of challenges for existing players and presenting new opportunities for emerging firms. We discuss some of the key challenges affecting the active management industry in this new environment. While our list is not meant to be exhaustive, we focus on the main trends that will drive the adoption of text mining techniques in the coming years. We also provide the motivation for firms to leverage natural language processing (NLP) to capitalize on these trends.

Low Expected Returns

The driving focus for many investors since the Global Financial Crisis (GFC) has been the search for returns. Bond yields collapsed following the GFC, and concerns about economic growth suppressed expectations around equity returns. With prospects for returns expected to be much lower versus historical norms, asset owners and asset managers widened their search for high-yielding and high-returning assets. At the end of 2021, US 10-year government yields hovered near all-time lows, at 1.5%, and the price-to-earnings ratio of the S&P 500 Index was at 25, higher than historical averages. Although inflationary concerns caused a rise in rates and a significant drawdown in equity markets over the first nine months of 2022, below-average yields and above-average equity valuations persist across many countries, implying that future returns will likely be on the low end of long-term trends.

Over the past decade, investors are increasingly taking on more risk in an effort to enhance returns. Private markets and structured products are becoming more popular in the asset allocations of many investors. While these historically niche areas are becoming more mainstream, the investment, operational, and counterparty risks associated with them may still not be fully understood. Nevertheless, the low expected returns in the current environment are pushing asset managers to find new sources of returns and differentiation.

Active Managers Have Struggled

While investors are searching for higher returns, active managers, overall, have not delivered on their promises. Over the past decade, active managers have underperformed their respective benchmarks. **Exhibit 1** shows the percentage of US large-cap equity managers outperforming the broad US market as measured by the Russell 1000 Index. During any given year since the GFC, about one-third of the managers have beaten their benchmarks, suggesting that over longer horizons, even fewer managers are consistently beating the markets and providing value for their clients.

As a result of these struggles, management fees have collapsed, and significant assets have moved from high-fee, active to low-fee, passive strategies. Specifically, index products at the largest asset managers have swelled over the past decade, adding further to the headwinds for active management. One only needs to witness the enormous growth of such popular products as the SPDR S&P 500 ETF Trust (SPY) or the Vanguard 500 Index ETF (VOO) to gauge investor preferences. Many believe that these trends are set to persist unless active managers can reverse their recent headwinds.

Big Data and Data Science Present Opportunities

Given these challenges, asset managers are looking to provide higher and more consistent returns for their clients. For long-only managers, market returns dominate total portfolio returns; most of these managers have a beta close to 1 against their benchmark, and as a result, portfolio returns will largely mimic the returns of the broader market. Managers may look outside their stated

Exhibit 1. Percentage of Funds Outperforming the Russell 1000 Index, 2003–2021

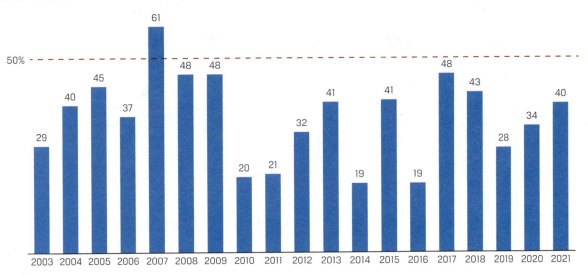

Source: Bank of America.

benchmarks to enhance their returns. For example, equity managers may include IPOs (initial public offerings) and SPACs (special purpose acquisition companies) to potentially increase returns, while bond managers may include securitized instruments or other higher-yielding assets to enhance performance. All these strategies look "outside the benchmark" for investment opportunities and attempt to enhance the total returns of the portfolios.

Managers look to provide a consistent edge above and beyond the broad markets by attempting to uncover differentiated insights around potential investments. They endeavor to gain a deeper understanding of their investments, giving them more confidence in the companies or the securities they are interested in. Examples include a consumer analyst having a better sense of customer preferences for a certain brand or a tech analyst being able to forecast the technology stack favored by companies in the future. Other examples may include a systematic process that leverages unique data sources or uses sophisticated algorithms to synthesize data. These insights can give organizations the confidence they need to bolster their convictions and deliver stronger performance for their clients.

To do this, portfolio managers are increasingly turning to new data sources and more sophisticated techniques to provide the edge they need to survive.

Alternative Data

Traditional data normally refers to structured data that managers have been consuming for decades. These data can easily be shown in a Microsoft Excel spreadsheet in two dimensions: Typically, time is used as one dimension, and some market or company variable is used as the other dimension. Over the past decade, new data sources have emerged to complement the traditional data sources. The four "Vs" in **Exhibit 2** can be used to describe the "bigness" of the new data. Volume refers to the exponential growth in the amount of data available. Velocity describes the speed at which data are produced and consumed. Variety describes the range of data types and sources. Finally, the fourth V, veracity, is critical because having more data is not necessarily useful unless the data are verifiable and deemed to be accurate. The data collected on smartphones illustrate the 4 Vs. Data are being created constantly on smartphones as users' apps track their various activities (volume). These data may come in text, audio, or video formats (variety). As messages and notifications are received, the user may interact with or respond to the prompts (velocity). For these data to be useful, phone manufacturers and app developers create algorithms to cleanse, store, and enrich the data (veracity). These forces are playing out across all sectors of the economy.

Asset managers have had success in collecting and incorporating these new data into their investment processes. Initial use cases include summarizing customer reviews and comments on social media and other platforms. For example, when Starbucks introduced its new rewards program in February 2016, many customers took to Twitter to protest the changes. **Exhibit 3** shows that there were significantly more "angry" and "dislike" tweets after the initial announcement and even following the rollout about one month later. Portfolio managers holding Starbucks in their portfolios could have used these trends to study the potential impact of the loyalty program changes before

Exhibit 2. The Four Vs of Alternative Data

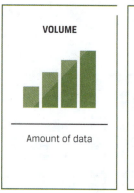

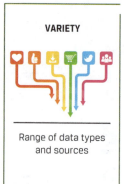
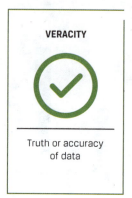

Exhibit 3. Tweets Relating to "Starbucks Rewards," 1 February 2016–25 April 2016

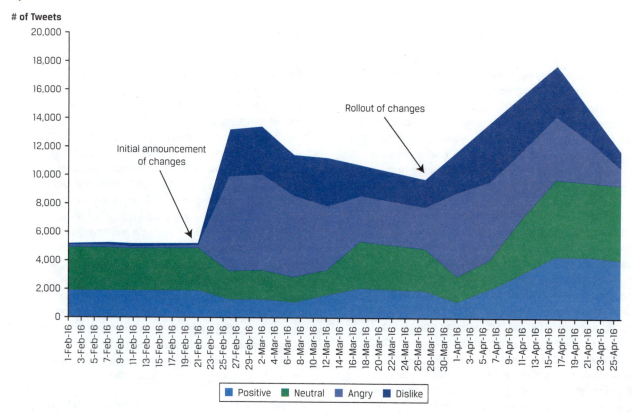

Source: AllianceBernstein.

the company officially reported the financial impact, likely in April 2016 to cover Q1 2016 performance. Reading and summarizing the sentiment of the tweets can give asset managers an early indication of the impact of the rewards program changes. In this case, Exhibit 3 suggests that the negative tweets had largely disappeared in April, and thus, the changes were unlikely to have a significant impact on Starbucks' financial performance.

Other applications with Twitter include measuring voting intentions during elections and monitoring product rollouts and advertising campaigns. Beyond Twitter, product review sites and message boards may be useful for customer feedback on brands and trends. In many of these early use cases, ingesting, cleansing, and interpreting text data were key ingredients to success. Specifically, measuring sentiment and intentions across thousands and millions of textual data requires sophisticated tools. This area is well suited for NLP.

With the evolving geopolitical and regulatory risks, companies are also looking to new data sources from governments. News and tweets can provide real-time insights into government policies and priorities, while public data sources containing infrastructure projects, shipping routes, energy consumption, enforcement actions, health data, and government spending can influence investment decisions across asset classes. Asset managers are increasingly leveraging these new datasets to enrich their understanding of the world and their impact on financial markets.

Artificial Intelligence and NLP

Artificial intelligence (AI) is the study of emulating human understanding and reaction to various situations. Machine learning (ML) is a branch of AI focused on machines learning to think by training on data. NLP is a specific form of ML that focuses on understanding and interpreting textual and spoken data. It uses linguistics, computer science, and statistics to create models that can understand text and respond to text.

NLP is a natural tool for the asset management industry because many activities of asset managers are driven by text data. Indeed, many of the alternative data trends require NLP capabilities to fully leverage their potential.

Before we discuss the applications of NLP in finance, an examination of NLP's successes and challenges in other industries can yield some insights into the evolution and adoption of these tools in our industry.

NLP Evolution and Applications

NLP research started prior to the 1950s, but the Turing test, developed by Alan Turing in 1950, was one of the first attempts to emulate human language understanding (Turing 1950, p. 457). It tests a machine's ability to "exhibit intelligent behavior" indistinguishable from humans. Initially, most of the algorithms to process language were based on predefined rules.

With the development of faster machines and the introduction of WordNet and the Penn Tree Bank in the 1980s, NLP gained prominence among researchers in computer science and in linguistics. More recently, language models incorporating neural networks, such as word2vec, allowed a vast cadre of researchers to train NLP models across different domains.

Recent NLP research relies on underlying language models to process text. A language model is a probability distribution over sequences of words. These probabilities are typically generated by training the language model on text corpora, including books, articles, news, and other forms of written text. Traditional language models include n-gram and recurrent neural network (RNN) models.

An n-gram model is a type of probabilistic model that predicts the most probable word following a sequence of n words. Since training corpora are typically limited, there may be many n-grams with zero probability (combinations of words that have never been seen before), especially as n increases. To overcome this scarcity issue, word vectors and mathematical functions can be used to capture history from text sequences and are commonly used in RNN language models.

Later implementations of RNNs use word embeddings to capture words and their positions in sequential text. These features allow RNNs to process text of varying lengths and retain longer word histories and their importance. The introduction of long short-term memory (Hochreiter and Schmidhuber 1997) in the 1990s further improved on traditional RNNs with additional capabilities to maintain information over long periods of time.

While RNNs form the backbone of many language models, there are limitations. Specifically, since text is processed sequentially, it is time consuming to train and apply these models. Moreover, when sequences are exceptionally long, RNN models may forget the contents of distant positions in sequences. Attention mechanisms (Vaswani, Shazeer, Parmar, Uszkoreit, Jones, Gomez, Kaiser, and Polosukhin 2017) are commonly used to overcome this memory issue by capturing word positioning and relevance regardless of their location in sequences and allowing the neural network models to focus on the most valuable parts of the sequences. Based on attention mechanisms, transformer-based models were introduced in 2017; they vastly improved the performance of language models across various tasks. Some of the most well-known transformers include the Bidirectional Encoder Representations from Transformers or BERT (Devlin, Chang, Lee, and Toutanova 2018), Google's T5 (Raffel, Shazeer, Roberts, Lee, Narang, Matena, Zhou, Li, and Liu 2020), and OpenAI's GPT3 (Brown, Mann, Ryder, Subbiah, Kaplan, Dhariwal, Neelakantan, Shyam, Sastry, Askell, et al. 2020).

The parameters in modern NLP models are typically initialized through pretraining. This process starts with a base model, initializes the weights randomly, and trains the model from scratch on large corpora. To adjust a pretrained model for specific problems and domains, researchers fine-tune their models by further training them on the desired domain and making small adjustments to the underlying model to achieve the desired output or performance. Fine-tuning is a form of transfer learning where model parameters are adjusted for a specific task.

NLP models have been applied successfully in a variety of settings and already play important roles in our everyday lives.

Spam detection is one of the most important and practical applications of machine learning. Spam messages usually contain eye-catching words, such as "free," "win," "winner," "cash," or "prize," and tend to have words written in all capital letters or use a lot of exclamation marks. Language models can be fine-tuned to search for these common spam features to identify unwanted messages. Another popular approach for spam detection leverages supervised learning and the naive Bayes algorithm by first annotating messages as either "spam" or "not spam" and then training a model to learn from the annotations to classify new messages.

NLP models use *part-of-speech tagging* techniques that identify the nouns, verbs, adjectives, adverbs, and so on in a given a sentence. These methods enable the language models to fully understand and interpret the text.

Topic modeling using such techniques as latent Dirichlet allocation, or LDA (Blei, Ng, and Jordan 2003), have been applied extensively to extract key themes and topics in a series of sentences or texts and thus provide the ability to summarize documents quickly.

As noted earlier, data have exploded in terms of volume, velocity, and variety. Social media platforms, online forums, and company websites provide a plethora of text-based datasets that are waiting to be mined. *Sentiment analysis* can be used to analyze how different segments of the population view certain products, events, policies, and so on.

Machine language translation can be modeled as a sequence-to-sequence learning problem—that is, a sentence in the source language and another sequence returned in the translated target language. RNNs can be used to encode the meaning of the input sentence and decode the model calculations to produce the output.

Not long ago, *voice user interfaces* (VUIs) were in the realm of science fiction, but voice-enabled agents are becoming commonplace on our phones, computers, and cars. Indeed, many people may not even be aware that NLP provides the foundation for these systems. Under the hood, audio sound waves from voice are converted into language texts using ML algorithms and probabilistic models. The resulting text is then synthesized by the underlying language models to determine the meaning before formulating a response. Finally, the response text is converted back into understandable speech with ML tools.

One of the most exciting innovations in VUIs today is *conversational AI* technology. One can now carry on a conversation with a cloud-based system that incorporates well-tuned speech recognition, synthesis, and generation into one system or device. Examples include Apple's Siri, Microsoft's Cortana, Google Home, and Amazon's Alexa. The home assistant devices in this category are quite flexible. In addition to running a search or providing the weather, these devices can interface with other user-linked devices on the internet to provide more comprehensive responses. Finally, these technologies leverage cloud-based tools for speech recognition and synthesis to integrate conversational AI into many aspects of our everyday lives.

The goal behind a *question answering* (QA) system is to respond to a user's question by directly extracting information from passages or combinations of words within documents, conversations, and online searches. Almost all the state-of-the-art QA systems are built on top of pretrained language models, such as BERT (Liu, Ott, Goyal, Du, Joshi, Chen, Levy, Lewis, Zettlemoyer, and Stoyanov 2019; Joshi, Chen, Liu, Weld, Zettlemoyer, and Levy 2020; Rajpurkar, Zhang, Lopyrev, and Liang 2016). Compared with systems that require users to scan an entire document, QA systems are more efficient because they attempt to narrow down answers quickly. Nowadays, QA systems are the foundation of chatbots, and some QA systems have extended beyond text to pictures. In some respects, QA systems can be viewed as the most generic of all the NLP solutions because the input questions can include translations, key topics, part-of-speech tags, or sentiment analysis.

NLP in Finance and Asset Management

In this section, we discuss how NLP is used in finance and asset management.

Decision-Making Framework

Given the success of NLP in solving a wide swath of problems, we now discuss its applications in finance. We start with the basic decision-making framework because it directly addresses the challenges that lead organizations toward NLP. **Exhibit 4** describes the broad actions we normally take to make decisions, regardless of whether those decisions are in finance or in everyday life. As we will see, this framework informs where NLP can be impactful.

- Gather data: Investors want to have a comprehensive view of all the data that may affect their decisions. Analysts collect financial information as well as competitor, supplier, and customer data. These data can come in many forms; alternative data sources have expanded the breadth of available data on potential investments. Whereas before, analysts would gauge real-time buying trends by visiting physical stores, they can now see more comprehensive data through geolocation or footfall data. This type of data is more

Exhibit 4. Traditional Decision-Making Framework

comprehensive because it covers many locations rather than just a hand-picked few and it tracks the trends consistently rather than for a subset of hours over a week. Ultimately, investors collect and monitor as much data as they can for their decision-making process.

- Extract insights: With reams of data at their fingertips, investors need to decide how to synthesize the data to make informed decisions. Doing so normally involves two steps: (1) determining what the data are saying and (2) deciding how to weigh each of the data points in the eventual answer.

Financial data and figures are relatively easy to interpret. Trends and other statistics can be calculated from the data to predict future performance. It is much more difficult to interpret nonfinancial data. For example, interpreting a written customer review on a website may be difficult because the source and intention of the review are both unclear. Even if we assume the review is objective and without bias, does it contain new and useful information? We normally overcome these issues by using the law of large numbers: By collecting sufficiently large sample sizes, we hope to dilute the effects of outliers and biases.

Once interpretations are extrapolated, weighing the data in the context of all the other data surrounding a potential investment is paramount. In the absence of empirical evidence, investors may use heuristics; they may assign higher weights to more recent data or data that they believe are more reliable or predictive. Asset managers tend to emphasize data that have been predictive in the past or somehow correlated with historical outcomes. These heuristics can be extremely helpful, but investors may have behavioral biases that could lead them to suboptimal results. For example, they may be biased by their connection to the CEO of a company, or they may not remember the full earnings report from last year to adequately compare the current results.

ML can overcome these issues by systematically learning from the data and monitoring the outcomes. It can be used to help weigh the data to ensure biases are mitigated and predictions are robust. Our use cases later in the article will explain these ideas in more detail.

Once the data are synthesized, investors can make their decisions using their decision-making framework.

By monitoring the outcomes (i.e., the accuracy of predictions or the impact of recommended actions), investors can then feed these new data back into the decision-making framework to improve future decisions. This iterative feedback mechanism is critical for ongoing success. ML models are trained by data and humans, so by incorporating feedback on the success or failure of the predictions, these same models can be improved. We believe this is a significant benefit of ML models. They can be trained to learn from new data and past decisions, whereas humans may be slower (or unable) to adapt to new data or incorporate failures into the decision-making framework.

NLP has a natural place in this decision-making framework because it offers a systematic approach to scan a broad set of documents and leverages ML techniques to extract insights. Reading, understanding, and synthesizing multiple documents accurately and efficiently offer clear benefits for NLP approaches.

Common NLP Tasks

We now discuss some of the common tasks relating to NLP in finance. Many of these applications were discussed in the prior section, but we will include additional comments on their uses in our industry.

Summarization

News aggregators use this technique to summarize long articles to send digestible content to inboxes. We may also wish to summarize corporate filings or presentations for quick consumption. The key challenge with this task is understanding and capturing the key relevant points of the large document. This challenge is made more difficult because different investors may weigh the content of the text differently, and as a result, the optimal summary depends on the user or usage.

Topic extraction

The key themes and topics in an article can be extracted using supervised, semi-supervised, or unsupervised methods. In the supervised approach, the model is trained to look for specific keywords related to a predefined theme, whereas the unsupervised approach attempts to infer the themes being discussed. The semi-supervised approach is a hybrid approach in which seed words can be used as starting points to identify themes. One example is in the context of central bank statements. Common themes debated during central bank meetings in the United States include inflation and growth. We may seed the topic modeling process with these words and then apply various language techniques to find new words and phrases resembling these themes to derive the final topics from the documents.

Search/information retrieval

We may be interested in looking for specific terms or references from the text. Examples may include competitor or product references in a document. An analyst for Apple may be interested in finding all references to the iPhone in corporate documents or news articles.

Question answering

Similar to the search task, we are interested in finding information in a document. However, the QA task is focused on answering specific questions rather than returning references to those questions. In the previous example regarding the Apple analyst, he may be interested in the actual iPhone units sold rather than simply references to the phone. Another example may be extracting the interest rate or the covenants in a loan document. A specific application of this question answering task is the chat box, where specific and relevant responses are needed to reply to questions.

Sentiment analysis

Should the text be viewed positively or negatively? This will again depend on the user and application. For example, certain words, such as "debit," "liability," and "resolve," may have different meanings depending on the context. The first two terms are normally viewed as negative words in common parlance but tend to be more neutral in a financial setting since they are common terms in financial statements. "Resolve" may be viewed as positive in most settings, but "did not resolve" should be viewed as negative.

Named entity recognition

Extracting entity names from text is a common but important task. Entities include countries, organizations, companies, individuals, places, and products. By identifying the entities in a document, investors can link the article to other information on the entities and thereby create a comprehensive view before making decisions. Client interactions are no different: Determining client-relevant text is critical to a complete understanding of a client. While this type of data is critical, the problem is difficult; for example, separating articles regarding the technology company Apple and the fruit apple is not trivial.

Typical NLP Pipeline

With these applications in mind, we discuss the infrastructure required to incorporate NLP at scale. The NLP pipeline depicted in **Exhibit 5** presents a high-level overview of the key components in NLP analysis that mainly handle text inputs. Note that the original data need to be converted to machine readable text. For example, speech to text is required for audio and video sources. The original data can come from a variety of external and internal sources, such as corporate statements, central bank statements, news, social media, web content, internal documents, and video/audio meeting transcriptions. A data lake is typically needed to handle large amounts of input data. Depending on the size, structure, and usage of the data, they can be stored in different types of databases. Data with clear structure or schema can typically be stored using SQL relational databases. Unstructured data can be stored in nonrelational databases, such as MongoDB. Today, graph databases are becoming more popular in handling exceptionally large sets of structured, semistructured, or unstructured data.

The NLP engine shown in Exhibit 5 depicts the tools for text processing and is composed of two components. The first part focuses on processing raw text. Different use cases require different preprocessing procedures. For example, "case handling" refers to the conversion of all characters to uppercase/lowercase. This process is nuanced because "us" can refer to the United States if written in uppercase or the pronoun "us" if lowercase is used. In addition, while the removal of irregular punctuation and characters from formal documents, such as corporate filings, may be warranted, some characters may carry valuable information in other domains, such as emojis in social media data. Expansion/contraction refers to the process of expanding contractions into separate words, such as replacing "isn't" with "is not." This procedure will affect the final list of tokenized words (the result of splitting text into smaller units). Stop words, such as "the," "a," and "is," are not informative and are typically removed to reduce the size of the vocabulary. Depending on the application, stemming or lemmatization may be applied to reduce words to their root or stem forms. In the tokenization procedure, text in a document can be broken down into sentences, and these sentences can be further split into words or subwords. In some situations, subwords may be more robust when dealing with rare words.

The second part of the NLP engine contains tools to process and transform the cleansed text into usable information that can be consumed by the end applications or users. For example, we can analyze a sentence by splitting it into its parts and describing the syntactic roles of the various pieces. Named entity recognition is a commonly used parsing technique to identify persons, locations, and organizations from the text. Text vectorization—using

Exhibit 5. NLP Pipeline

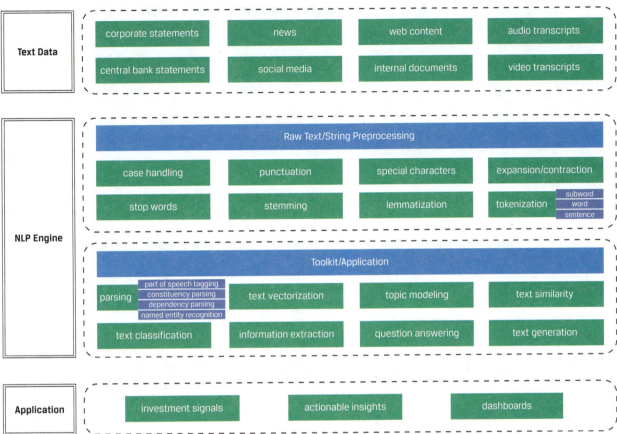

vectors to represent text—is commonly used for feature engineering. Popular techniques for text vectorization include one-hot encoding, term frequency–inverse document frequency (TF–IDF), word embeddings using word2vec (Mikolov, Chen, Corrado, and Dean 2013) and GloVe (Pennington, Socher, and Manning 2014), and word/sentence embeddings with deep learning language models. As an example, representing documents through bag-of-words approaches using one-hot encoding allows us to compute statistics describing the words in the document. These statistics can be enhanced to carry more information by assigning weights to the various words using such methods as TF–IDF. Word embeddings using word2vec or GloVe allow us to represent individual words using numerical vectors. Deep learning language models, such as BERT and GPT-3, can represent words and sentences using numerical vectors containing rich contextual information, such as positioning within sentences. These models are very efficient and powerful and have a wide range of applications.

Asset managers should modularize their tools to leverage these tools on diverse types of documents. For example, text summarization tools should be abstracted so they can be used for news articles, corporate filings, and internal emails. By modularizing the code, the various NLP techniques can be applied broadly across different types of documents. Depending on the size of the data and the specific algorithms used, different infrastructure may be needed. For example, to create sentence embeddings from many documents, a single GPU (graphics processing unit) processor can be substantially faster than parallelizing multiple CPUs (central processing units). For even larger corpora, such as global news articles, large clusters of machines may be needed to create deep learning models.

The output from the NLP engine can be consumed in different ways. For example, the NLP signals can be used directly to prompt an investment action or as part of a broader strategy. There may also be value in showing the results in a dashboard where users can interact with the original documents and the output. This transparency gives the users confidence in the signals because they can easily review the results on their own. In addition, asset managers may leverage these dashboards to solicit feedback from their users to improve their algorithms. One idea may be to give users the ability to highlight certain text and annotate the sentiment of the text to further fine-tune their models.

NLP Applications in Asset Management

In this section, we examine several applications of NLP in the asset management industry.

Deciphering Sentiment in Social Media Posts

Let us start with a simple example of applying NLP to social media posts to track sentiment. When the iPhone X was launched in late 2017, there were questions about its adoption and success. Investors and analysts turned to social media posts and reviews to gauge the sentiment of the iPhone X, as well as its competitors, during the rollout.

Investors were interested in understanding the features consumers valued in smartphones and whether the iPhone X's new features (Face ID, lack of a home button, etc.) were resonating with consumers.

One common approach to this question was to scrape smartphone reviews among various websites to assess consumer feedback. A simple word cloud, such as the one shown in **Exhibit 6**, is a quick way to uncover the key topics and themes.

The larger words represent the most frequently used words in the reviews. While some words are meaningless ("much" and "use") or expected ("Apple"), it may have been reassuring to see that "Face ID" was being highlighted and such words as "amazing" and "love" were being used to describe the new phone.

Investors can also analyze the sentiment across the reviews to gauge consumer feedback on the various smartphone models. VADER (Valence Aware Dictionary and sEntiment Reasoner) is well suited for this purpose given its ability to measure polarity and intensity of social media posts (Hutto and Gilbert 2014). **Exhibit 7** shows a snapshot of the reviews soon after the iPhone X was introduced. While most of the consumers were "neutral" on the new phone, it seemed that the iPhone X was lagging its predecessors in terms of positive reviews.

Investors may have also wanted to determine the features that were most prevalent in reviews to assess the appeal of the iPhone X's new features since those enhancements were likely going to drive adoption. This analysis typically requires the determination of the key features differentiating the phones (system, screen, battery, price, etc.) and the creation of a list of keywords used to describe those features. For example, such terms as "iOS" and "Android" are associated with the "system" feature. **Exhibit 8** suggests that the new features in the iPhone X were leading to many positive reviews.

This simple example illustrates the basics of NLP analysis. Once the raw data from social media posts and customer reviews are ingested, simple tools can be used to analyze the data to provide insights into investment controversies. In late 2017, investors were assessing the launch of the iPhone X, and by monitoring and

Exhibit 6. Word Cloud for iPhone X Reviews

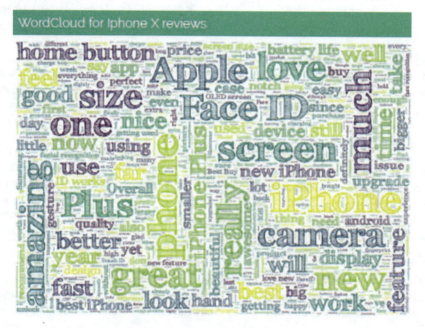

Source: AllianceBernstein.

Exhibit 7. Consumer Sentiment by Phone

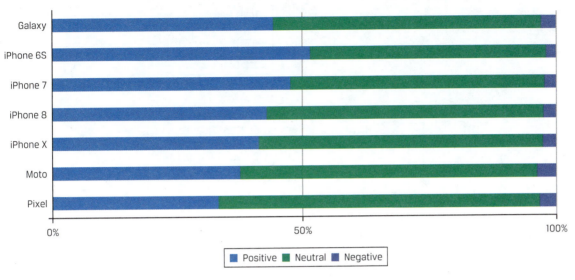

Source: AllianceBernstein.

Exhibit 8. Percentage of Feature Mentions in Positive Reviews

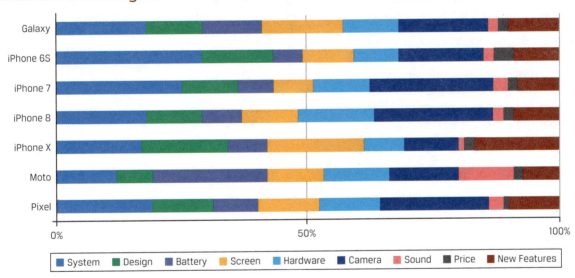

Source: AllianceBernstein.

aggregating the social media posts, they were likely able to discern the positive adoption of the new features and thus conclude that the new phone was likely to achieve the success of the prior models.

Extracting Themes to Highlight Important Topics and Trends

Our industry deals with vast amounts of documents. Often, analysts are tasked with synthesizing and summarizing enormous documents or extracting important sections or figures from these documents. **Exhibit 9** highlights some of the key tasks when dealing with large documents.

Topic modeling can streamline the analysis of large documents by identifying and extracting the key topics or themes in the data. The evolution of these topics from the corpora may also provide insight into the importance of the themes over time.

In the following example, the BERTopic package (Grootendorst 2022) is used to generate topic representations by converting each document to its embedded

Exhibit 9. Synthesizing Large Documents

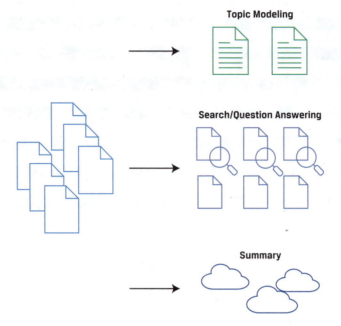

representation, clustering the documents, and then extracting keywords to represent the derived themes.

We applied BERTopic to about 260,000 Apple headlines from October 2019 to September 2022 to extract the top topics from the text. Since the topics were generated programmatically, we inferred the true themes for each of the topics from the generated keywords and used them as labels in **Exhibit 10**. For example, we created a theme called "Stock Market" because the important keywords for the topic are "sp," "500," "nasdaq," and "dow." Similarly, the "Covid" theme has references to "infection," "contact," and "tracing." Deciphering intuitive and interpretable themes from the BERTopic output is a crucial step when using topic modeling tools.

The topics we inferred from the Apple news articles ("Apps," "Covid," "Inflation Concerns," "Stock Market," and

Exhibit 10. Top Five Topics from Apple News Articles, October 2019–September 2022

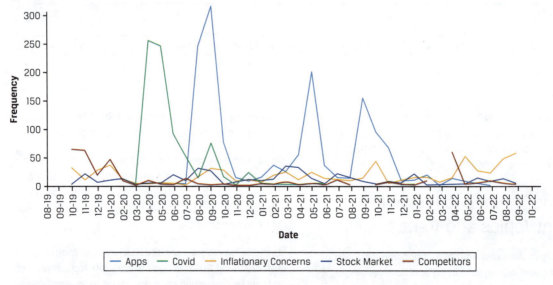

Source: AllianceBernstein.

"Competitors") are intuitive and distinct. Note that "Covid" was unsurprisingly the key topic in the first half of 2020, but its importance has waned since then. Instead, inflationary concerns are dominating more recent Apple news headlines. **Exhibit 11** provides the sample code to extract key themes from text.

Topic modeling is particularly powerful in uncovering the key themes or ideas across a set of documents. It can also be used to explain the evolution of topics over time to understand their importance in a specific area. In the Apple example, investors can extract the key themes and the associated keywords from market news to drive their research and perspective on the company. In another example, we applied topic modeling on central bank statements to uncover the emphasis of the Federal Open Market Committee (FOMC) on its two goals—price stability and sustained economic growth. By parsing central bank statements, we could assess the FOMC's trade-off between these two goals to gain insights into their policies at upcoming meetings.

Exhibit 11. Sample Code: Extracting Key Themes

Load in time series data - Apple headlines

```
1  import pandas as pd
2  apple_news = pd.read_csv("./apple_news.csv").dropna()
3  apple_news = apple_news.drop_duplicates( keep='last')
4  apple_news['date']= pd.to_datetime(apple_news['date'])
5  apple = apple_news.groupby(['date'])['text'].apply(lambda x: ' '.join(x)).to_frame().reset_index()
6  timestamps = apple.date.to_list()
7  apple_news_list = apple.text.to_list()
8  apple_news.head(3)
```

	date	text
0	2019-09-22 11:00:00	Apple (AAPL) Valuation Rose While Independent ...
1	2019-09-22 11:00:00	Do Directors Own Apple Inc. (NASDAQ:AAPL) Shares?
2	2019-09-22 11:45:00	Global tax authorities discuss targeting multi...

Calculate headline embeddings and create clusters over time

```
1   from bertopic import BERTopic
2   # Initialize the model
3   topic_model = BERTopic(verbose=True)
4   # calculate headline embeddings
5   topics, probs = topic_model.fit_transform(apple_news_list)
6   # create clusters over time
7   topics_over_time = topic_model.topics_over_time(apple_news_list, topics, timestamps, nr_bins=36)
8   top_topics = topics_over_time[topics_over_time['Topic'].isin(range(5))]
9   top_topics = top_topics.set_index('Timestamp')
10  top_topics_pivot = top_topics.pivot_table(index='Timestamp',columns='Topic',values='Frequency',aggfunc='sum')
```

Visualize the top 5 topics over time

```
1   import matplotlib.pyplot as plt
2   import matplotlib.dates as mdates
3   fig = plt.figure(figsize=(25,10))
4   ax = plt.axes()
5   # re-name topic names
6   plt.plot(top_topics_pivot[0], label='Apps', color='purple',linewidth=3.0)
7   plt.plot(top_topics_pivot[1], label='Covid', color='black',linewidth=3.0)
8   plt.plot(top_topics_pivot[2], label='Inflationary Concerns', color='blue',linewidth=3.0)
9   plt.plot(top_topics_pivot[3], label='Stock Market', color='green',linewidth=3.0)
10  plt.plot(top_topics_pivot[4], label='Competitors', color='red',linewidth=3.0)
11  # change background color and date format
12  ax.set_facecolor("white")
13  ax.xaxis.set_major_locator(mdates.MonthLocator())
14  ax.xaxis.set_major_formatter(mdates.DateFormatter('%m-%y'))
15  # add axes labels and a title
16  plt.title('Top 5 Topics Over Time\n', fontsize=18)
17  plt.xlabel('\n Date', fontsize=16)
18  plt.ylabel('\n Frequency', fontsize=16)
19  # display plot with legend
20  plt.legend(title='Topic_Name')
21  plt.show()
```

Searching for Key Themes and Question Answering

While topic modeling can provide a good overview of a set of documents, investors may be interested in extracting relevant sections or targeted data points from specific documents. We provide an example of these tasks using environmental, social, and governance (ESG) documents. Because ESG-oriented strategies have become more mainstream, asset managers are looking for ways to assess ESG-related activities in their investment companies and to monitor their progress toward their goals. Corporate and social responsibility (CSR) reports are used by companies to communicate their ESG efforts and their impact on the environment and community. These reports describe the company's relations with its full range of stakeholders: employees, customers, communities, suppliers, governments, and shareholders. Though corporations are currently not mandated to publish CSR reports annually, more than 90% of the companies in the S&P 500 Index did so for 2019.

In the following example shown in **Exhibit 12**, we parse sentences from a CSR report in the automotive industry and leverage a semantic search model that uses predefined keywords to rank and select parsed sentences. This example searches for sentences related to "GHG [greenhouse gas] Emissions." We embed this phrase into a vector and use it to compare against the embedded representation of the document text. Our example uses only one comparison sentence ("text" variable in the sample code below) for simplicity, but we can apply the same process for multiple candidate sentences, sort similarity scores across all of them, and then select the most similar ones from the process.

Exhibit 12. Sample Code: Searching for ESG Themes in a CSR Report

Load packages and the USE model

```
1  import numpy as np
2  import tensorflow as tf
3  import tensorflow_hub as hub
4  module_url = "https://tfhub.dev/google/universal-sentence-encoder/4"
5  use_model = hub.load(module_url)
```

Specify the keyword and text, and calculate embeddings separately

```
1   keyword = "GHG Emissions"
2   keyword_vec = use_model([keyword])[0]
3
4   text =['''Energy indirect (Scope 2) GHG emissions Baseline year 2010,
5   which was the first full year of operation as the new
6   General Motors Company and includes all facilities under GM operational control.
7   Calculation includes CO2, CH4 and N20.
8   Reporting is based on GHG Protocol, and the source of emission factors is regulatory or IPCC.
9   2020 GHG emissions are as follows:Gross location based indirect emissions: 3,087,816 Metric tons CO2e
10  Gross market based indirect emissions: 2,599,822 Metric tons CO2e''']
11  sentence_embeddings = use_model(text)
```

Calculate the cosine similarity

```
1  def calculate_cosine_similarity(u, v):
2      return np.dot(u, v) / (np.linalg.norm(u) * np.linalg.norm(v))
3  score = calculate_cosine_similarity(keyword_vec, sentence_embeddings[0])
```

Print out results

```
1  print("Query = ", query,end='\n\n')
2  print("Sentence = ", text[0],end='\n\n')
3  print("Similarity Score = ", round(score,2))
```

Query = GHG Emissions

Sentence = Energy indirect (Scope 2) GHG emissions Baseline year 2010, which was the first full year of operation as the new
General Motors Company and includes all facilities under GM operational control. Calculation includes CO2, CH4 and N20.
Reporting is based on GHG Protocol, and the source of emission factors is regulatory or IPCC. 2020 GHG emissions are as follows:
Gross location based indirect emissions: 3,087,816 Metric tons CO2e Gross market based indirect emissions: 2,599,822 Metric tons CO2e

Similarity Score = 0.46

Theme searches can direct researchers to relevant sections of the text quickly, thus simplifying the process to extract insights from documents. One caveat is that semantic searches initially start as unsupervised learning processes and may need to be enhanced by creating classification models based on labeled feedback. These resulting supervised learning models ensure important sections are not missed during the search process. Indeed, creating a comprehensive list of keywords and fine-tuning the model on annotated search results are common methods to minimize false negatives (incorrectly labeling a section as not important).

While finding relevant and related text improves both the efficiency and effectiveness of researchers, more direct approaches to narrow down the answers to queries may be even more impactful. Question answering is designed for exactly this purpose. The goal of QA is to build systems that automatically extract answers from a given corpus for questions posed by humans in a natural language. In the following example in **Exhibit 13**, we feed the question "What is the goal by 2035?" and a representative passage from a CSR report into the RoBERTa model (Liu et al. 2019), an optimized model leveraging BERT. The model can extract the exact answer from the passage—"source 100% renewable energy globally"—thus directly answering the original question. In real-life examples, passages and documents are much longer but the same approach can be used to find the best answer to the question.

These techniques have broad applications across the asset management industry; research analysts, risk managers,

Exhibit 13. Sample Code: Question Answering for ESG Metrics

Load packages and the RoBERTa models

```python
import torch
from transformers import AutoTokenizer, AutoModelForQuestionAnswering
tokenizer = AutoTokenizer.from_pretrained("vanadhi/roberta-base-fiqa-flm-sq-flit")
model = AutoModelForQuestionAnswering.from_pretrained("vanadhi/roberta-base-fiqa-flm-sq-flit")
```

Specify the question and text, and calculate embedding inputs using the tokenizer

```python
question ="What is the goal by 2035?"

text = '''We're committed to achieving this vision in a timeframe that aligns with climate science.
That's why GM has announced plans to become carbon neutral in our global products and operations by 2040.
Making progress toward these goals will address the most significant sources of
carbon emissions that we may be able to impact, including vehicle emissions, which currently represent 75% of the
emissions we are trying to reduce, and our manufacturing operations, which are responsible for 2%. To reach carbon
neutrality in our operations, we have a goal to source 100% renewable energy globally by 2035, five years earlier than
our previous commitment made in 2020 and 15 years sooner than our original target.'''

inputs = tokenizer(question, text, return_tensors='pt')
```

Feed input embeddings into the model, and extract an answer from the text

```python
outputs = model(**inputs)
start_scores = outputs.start_logits
end_scores = outputs.end_logits
answer_start = torch.argmax(start_scores)
answer_end = torch.argmax(end_scores) + 1
answer = tokenizer.convert_tokens_to_string(
    tokenizer.convert_ids_to_tokens(inputs["input_ids"][0][answer_start:answer_end]))
```

Print out results

```python
print('Question: '+ question, end='\n\n')
print('Context: '+ text, end='\n\n')
print('Answer: '+answer)
```

Question: What is the goal by 2035?

Context: We're committed to achieving this vision in a timeframe that aligns with climate science.
That's why GM has announced plans to become carbon neutral in our global products and operations by 2040.
Making progress toward these goals will address the most significant sources of
carbon emissions that we may be able to impact, including vehicle emissions, which currently represent 75% of the
emissions we are trying to reduce, and our manufacturing operations, which are responsible for 2%. To reach carbon
neutrality in our operations, we have a goal to source 100% renewable energy globally by 2035, five years earlier than
our previous commitment made in 2020 and 15 years sooner than our original target.

Answer: source 100% renewable energy globally

compliance officers, and operations staff are constantly scouring documents for key figures and specific items within documents. Examples include financial statement analysis, ESG monitoring, regulatory reporting, and fund prospectus reviews. While these tools can be extremely powerful, they need careful calibration and fine-tuning before they can be used widely across the financial services industry. In our experience, creating a step to extract relevant sections *before* the QA process, as in the prior use case, is essential to success. This step ensures that the appropriate sections of the document are being searched for the answers.

Uncovering Risks in Corporate Filings

We now delve further into the actual text and language used in documents to uncover insights for investment research. We scan corporate filings for potential risks using text mining techniques. Since the Securities and Exchange Commission (SEC) requires publicly traded companies to file reports disclosing their financial condition, investors can parse these reports for significant disclosures, changes, and trends.

In an influential paper, Cohen, Malloy, and Nguyen (2019) found that significant changes in sequential 10-Ks convey negative information on future firm performance. Since 10-K filings are typically long and complicated, leveraging NLP techniques to extract information systematically can greatly improve the comparison of year-over-year (YOY) changes. Cohen et al. used several bag-of-words approaches to measure document changes, including the cosine similarity between vectors representing the documents. The following example in **Exhibit 14** leverages doc2vec (a generalized version of word2vec that represents whole documents as vectors) to model the changes of the management discussion and analysis (MD&A) section in 10-K forms.

Corporate filings, including 10-Ks, can be scraped from the SEC's websites. Text from the MD&A section is extracted and doc2vec is used to represent the text in each of the filings. Specifically, the words in the MD&A sections are represented by numerical vectors using the doc2vec algorithm. To gauge YOY changes, we compute the cosine similarity of the two vectors representing the sequential filings. High cosine similarity suggests the text from the two filings is largely the same, whereas low cosine similarity suggests substantial differences in the underlying reports.

A typical long–short backtest can be used to determine the predictive efficacy of this NLP feature. **Exhibit 15** shows the performance of a monthly-rebalanced long–short strategy, with the long side representing the companies with the most similar YOY filings and the short side containing the companies with the most dissimilar filings. The backtest shows compelling results throughout the study period, with the strongest results in more recent years. Our results suggest that simple calculations using vectorized representations of documents can uncover risks and opportunities from corporate filings. The NLP process in this example "reads" the documents and looks for differences in the text, emulating the tasks commonly performed by research analysts.

Broadening Insights on Earnings Call Transcripts

Earnings calls provide forums for companies to convey important financial and business information to the investment community and the public. Human analysts scour individual calls for insights into company operations, but doing so systematically across a wide swath of companies can be time consuming and error prone. NLP tools can be leveraged efficiently and effectively to address these issues.

Earnings calls typically consist of a presentation section and a question-and-answer (Q&A) section. Company executives are the sole participants in the first section, whereas both corporate executives and analysts from the investment community interact during the Q&A section. Investment signals can be mined on the different sections and the different types of speakers—namely, CEOs, other executives, and analysts—to study potential differences among them.

A variety of NLP approaches can be used to generate investment signals from earnings call transcripts. Bag-of-words approaches using predefined dictionaries and context-driven language models are common techniques. We describe three categories of features in our analysis of the transcripts—document attributes, readability scores, and sentiment scores.

Document attributes refer to features derived from the characteristics of the call. Examples include the number of words, sentences, questions, and analyst participants in a call.

Readability scores use a variety of methods to assess the difficulty of the text and document. These metrics tend to focus on two areas: the use of difficult-to-understand words and the length of sentences. Easily understood messages (texts with low readability scores) may be quickly incorporated into market prices and will therefore have a negligible impact on potential mispricing. Complex messages (texts with high readability scores) may be used by company executives to obfuscate bad news or less-than-stellar results.

Sentiment scores can be derived from the underlying text using different formulations. The most basic method to assess sentiment is to count the number of positive and negative words based on a specific dictionary, such as Harvard IV-4, VADER (Hutto and Gilbert 2014), and Loughran–McDonald (Loughran and McDonald 2011). This approach, commonly called bag of words or dictionary

Exhibit 14. Sample Code: Determining Changes in Corporate Filings

Load packages

```
1  import pandas as pd
2  import numpy as np
3  from nltk.tokenize import word_tokenize
4  from gensim.models.doc2vec import Doc2Vec, TaggedDocument
```

Prepare data

```
1  df = pd.read_csv('df_AAPL_10K_MDA.csv')
2  train = list(df[~df['heading'].str.contains('highlights')]['sectionText'].dropna())
3  test = list(df[df['heading'].str.contains('highlights')]['sectionText'].values)
4  print("There are {} pieces of text used for model training and {} pieces of text used in test"\
5        .format(len(train), len(test)))
```

There are 248 pieces of text used for model training and 9 pieces of text used in test

Train a doc2vec model based on training data

```
1  # Tokenize and tag each document
2  train_tokenized = [word_tokenize(doc.lower()) for doc in train]
3  train_tagged = [TaggedDocument(d, [i]) for i, d in enumerate(train_tokenized)]
4
5  # Train doc2vec model
6  '''
7  vector_size = Dimensionality of the feature vectors.
8  window = The maximum distance between the current and predicted word within a sentence.
9  min_count = Ignores all words with total frequency lower than this.
10 alpha = The initial learning rate.
11 '''
12 model = Doc2Vec(train_tagged, vector_size = 32, window = 3, min_count = 1, epochs = 100)
```

Get the results on the test data

```
1  # tokenzize test docs
2  test_tokenized = [word_tokenize(doc.lower()) for doc in test]
3
4  # get the vector representation for the test docs
5  test_vectors = [model.infer_vector(doc) for doc in test_tokenized]
6  n = len(test_vectors)
```

Calculate the cosine similarity and print out results

```
1  def calculate_cosine_similarity(u, v):
2      return np.dot(u, v) / (np.linalg.norm(u) * np.linalg.norm(v))
3
4  YoY_sim = []
5  for i in range(len(test_vectors)-1):
6      YoY_sim.append(calculate_cosine_similarity(test_vectors[i], test_vectors[i+1]))
7
8  print(pd.Series(YoY_sim, index=[str(year-1)+'-'+str(year) for year in range(2014, 2022)]).round(2))
```

```
2013-2014    0.93
2014-2015    0.94
2015-2016    0.88
2016-2017    0.94
2017-2018    0.95
2018-2019    0.79
2019-2020    0.59
2020-2021    0.90
```

based, is intuitive and interpretable, but it has limitations. For example, it cannot handle negation or words that may have different meanings in different settings. Context-driven language models can overcome the issues of dictionary-based approaches. With the development of advanced algorithms and improvements in computational power, transformer-based models, such as BERT, have proven to be effective in encoding and decoding the semantic and syntactic information of natural languages. The sample code in **Exhibit 16** uses FinBERT (Huang, Wang, and Yang, forthcoming), a BERT-based model pretrained on financial text, to score sentiment on a series of input sentences.

Exhibit 15. Performance of Similarity Score on US Large-Cap Companies, 2004–2019

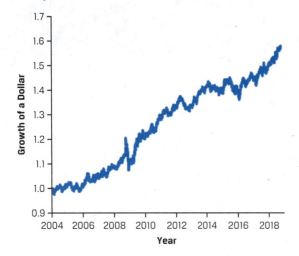

Source: AllianceBernstein.

We assess the ability of our features to differentiate between outperforming and underperforming stocks using a monthly rebalanced strategy. At the beginning of each month, we form portfolios based on the available features as of that date and track the difference in subsequent returns between the top and bottom quintiles over the following month. **Exhibit 17** shows a histogram of information ratios (IRs) for various features on US large-cap companies over the period 2010–2021. Approximately 20% of the IRs in our research are greater than 0.5 for the US companies, suggesting there is promise in the features. We found similarly encouraging results for features created in other stock and bond universes.

We now analyze the differences between dictionary-based and context-driven approaches to derive sentiment. Conceptually, the context around words should be an important driver when assessing sentiment. While "grow" may typically be viewed as positive, "competitors growing" or "economic headwinds growing" should be scored negatively. **Exhibit 18** shows the dollar growth of the strategies based on representative sentiment scores generated through these two approaches. The context-driven approach based on BERT has performed better recently, suggesting that it has been able to better discern sentiment in financial text. Additionally, there has been evidence suggesting company executives are adapting to the rise of machines listening to their comments by changing the words they use in their communications. In other words, company executives may be choosing their words carefully since they know NLP techniques are being used to analyze their comments. Thus, dictionary-based approaches may not be as useful going forward, and context-driven approaches may be more robust in overcoming these behavioral changes.

These high-level results suggest that the generated NLP signals from earnings call transcripts may be useful for portfolio managers. Applications include the usage of these signals in systematic strategies or to complement fundamental processes. Additionally, similar techniques can be applied to other types of corporate filings and statements to extract insights from those documents. These tools give investors the ability to analyze large amounts of documents methodically and potentially save them from doing the work manually.

Deepening Client Insights to Prioritize Sales Efforts

With continued economic and market uncertainty, sales teams need to quickly digest and synthesize client information and updates to assess their needs. We can leverage NLP to help these sales teams deepen client insights and prioritize sales efforts using publicly available data.

The data sources include client presentations, quarterly/annual reports, meeting minutes, announcements, and news. It is time consuming for any sales team to monitor all the media outlets for information across a broad set of prospects and clients. NLP techniques can be leveraged to collect, process, and synthesize the data and alert the sales team with timely and actionable prompts.

Exhibit 19 illustrates this process. First, public data can be obtained through web scraping. For example, data scraping pipelines can be built to detect document changes on various websites. We can also monitor major news outlets to track mentions of specific keywords, such as names of organizations, themes, and topics. The scraped data are populated into a database before being fed into the NLP engine. Based on the specific use case, the NLP engine (more details are shown in Exhibit 5) aims to further prepare the data and applies the applicable algorithms to extract the relevant information. As a final step, notifications and prompts are sent to the sales team for further action.

In summary, using NLP to effectively process and synthesize information can inform and improve sales outreach by surfacing timely alerts and relevant intelligence from publicly available data sources.

Identifying Entities within Documents

Across many of the use cases discussed above, entity names and identifiers need to be extracted from the text to tie the documents back to specific people or organizations.

Exhibit 16. Sample Code: Extracting Sentiment from Text

Load packages and the finBERT models

```
from transformers import BertTokenizer, BertForSequenceClassification
from transformers import pipeline
import pandas as pd

finbert = BertForSequenceClassification.from_pretrained('yiyanghkust/finbert-tone',num_labels=3)
tokenizer = BertTokenizer.from_pretrained('yiyanghkust/finbert-tone')

nlp = pipeline("sentiment-analysis", model=finbert, tokenizer=tokenizer)
```

Predict the sentiment of sentences

```
sentences = ["there is a shortage of capital, and we need extra financing.",
             "growth is strong and we have plenty of liquidity.",
             "there are doubts about our finances.",
             "profits are flat."]
results = nlp(sentences)
```

Check the results

```
%%capture
[results[i].update({'sentence': sentences[i]}) for i in range(len(sentences))]
output = pd.DataFrame(results)[['sentence', 'score', 'label']]
output['score'] = output['score'].round(3)
```

```
output
```

	sentence	score	label
0	there is a shortage of capital, and we need extra financing.	0.995	Negative
1	growth is strong and we have plenty of liquidity.	1.000	Positive
2	there are doubts about our finances.	1.000	Negative
3	profits are flat.	0.994	Neutral

Named entity recognition refers to the task of identifying the entities (person, place, country, company, financial instrument, etc.) within documents. **Exhibit 20** provides a simple example using spaCy to identify the various entities in a news title.

Successfully Leveraging NLP

While our use cases demonstrate that significant advances have been made, NLP is still relatively new in finance. We discuss the key technical and business challenges next.

Overcoming Technical Challenges

Broadly, technical challenges, such as breaking down sentences and tagging the parts of speech within sentences, are common across all NLP applications. Linguists and computer scientists are researching and creating new insights to improve on these capabilities, especially across different languages.

Context-specific tools for the financial services industry are being developed. Dictionaries are extremely useful and improve language understanding, especially for specialized domains. One complexity lies in robust dictionaries across different languages. We found that a simple translation of the Loughran–McDonald dictionary to Chinese is not robust because some words do not carry the same meanings in Chinese and there are additional Chinese words that are more meaningful for Chinese investors.

Even context-specific language models, such as BERT, will need to learn from new financial domains. While FinBERT-type models have been trained on financial text, further training and fine-tuning is likely required to improve

Exhibit 17. Number of NLP Features across Different Information Ratio Levels

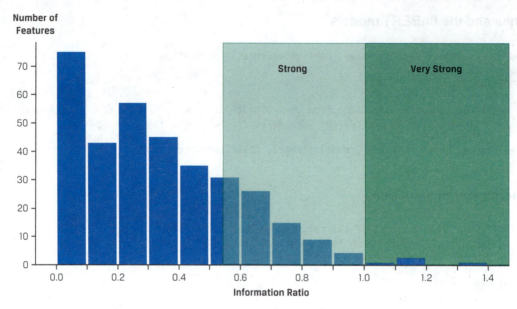

Source: AllianceBernstein.

Exhibit 18. Performance of Context-Driven vs. Dictionary-Based Approaches, 2010–2021

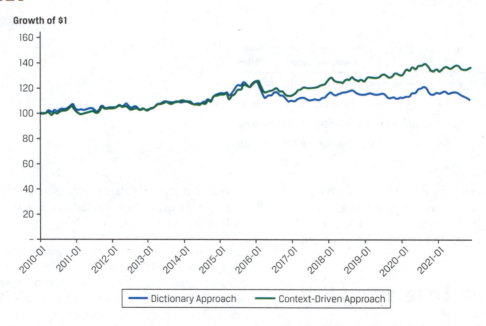

Source: AllianceBernstein.

performance in specialized areas, such as securitized assets, regulatory filings, fund disclosures, and economic forecasts. In securitized assets, for example, such common English words as "pool" and "tranche" have vastly different meanings, and language models will need to be trained with these new words before machines can systematically understand and synthesize text as humans do.

Named entity recognition (NER) is an important task in finance. Even though we provided a simple example among our use cases to apply spaCy's NER model on written text, the model is not perfect. For example, spaCy's model incorrectly tags companies with names containing common English words. For example, numerous articles containing the words "state" or "street" may be classified under

Exhibit 19. Overview of Process to Deepen Client Insights

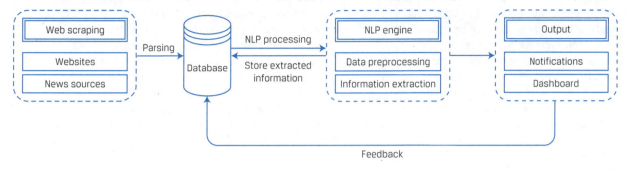

Exhibit 20. Sample Code: Identifying Entities within Documents

Import packages and the model

```
1  import spacy
2  import en_core_web_trf
```

```
1  spacy_model_name = 'en_core_web_trf'
2  if not spacy.util.is_package(spacy_model_name):
3      spacy.cli.download(spacy_model_name)
4  nlp = spacy.load(spacy_model_name)
```

Identify entities in text

```
1  text = "Elon Musk pulls out of $44bn deal to buy Twitter."
2  doc = nlp(text)
```

```
1  for entity in doc.ents:
2      print(entity.text, entity.label_)
```

Elon Musk PERSON
$44bn MONEY
Twitter ORG

the company "State Street." These limitations encourage researchers to further fine-tune and improve their NER models. One approach is to leverage threshold-based matching techniques to achieve the desired accuracy. By increasing the threshold to accept matches using NLP-based similarity metrics, we can improve the accuracy of the models. However, this increased accuracy comes at a cost: We may have more false negatives because our model may be less forgiving of misspellings and short names. As a result, researchers should assess the trade-offs between false positives and false negatives in their applications.

Another approach to improve NER involves applying additional code to the results from the spaCy model. This allows more flexibility for researchers to customize their requirements and insights for identifying entities. This approach may be helpful to deal with the difficulties in identifying such companies as AT&T, where its ticker (T) and acronyms are quite common in normal language usage.

Overcoming Business Challenges

On top of these technical challenges, various business issues slow or hinder the adoption of NLP across asset managers. In our view, the biggest hurdle is data—data quality and accessibility. Until recently, data had not been viewed as an asset, and as a result, the quality of data is varied and in many cases, unknown. We see many companies creating data organizations to tackle these issues, with the emergence of the chief data officer as an important executive and driver of business prioritization.

With the appropriate focus and resourcing, firms can leverage data as an asset, feeding data into dashboards and models that ultimately help with faster and better decision making. This is particularly true for NLP pipelines and tools because the existing policies around these data are likely nonexistent, which presents an opportunity for organizations to design governance processes from scratch. In addition, firms will need to be nimble in their governance and policies because of the nascent and evolving regulatory frameworks; regulators are struggling to keep up with the breadth and complexity of data and the uses of data across commercial platforms, but we expect improved guidance in the future.

Data accessibility is also a big hurdle: Data scientists face challenges in finding and ingesting the required data for analysis and modeling. With regard to external data, asset managers can choose to create their own datasets or partner with vendors. Our view is that the most innovative and impactful data sources will be harder to obtain, and as a result, asset managers will need to develop their own pipelines to ingest these data. This may involve web scraping and capturing various forms of communication (html, different text file formats, audio, and video). Fortunately, many open-source tools exist to handle these situations.

As datasets become widely used and commoditized, vendor solutions are likely feasible and cost effective. For example, about 10 years ago, asset owners creating NLP signals from corporate filings, such as 10Ks and 10Qs, and earnings call transcripts developed pipelines to scrape, clean, and ingest the documents directly from the SEC's EDGAR website. Today, various vendors offer data solutions that significantly simplify the pipelines to leverage corporate filings. Another example is ESG data: Currently, there is little consistency in ESG metrics, standards, reporting formats, and disclosure frequencies. This means that asset managers are developing bespoke NLP pipelines to process the various documents and metrics on company websites, disclosures, and presentations. Over time, requirements will evolve because we expect this space to consolidate considerably over the next few years and vendors will emerge to develop solutions around ESG data collection, analysis, and reporting.

Transforming Culture

An organization's culture may be another important hurdle in its transformation. Organizations aspire to learn, innovate, and adapt, but cultural norms and human behavior can sometimes impede progress. We see this repeatedly across the industry.

Successful portfolio managers at all organizations typically have successful track records and significant assets under management from clients who have bought into their capabilities. Although these portfolio managers strive to outperform and deliver for their clients, one clear tendency is for teams to continue doing what has been successful.

Investment teams operate on clearly articulated investment philosophies that have been honed over many years. They apply these philosophies using disciplined investment processes to uncover insights and opportunities. These structures have brought the team historical success, so changing or overriding these processes will be extremely difficult. This is the challenge that new data sources and more advanced techniques, such as NLP, face—overcoming the entrenched mindset that may come with historical success. This issue is compounded because clients expect investment teams to continue with processes that have worked and brought them success. However, with the financial markets, competitors, data sources, and investment tools changing rapidly, successful teams will need to evolve to survive.

To help organizations in their transformation, data scientists should leverage techniques to augment rather than replace existing processes, which is best achieved through pilot projects focused on real problems. Projects should be driven by investment controversies, sales opportunities, or operational gaps. By partnering with the decision makers, data scientists can achieve shared outcomes that are valued by all parties, thus ensuring adoption and success. NLP projects focused on addressing inefficiencies, such as gathering data, updating tables, and systematically making data more accessible, can deliver value and encourage adoption. Our use cases discussed in the earlier sections are examples where we have seen success because they address existing gaps that can be addressed through data science techniques.

Once investors, sales teams, and operations functions understand the value and capabilities of data science, they will be more open to further exploration. For example, once the investment teams have access to the corporate filings on a common platform (such as a dashboard), it is natural to extend the capabilities to synthesize the documents. Sentiment analysis and topic extraction are examples of common extensions once the data are in place. Indeed, to ensure adoption and success, asset managers should engage with end users to implement these ideas. We find that summarization, topic modeling, and question answering projects have the highest probability of success because they address common inefficiencies or manual processes.

Asset managers may see opportunities to leverage NLP to achieve efficiencies in operational processes. Indeed, as we discussed in our use cases, our techniques can be applied across various parts of the organization. While this may be low-hanging fruit, cultural norms and mindsets may make it difficult for innovative ideas to be adopted quickly. Employees may be concerned about their roles and livelihood when new technology is introduced: What is their place once the new techniques are incorporated? What incentive do they have to adopt the new technologies and potentially eliminate the need for their roles? As a result, asset managers need to assess cultural barriers when trading off the operational savings versus the likelihood of success.

Developing Clear Success Metrics

Companies of all stripes are intrigued by the potential of new data, new techniques, and new technologies in their organizations. However, it is important to define clear success metrics on these new initiatives. For organizations starting their exploration, modest goals are likely appropriate. For example, getting one investment team to adopt and thus champion the successes may be a realistic and achievable goal. For more advanced organizations, developing common infrastructure and tools while nurturing talent may be the appropriate goals. In all cases, however, we suggest organizations take long-term views on their projects and articulate short-term milestones that create awareness, maximize adoption, and develop competencies.

Attracting and Developing Talent

There will be a talent gap. Existing employees may not possess the required data science or NLP skills, so companies will need to hire external talent. Creating a "Center of Excellence" that aims to raise the capabilities across the organization is one way to bridge the talent gap. While exact structures may differ from firm to firm, we believe it is important to have a dedicated centralized team that keeps abreast of industry developments, creates new capabilities, shares best practices, builds common infrastructure, and develops talent. Achieving these outcomes will be maximized with a centralized team with the mandate to raise the competencies of the entire organization.

This central hub acts as a critical link among all the teams in the organization, ensuring that the latest insights and capabilities are shared broadly. With this core team in place, organizations now have different approaches to build out their data science capabilities. On the one hand, augmenting the centralized team with embedded data scientists within business functions ensures that there is domain expertise and the business units are accountable for the success of the teams. On the other hand, consolidating all the data scientists in one centralized team ensures there are efficiencies and few overlaps on projects, but the researchers may be more removed from the end users. Ultimately, the optimal structure will depend on the organization's existing norms, culture, and goals, but having a Center of Excellence is essential to long-term success.

The Road Ahead

NLP has tremendous potential in asset management. Our use cases highlight existing areas where NLP is already having an impact. We expect growing adoption across more functions in asset management organizations as three trends take hold: (1) availability of and improvements in open-source models, training data, tools, and vendor options, (2) fine-tuned models with proprietary insights, and (3) development of non-English capabilities.

Improved Tools

Even though there were over 70,000 models and counting as of late 2022 on Hugging Face (a popular NLP platform), we expect to see continuous innovation in training and fine-tuning techniques. Models will be trained for specific tasks, thus improving their performance across various activities. For example, customized BERT models may be developed for different fixed-income sectors, such as collateralized loan obligations, mortgages, private credit, and municipal bonds, among others. Semantic improvements will also be made, as machines are taught to further understand the nuances of language.

Asset managers are also exploring the use of audio and visual cues to augment the text-driven features we have discussed. By combining the tonal variations of spoken text, the facial and bodily expressions of the speakers, and the actual text used, researchers hope to have a more comprehensive understanding of the intended communication. Indeed, in our day-to-day interactions, we incorporate all these elements (tone, delivery, body language, and content) to discern the message and its nuances. Interestingly, techniques such as the ones discussed in this chapter can be extended to capture audio and visual features. For example, different aspects of the audio message can be embedded using BERT-type models, and these embeddings can be compared and manipulated to tease out changes in emotions and reactions.

We have seen an explosion in the breadth of vendor offerings to solve specific NLP tasks in investment, compliance, and operational activities. Specifically, document processing such as that in our use cases on theme searches and question answering is becoming more mainstream. Vendors have developed customized solutions for specific applications across the industry (ESG documents, regulatory filings, shareholder documents, etc.). While customized solutions are the natural starting points, we expect more consolidation to occur and more generalized and robust solutions in the future. For example, QA techniques will be more powerful and able to handle diverse types of questions across different documents. To draw an analogy from another domain, the Google search engine has evolved over time and is now able to handle specific queries rather than simply return generalized results. Searching for the "score from yesterday's Yankees game" returns the actual score rather than links to the team website or a list of baseball scores. We expect these capabilities to materialize for the asset management industry, giving researchers the ability to answer specific questions and synthesize ideas quickly.

Proprietary Models

We have seen various instances of asset owners injecting their own insights into language models to improve the base models. There are two common approaches—proprietary dictionaries and proprietary phrase annotations. As discussed earlier, various public dictionaries exist to score sentiment on sentences and documents. Having said that, investment teams can create custom dictionaries to score documents based on their own preferences, thereby tailoring the NLP algorithms for their specific use cases. This customization enables asset managers to synthesize documents using their own views and insights and build trust in the underlying algorithms.

Beyond customized dictionaries, investment teams can also label or annotate words, phrases, and sentences to improve language models, such as BERT. Our own research suggests language models can be more accurate on sentiment classification and other NLP tasks with feedback from human annotators. The following two sentences are from a telecom company that FinBERT scores as positive.

Sentence 1: "It does seem as though your competitors are healthfully ramping up their efforts to try and improve service quality."

Sentence 2: "Churn in handsets remains below 0.9%, but it sure looks like it was up a lot year over year."

From a sentiment perspective, we view these sentences as negative when the broader context is considered. In the first sentence, a company's competitors performing better is typically negative for the company, but FinBERT focuses on the "ramping up" and "improve service quality" to determine its positive sentiment.

As for the second sentence, higher "churn" for a telecom company should be viewed as a negative even though such models as FinBERT normally view "up a lot year over year" as positive. These examples illustrate the need for language models to be further trained on specific domains for them to be effective.

By manually labeling these sentences and using them to fine-tune FinBERT, we found marked improvement in the model's performance. We expect more firms to use manual annotations to improve the base models and to engender more trust in the models.

While we largely used the investment arena for our discussion on proprietary dictionaries and phrases, the same concepts can be leveraged in other parts of the organization. Sales teams can customize NLP tools for their client outreach using the same methods to optimize client interactions and sales effectiveness.

Language Expansion

Finally, we expect to see substantial progress in the development and advancement of non-English language models. While many of the NLP developments started with English documents, there has been both academic and practitioner interest in other languages. Specifically, as firms look for an edge in NLP, one fruitful path may be using documents in local languages rather than using the translated English versions. Local documents may reveal tone and semantic references that are discernible only in the original language.

Conclusion

As NLP tools mature in the asset management industry, organizations will be able to apply these tools to a wide range of problems. We are already seeing early successes in investments, distribution, and operations, and we expect this momentum to continue. As decision makers become more comfortable with the new tools and models, adoption will accelerate and efficiency gains will accrue quickly. Over time, with appropriate engagement and training by humans, the NLP tools will become more transparent and effective and users will readily incorporate these tools into their arsenal.

Ultimately, these NLP tools improve our decision making, and that alone should ensure their adoption and success.

References

Blei, David M., Andrew Y. Ng, and Michael I. Jordan. 2003. "Latent Dirichlet Allocation." *Journal of Machine Learning Research* 3: 993–1022.

Brown, Tom B., Benjamin Mann, Nick Ryder, Melanie Subbiah, Jared Kaplan, Prafulla Dhariwal, Arvind Neelakantan, Pranav Shyam, Girish Sastry, Amanda Askell, et al. 2020. "Language Models Are Few-Shot Learners." Cornell University, arXiv:2005.14165 (22 July).

Cohen, Lauren, Christopher J. Malloy, and Quoc Nguyen. 2019. "Lazy Prices." Academic Research Colloquium for Financial Planning and Related Disciplines (7 March).

Devlin, Jacob, Ming-Wei Chang, Kenton Lee, and Kristina Toutanova. 2018. "BERT: Pre-Training of Deep Bidirectional Transformers for Language Understanding." Cornell University, arXiv:1810.04805 (11 October).

Grootendorst, M. 2022. "BERTopic: Neural Topic Modeling with a Class-Based TF-IDF Procedure." Cornell University, arXiv:2203.05794 (11 March).

Hochreiter, Sepp, and Jürgen Schmidhuber. 1997. "Long Short-Term Memory." *Neural Computation* 9 (8): 1735–80.

Huang, Allen, Hui Wang, and Yi Yang. Forthcoming. "FinBERT: A Large Language Model for Extracting Information from Financial Text." *Contemporary Accounting Research*.

Hutto, Clayton J., and Eric Gilbert. 2014. "VADER: A Parsimonious Rule-Based Model for Sentiment Analysis of Social Media Text." *Proceedings of the Eighth International AAAI Conference on Weblogs and Social Media* 8 (1): 216–25. https://ojs.aaai.org/index.php/ICWSM/article/view/14550/14399.

Joshi, Mandar, Danqi Chen, Yinhan Liu, Daniel S. Weld, Luke Zettlemoyer, and Omer Levy. 2020. "SpanBERT: Improving Pre-Training by Representing and Predicting Spans." *Transactions of the Association for Computational Linguistics* 8: 64–77.

Liu, Yinhan, Myle Ott, Naman Goyal, Jingfei Du, Mandar Joshi, Danqi Chen, Omer Levy, Mike Lewis, Luke Zettlemoyer, and Veselin Stoyanov. 2019. "RoBERTa: A Robustly Optimized BERT Pretraining Approach." Cornell University, arXiv:1907.11692 (26 July).

Loughran, Tim, and Bill McDonald. 2011. "When Is a Liability Not a Liability? Textual Analysis, Dictionaries, and 10-Ks." *Journal of Finance* 66 (1): 35–65.

Mikolov, Tomas, Kai Chen, Greg Corrado, and Jeffrey Dean. 2013. "Efficient Estimation of Word Representations in Vector Space." Cornell University, arXiv:1301.3781 (7 September).

Pennington, Jeffrey, Richard Socher, and Christopher D. Manning. 2014. "GloVe: Global Vectors for Word Representation." *Proceedings of the 2014 Conference on Empirical Methods in Natural Language Processing (EMNLP)* (October): 1532–43.

Raffel, Colin, Noam Shazeer, Adam Roberts, Katherine Lee, Sharan Narang, Michael Matena, Yanqi Zhou, Wei Li, and Peter J. Liu. 2020. "Exploring the Limits of Transfer Learning with a Unified Text-to-Text Transformer." Cornell University, arXiv:1910.10683 (28 July).

Rajpurkar, Pranav, Jian Zhang, Konstantin Lopyrev, and Percy Liang. 2016. "SQuAD: 100,000+ Questions for Machine Comprehension of Text." *Proceedings of the 2016 Conference on Empirical Methods in Natural Language Processing* (November): 2383–92.

Turing, Alan Mathison. 1950. "Computing Machinery and Intelligence." *Mind* LIX (236): 433–60.

Vaswani, Ashish, Noam Shazeer, Niki Parmar, Jakob Uszkoreit, Llion Jones, Aidan N. Gomez, Łukasz Kaiser, and Illia Polosukhin. 2017. "Attention Is All You Need." In *Advances in Neural Information Processing Systems 30*, edited by I. Guyon, U. V. Luxburg, S. Bengio, H. Wallach, R. Fergus, S. Vishwanathan, and R. Garnett, 5998–6008.

5. ADVANCES IN NATURAL LANGUAGE UNDERSTANDING FOR INVESTMENT MANAGEMENT

Stefan Jansen, CFA
Founder and Lead Data Scientist, Applied AI

Introduction

Investors have long sifted through documents searching for facts that corroborate fundamental analysis, support forecasts, or provide insight into market dynamics. Given the importance of language for communication, it is not surprising that 80%–90% of information is available only in unstructured forms, such as text or audio, making it much harder to work with than tabular data that conform to database and excel formats (Harbert 2021). However, such data can enable more valuable, differentiated insights than numerical data in widespread use alone.

Text data sources relevant for investors depend on the asset class and investment horizon. They can be very diverse, ranging from regulatory filings and research reports to financial news and social media content. In addition, legal contracts may play an essential role for, for example, debt or real estate investments. Substantial improvements in speech recognition enable real-time processing of audio data, such as earnings calls, adding speaker tone, and other verbal nuances, which may uncover hidden insights. Similar advances in machine translation expand this universe to any common language. Over the last two decades, *electronic access to text data* with information affecting investment decisions in real time has increased by orders of magnitude. Automated downloads of corporate 10-K and 10-Q SEC filings, for instance, multiplied almost 500 times, from 360,861 in 2003 to around 165 million in 2016 (Cao, Jiang, Yang, and Zhang 2020). Machines have been driving part of this data explosion: In 2015, the Associated Press (AP) was already generating over 3,000 stories automatically on US corporate earnings per quarter, a tenfold increase over previous human production. The output had grown by more than 50% by 2017, while other outlets followed the AP's lead.

Unsurprisingly, the resulting data deluge has accelerated research into *natural language processing* (NLP), the AI discipline that cuts across linguistics and computer science and focuses on the ability of machines to make sense of text data. Practical goals are to automate and accelerate the analysis of text data or augment the capabilities of humans to do so. In 2016, J.P. Morgan deployed technology that could read 12,000 documents to extract 150 attributes relevant for human review in seconds, compared to 360,000 person-hours per year needed previously, all while being more accurate. NLP *use cases* vary from matching patterns and summarizing documents to making actionable predictions. They include standardizing and tagging investment targets across a large body of documents, scoring news sentiment or environmental, social, and governance (ESG) disclosures, flagging compliance issues, and forecasting market prices. *Sustained R&D* has improved applications that help manage and exploit the explosion of unstructured language data in versatile ways to create value along the investment process. These applications can boost analyst productivity by imposing structure on documents and their content, focus the attention of portfolio managers by prioritizing news flow, and facilitate risk management by detecting material events in real time. They can also support investment decisions by generating alpha signals.

The most impressive improvements build on *breakthroughs in machine learning (ML)*, particularly deep learning, where new language models have dramatically boosted performance on various tasks. However, organizations with a range of resources can leverage NLP applications because cloud-based application programming interfaces (APIs), high-quality open-source building blocks, and a growing vendor ecosystem have simplified the adoption or development of NLP solutions. At the other end of the spectrum, cutting-edge systems that generate proprietary alpha signals require an in-house team of specialists. This chapter describes NLP applications used by analysts and discretionary or systematic portfolio managers and characterizes emerging applications under development at leading quantitatively oriented funds. I begin by explaining key challenges facing NLP by machines and how recent advances have addressed them much better than earlier approaches. Then, I outline various categories of NLP applications and how they are used throughout the investment process. Finally, I illustrate three popular financial NLP use cases in more detail.

Challenges Faced by NLP

Making sense of language, never easy for machines, is even harder in finance.

Human language has many characteristics that make it *notoriously hard for machines* to process, interpret, and act on. It builds on complex grammatical rules, idiomatic usage, and contextual understanding—all of which humans take a significant amount of time to learn. Common challenges in interpreting language require decisions between multiple meanings for the same word, which may require context not provided in the document but instead assumed to be known to the reader. An early machine translation attempt illustrates how this process can go wrong: "out of sight, out of mind" translated into Russian and back to English produced "invisible, insane" (Pollack 1983).

A key challenge particular to machines is the requisite *conversion of text into numbers* suitable for digital computation. The output tends to simplify the intricate structure of language by omitting or weakening critical relationships among words, phrases, and sentences. As a result, algorithms have struggled for a long time to recover the meaning of statements and documents.

Popular applications such as sentiment analysis used relatively *simplistic, error-prone approaches*: They relied on the presence of specific words or language patterns defined by humans to evaluate statements or flag events, as we will see in more detail later. Such methods are transparent and intuitive but often have limited flexibility and sensitivity compared to language models with more sophisticated understanding.

Additional challenges emerge with *domain-specific uses of language*, as in finance. The need to account for the distinct semantics of technical terms and incorporate specialized vocabulary limits the transfer of applications that have proven helpful in other areas, such as online search, marketing, and customer service.

Sentiment analysis, for instance, one of the most popular financial NLP applications, is used across industries to evaluate customer feedback. However, as we will see in more detail, investor communication differs too much for results to carry over. These differences also limit the data that specialized applications can learn from. As a result, *text-based applications in finance are lagging* substantially behind developments in other domains.

Progress of NLP Applications in Investments

Notwithstanding these hurdles, ML applications for text data have advanced dramatically, driven by the familiar trifecta of more data, faster computation, and better algorithms. Paralleling critical developments in other AI disciplines over the last two to three decades, NLP has gradually abandoned techniques based on rules crafted by domain specialists, such as linguists, in favor of statistical models that *learn relevant patterns directly from text data*.

Over the last 5–10 years, language models based on novel deep neural network architectures have evolved to capture the nuances of language much more accurately than before. Recent breakthroughs involve using neural networks that learn how to *represent words as vectors* rather than individual integers (Mikolov, Sutskever, Chen, Corrado, and Dean 2013). These so-called embedding vectors contain hundreds of real numbers that reflect language usage in context because they are optimized to predict terms that are missing from a given piece of text. More specifically, the location of a vector captures much of a word's meaning in the sense of "know a word by the company it keeps" (Firth 1957). Not only are synonyms nearby, but even more complex relationships have vector equivalents: For example, the vector pointing from France to Paris would be parallel and of equal length to the one connecting Japan and Tokyo.

In another critical step forward, the *transformer architecture* abandoned recurrent neural networks, the hitherto dominant way to process text data due to its sequential nature, in favor of the attention mechanism (Vaswani, Shazeer, Parmar, Uszkoreit, Jones, Gomez, Kaiser, and Polosukhin 2017). This innovation allows modeling dependencies between words regardless of distance and parallelizing the training process. The benefits are step changes in scale: Models can learn from much longer sequences, benefit from dramatically larger datasets, and rely on many more parameters.

State-of-the-art implementations now reach or exceed *human-level performance* on various benchmark tasks from sentiment analysis to paraphrasing or question answering (Wang, Pruksachatkun, Nangia, Singh, Michael, Hill, Levy, and Bowman 2019). Google introduced machine translation systems based on neural networks that reduced errors by 60% in 2016. Recent machine translation systems produce outputs that humans have difficulty distinguishing from those of a professional translator (Popel, Tomkova, Tomek, Kaiser, Uszkoreit, Bojar, and Žabokrtský 2020).

These large-scale models require a massive amount of unlabeled data and computation to extract their intricate understanding of language, which would make this new technology cost prohibitive for most applications. Fortunately, the performance breakthroughs reflect an emerging paradigm in developing AI systems toward a new class of *foundation models* (Bommasani, Hudson, Adeli, Altman, Arora, von Arx, Bernstein, Bohg, Bosselut, Brunskill, et al. 2021). This new model class learns universal capabilities from broad data (including but not limited to text data) that transfer to specific tasks very cost effectively. Instances of this new model class have begun to generate computer code and prove mathematical theorems (Polu and Sutskever 2020). Multimodal models that integrate, for example, text and audio data add intent parsing to speech recognition to capture nuances of language; under active research for voice assistants, applications aiming to read between the lines of earnings call transcripts are also emerging. Model performance appears to scale reliably with input data and model size, and the foreseeable

Exhibit 1. The Transfer Learning Workflow

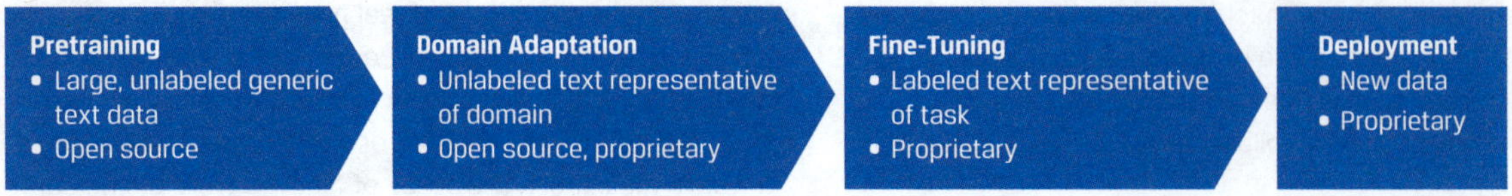

Pretraining
- Large, unlabeled generic text data
- Open source

Domain Adaptation
- Unlabeled text representative of domain
- Open source, proprietary

Fine-Tuning
- Labeled text representative of task
- Proprietary

Deployment
- New data
- Proprietary

ability to boost both makes substantial further advances likely (Srivastava, Rastogi, Rao, Shoeb, Abid, Fisch, Brown, Santoro, Gupta, Garriga-Alonso, et al. 2022).

This new paradigm enables so-called *transfer learning*, which renders developing applications for financial use cases much more cost effective and accurate (see **Exhibit 1**). Pretrained models are widely available via open-source platforms, reducing model development to adapting the model's language understanding to its domain-specific uses. This process can be proprietary and requires only unlabeled data relevant to the target application, such as earnings call transcripts, financial news, or research reports, which are often abundant. Fine-tuning the adapted model to a specific task, such as sentiment analysis or return prediction, requires labeled data, which may need human expertise. Still, it can be relatively small, measured in thousands of documents rather than (hundreds of) millions.

As a result, it has become easier to unlock investment insights hidden in unstructured text data. Established applications such as sentiment analysis have evolved to become more sophisticated and effective, while new applications are beginning to emerge.

Applications and Use Cases along the Investment Process

NLP applications aim to extract relevant information from language data and are thus very versatile. As a result, *use cases vary widely, depending on how investors use text data* throughout the investment process and where NLP can add value. The investment strategy, asset classes, holding periods, and degree of process automation further shape the specifics of suitable applications. The availability of human, technical, and financial resources affects the sophistication of applications and influences decisions about external sourcing and in-house development.

The most popular applications cover a spectrum from data management, research support, and idea generation to alpha signal generation:

- On one end of the spectrum are applications that aim to boost the *productivity of research analysts* faced with growing amounts of potentially relevant text data. NLP solutions that focus on efficiency range from tagging, intelligent search, text summarization, and document comparison to the discovery of topics based on ML that helps organize large numbers of documents.

- On the other end are applications that extract *predictive signals to generate alpha* using state-of-the-art deep learning models. The outputs can inform discretionary and systematic portfolio management decisions or feed into further models to drive an automated strategy.

Along this spectrum exist numerous applications that *quantify or score text content* for specific characteristics deemed insightful and complementary to the content alone. Well-known examples include the analysis of sentiment, which can be defined in various ways, as we will see later. Alternative targets include ESG scores that measure how well corporate communication aligns with certain concepts. Approaches have tracked the evolution of NLP technology, as I will discuss in more detail.

Various inputs and techniques underlie most NLP applications. *Data sources* are the starting point and have multiplied and diversified. They range from public sources, such as machine-readable SEC filings, to familiar aggregators, such as Bloomberg, S&P Global, or Refinitiv (now LSEG Labs). Primary news or social media sources are now offering data to investors, as do companies that generate text data. Web-scraping produces potentially more exclusive data but is more resource intensive. Vendors have emerged that collect and aggregate text data, such as earnings calls. Depending on the source format, additional data preparation may be required to make raw data machine readable using, for example, image recognition, OCR (optical character recognition), or PDF (portable document format) extraction.

Text preprocessing segments raw text into tokens and higher-order elements, such as paragraphs, sentences, and phrases. Another critical step to enable further analysis is tagging text elements with linguistic annotations and other metadata, in particular, entity information, to resolve references to investment targets. Alternatively, data providers also provide "machine-ready" news that incorporates some metadata.

Investment firms that seriously pursue NLP tend to build proprietary pipelines using open-source tools that convert text data into custom model inputs because of the high added value at this step. Like other AI disciplines, *open-source software* has played an essential role in pushing the NLP research frontier, facilitating widespread technology adoption, and developing applications. A central reason is that the NLP workflow has common steps that can share tools. The Python language community has been particularly active in this regard. A popular Python library for these tasks is spaCy.

As a result, the development cost of custom NLP applications has dropped significantly and has become accessible to medium-sized firms. Furthermore, vendors have emerged that provide specialized solutions for certain workflow aspects and end-to-end solutions for specific applications: The estimated value of the global NLP market was USD10 billion in 2019 and is projected to grow to USD33 billion by 2025 (Lewington and Sartenaer 2021).

An excellent example of the evolution and broadening availability of NLP solutions is *Kensho*, which aims to make advanced information processing capabilities available to market participants beyond leading quant hedge funds. The company started in 2012 and was acquired by Standard & Poor's in 2018, setting a record for AI-driven deals at USD550 million, exceeding the price paid by Google for DeepMind. Kensho had developed an application named Warren (after Warren Buffett) with a simple textbox interface that offered investment advice to complex questions posed in plain English. It could access millions of data points, including drug approvals, economic reports, monetary policy changes, and political events, and could reveal their impact on nearly any traded financial asset worldwide. The company also provides an automated contextual analysis of changes in news flow, earnings reports, and analyst ratings. Early adopters included Goldman Sachs, which primarily used it to advise investment clients who contacted its trading desks.

Solutions have since evolved to focus on unstructured data and cover several techniques and applications mentioned previously. Namely, the company transcribes earnings calls, extracts data from PDF documents, detects and resolves named entities, such as companies, and links them to established identifiers. It also offers ML solutions, such as fine-tuning text classifiers and high-quality training sets, including 5,000 hours of earnings call recordings for multi-modal modeling.

A *2020 survey of 20 customers* by the LSEG (London Stock Exchange Group) Labs (formerly Refinitiv) found that *65% had begun to use NLP applications*. Of this group, around one-third were just getting started, and another third were expending significant resources to identify use cases and deploy solutions. In contrast, the final third considered NLP fundamental and had already implemented the most advanced technologies, including deep learning models (Lewington and Sartenaer 2021).

An analysis of automated downloads of SEC filings further illustrates the *value different organizations place on NLP applications* (Cao et al. 2020). **Exhibit 2** displays the number of downloads over 2004–2017 by 13F filers. Among the most active consumers of machine-readable corporate filings are leading quantitative hedge funds, from Renaissance Technologies to D. E. Shaw. These institutions are the most likely to develop cutting-edge applications, such as the end-to-end training of models that combine text and other data sources to directly predict such outcomes of interest as returns for use in automated trading strategies. Institutions that heavily rely on research analysts, such as asset managers (but also quantitative hedge funds), certainly use productivity-enhancing NLP applications to efficiently process the large amounts of information contained in regulatory filings and other text documents.

I now proceed to describe applications that facilitate text data management to support the research process and lay the groundwork for more sophisticated applications. Then, I discuss how sentiment and other scoring tools have evolved with improved technology. Finally, I sketch applications on the horizon at the research frontier.

I illustrate these applications using publicly available datasets containing real-life financial news (see **Exhibit 3**). The financial phrasebank contains 4,840 sentences from English language news about companies trading on the Finnish stock exchange. Annotators have hand labeled each sentence as positive, neutral, or negative. I use the portion of the dataset where all annotators agree. The US financial news dataset consists of over 200,000 financial news articles on US companies sourced from various websites.

Getting Started: Organizing and Tagging Large Amounts of Text Data

The dramatic increase in text data volume generates new opportunities to detect a valuable signal but risks inundating the investment process with noise. To boost research analyst productivity and focus investment manager attention on critical events, tools that automate search, categorization, and the detection of relevant information are paramount.

The first steps toward this goal involve applying the initial stages of the NLP workflow described previously. More specifically, they include the following applications:

- **Named entity recognition (NER):** The automated tagging of objects of interest, such as corporations, people, or events

Exhibit 2. Downloads for Select 13F Filers, 2004–2017

Investment Firm	No. of Downloads	Type
Renaissance Technologies	536,753	Quantitative hedge fund
Two Sigma Investments	515,255	Quantitative hedge fund
Barclays Capital	377,280	Financial conglomerate with asset management
JPMorgan Chase	154,475	Financial conglomerate with asset management
Point72	104,337	Quantitative hedge fund
Wells Fargo	94,261	Financial conglomerate with asset management
Morgan Stanley	91,522	Investment bank with asset management
Citadel LLC	82,375	Quantitative hedge fund
RBC Capital Markets	79,469	Financial conglomerate with asset management
D. E. Shaw & Co.	67,838	Quantitative hedge fund
UBS AG	64,029	Financial conglomerate with asset management
Deutsche Bank AG	55,825	Investment bank with asset management
Union Bank of California	50,938	Full-service bank with private wealth management
Squarepoint	48,678	Quantitative hedge fund
Jefferies Group	47,926	Investment bank with asset management
Stifel, Nicolaus & Company	24,759	Investment bank with asset management
Piper Jaffray (now Piper Sandler)	18,604	Investment bank with asset management
Lazard	18,290	Investment bank with asset management
Oppenheimer & Co.	15,203	Investment bank with asset management
Northern Trust Corporation	11,916	Financial conglomerate with asset management

Exhibit 3. Reading the Financial Phrasebank

```python
def read_phrase_bank():
    """Load sentences and annotations and return unique values"""
    label_to_score = {'negative': -1, 'neutral': 0, 'positive': 1}
    file_path = Path('financial_phrase_bank',
'Sentences_AllAgree.txt')
    text = file_path.read_text(encoding='latin1').split('\n')
    df = pd.DataFrame([s.split('@') for s in text],
                    columns=['sentence', 'sentiment'])
    df.sentiment = df.sentiment.map(label_to_score)
    return df.dropna().drop_duplicates()
```

- **Linguistic annotation:** Labeling of text elements regarding their grammatical function and other aspects
- **Topic modeling:** The identification of themes present in documents for automated categorization

I illustrate how each works and can, in turn, add value to the investment process.

Programmatic Tagging of Content with NER

Named entity recognition detects real-world concepts of interest, such as companies, individuals, locations, or custom entities in the text, allowing for spelling and other variations to ensure robustness across various sources. Among many different uses, it also supports compliance processes—for example, in anti-money laundering—because it can quickly flag critical items that require further diligence (sanction lists, politically exposed persons, etc.).

It automatically *annotates documents with tags or metadata* to enable the real-time detection of such concepts. Furthermore, it permits the integration of different datasets, such as news data that refer to a company by name and price data that identify relevant securities by ticker. It also lays the foundation for analyzing relationships between different concepts, such as competitors or members of a supply chain, or for comparing information for a given object at other points in time.

NER implementations can rely on predefined dictionaries that map words to concepts or learn these mappings from manually labeled data. The following code snippet (see **Exhibit 4**) shows some of the annotations that spaCy provides out of the box—that is, without custom training—for a given sentence: It recognizes nationality, company names, and ticker/exchange symbols, as well as the date and monetary values.

NER is a *foundational tool* that forms the basis for many other applications. Any investment firm that aims to automate the processing of text documents will require its results, whether it aims to use interactive applications to augment analysts or to build more sophisticated ML models that use documents.

Linguistic Annotation: Parsing Dependencies among Sentence Elements

While NER detects items in isolation, linguistic annotations establish *functional relationships among text elements* in a sentence. This technique reverse engineers the connections between objects and actions using the grammatical structure and provides vital inputs into downstream efforts at recovering the meaning of the content.

The details are beyond the scope of this chapter, but the code snippet in **Exhibit 5** illustrates how spaCy annotates a fragment of the sample sentence from Exhibit 4.

It simultaneously identifies the grammatical roles of words, such as nouns, verbs, and prepositions; the dependencies among them (e.g., "company" is further defined by "Finnish metal products"); and coherent phrases.

Downstream applications can use these metadata and the resulting dependency parsing tree to screen sentences for specific patterns and phrases, such as "net loss narrowed," with more positive implications than the individual words in isolation might suggest (Marinov 2019). An example is custom sentiment analysis that encodes specific observations about meaningful statements.

Exhibit 4. Named Entity Recognition with spaCy

```python
import spacy
from spacy import displacy
nlp = spacy.load('en_core_web_trf')
phrases = read_phrase_bank()
sentences = phrases.sentence.tolist()
doc = nlp(sentences[331])
displacy.render(doc, style='ent', jupyter=True, options={'compact': True})
```

Finnish **NORP** metal products company Componenta Oyj **ORG** (HEL **ORG** : CTH1V **ORG**) said today **DATE** its net loss narrowed to EUR 500,000 **MONEY** (USD 680,000 **MONEY**) in the last quarter of 2010 **DATE** from EUR 5.3 million **MONEY** for the same period a year earlier **DATE** .

Exhibit 5. Grammatical Dependency Relations with spaCy

```
doc = nlp(sents[331])
displacy.render(doc, style='dep', jupyter=True, options={'compact':
True, 'distance': 100})
```

To leverage the potential value of linguistic annotations, organizations need a dedicated data science team with NLP expertise to further process the results. Hence, it would rarely be used outside larger investment organizations.

Automatic Discovery of Themes across Documents with Topic Modeling

A topic model aims to *discover hidden themes* across a body of documents and computes the relevance of these themes to each of them. The most popular technique is latent Dirichlet allocation, or LDA (Blei, Ng, and Jordan 2003). In this context, a theme consists of terms that are more likely to appear jointly in documents that represent this theme than elsewhere. The discovery process is fully automated given a target number of topics, which can be optimized using statistical goodness-of-fit measures.

The results share a drawback common to *unsupervised learning*: The lack of a ground truth benchmark implies the absence of objective performance metrics. In other words, the value of a particular set of topics identified by the model depends on how useful they are to the downstream application. Moreover, topics do not come with handy labels; each one corresponds to a list of words with associated weights (but humans tend to quickly grasp the concepts behind a topic upon inspection). These practical challenges notwithstanding, topic models are among the most effective tools for organizing large amounts of text in a meaningful and automatic way.

Investment firms use topic models as tools that *facilitate the research process*. They are useful because they summarize large amounts of text in a much more manageable number of themes that are easy to track over time. At the same time, the content of individual documents transparently relates to these topics. Analysts can use this information to compare how the relevance of topics changes over time or across related companies and quickly identify the relevant text passages. Implementations used to require custom developments but can now rely to a much greater degree on third-party APIs. As a result, this technology is becoming increasingly accessible to small and medium-sized firms.

Bryan Kelly, of AQR and Yale University, and co-authors illustrate a practical use of LDA by identifying 180 topics in over 800,000 *Wall Street Journal* articles covering 1984–2017 (Bybee, Kelly, Manela, and Xiu 2021). The authors maintain an interactive website (www.structureofnews.com) that illustrates how textual analysis can summarize the state of the economy. The uncovered *structure of economic news* shows several benefits of the topic model output:

- The documents most relevant for a given topic are easy to retrieve at any point in time because each text has a topic weight.

- The relative prevalence of themes also matters because it reflects the attention that news pays to them over time. In other words, the mix of topics at any time reflects the current state of the economy and does correlate with macroeconomic indicators. Moreover, it explains 25% of aggregate market returns when used as an input to a statistical model and predicts economic events, such as recessions, beyond standard indicators.

Two Sigma illustrates how LDA can add value when applied to *Federal Open Market Committee meeting minutes* to quantify the relative weight of various economic issues over time. The company's analysis shows how financial market topics gained relative weight, at the expense of growth-related themes, at the beginning of Alan Greenspan's tenure, underpinning the market's perception of the Greenspan put at the time (Saret and Mitra 2016).

Exhibit 6 illustrates the selection of a random sample of 25,000 financial news articles with 250–750 words each, the preprocessing of the text with spaCy to remove less informative terms, and the use of Gensim's LDA implementation to identify 15 topics.

We then use pyLDAvis to visualize the relative importance of the 15 topics interactively. **Exhibit 7** displays the vocabulary frequency for each theme compared to its frequency across all documents. Topic 5, for instance, discusses technology companies.

Exhibit 6. Latent Dirichlet Allocation Using Gensim

```python
df = pd.read_csv('us_news.csv', usecols=['content']).drop_duplicates()
df = df[df.str.split().str.len().between(250, 750)].sample(n=25000)

nlp = spacy.load('en_core_web_md')
preprocessed_docs = []
to_remove = ['ADV', 'PRON', 'CCONJ', 'PUNCT', 'PART', 'DET', 'ADP',
'SPACE', 'NUM', 'SYM']
for doc in tqdm(nlp.pipe(df.tolist(), n_process=-1)):
    preprocessed_docs.append([t.lemma_.lower() for t in doc
                    if t.pos_ not in to_remove and not
t.is_stop and t.is_alpha])
len(nlp.vocab) # 117,319 tokens
dictionary = Dictionary(preprocessed_docs)
dictionary.filter_extremes(no_below=5, no_above=0.2, keep_n=5000)
LdaMulticore(corpus=corpus, id2word=dictionary, iterations=50,

        num_topics=num_topics, workers=4, passes=25, random_state=100)
```

Exhibit 7. Topic Visualization Using PyLDAvis

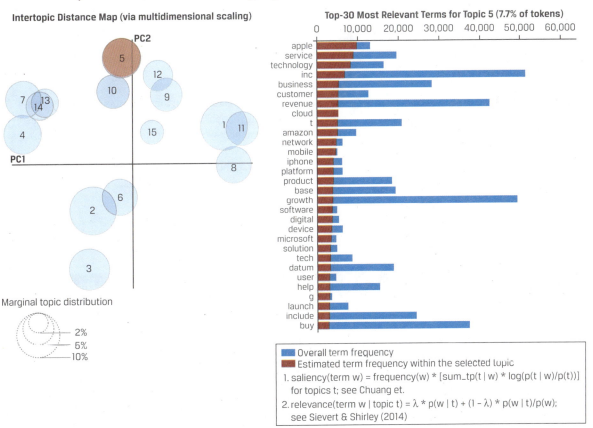

Sources: PyLDAvis using information from Chuang, Manning, and Heer (2012) and Sievert and Shirley (2014).

Scoring Text for Sentiment Analysis

The impact of news encoded in text data on prices has long motivated investors to design summary metrics that could anticipate the market's reaction to news content. Sentiment analysis is by far the most popular NLP application: Systematic attempts to score market sentiment regarding new information on an asset and to invest accordingly have been documented for almost 100 years (Cowles 1933). Computerized sentiment analysis at scale gained momentum after 2000.

Sentiment analysis is very popular because scores for news stories or corporate communications are available from various sources, including the ubiquitous Bloomberg terminal. Research analysts can use such scores to quantify and compare trends across a coverage universe, and portfolio managers can evaluate news flow quality "at a glimpse." Scores can also be used as trading signals (and are often promoted to this end).

However, there are many ways to derive such scores, as I will discuss later, not least because the term "sentiment" offers room for interpretation. Custom implementations tend to provide more valuable information because they control the definition of the outcome. However, they rely on supervised learning, which, in turn, requires costly human expertise to label data. It also requires in-house data science capabilities or trusted vendors.

Measuring Text Characteristics by Scoring Text Elements

Initially, practitioners relied on word lists developed in other disciplines, such as psychology, to score the positive or negative sentiment likely expressed by individual words. To evaluate the polarity of an entire document, they aggregated the sentiment scores.

In 2011, Loughran and McDonald demonstrated how the specific use of language in finance requires tailored approaches to avoid misinterpretation. For instance, investors tend to focus more on negative aspects. However, they face the challenge that corporate communication carefully controls positive and negative word frequencies in earnings calls and other disclosures (Loughran and McDonald 2011).

Beyond Sentiment: Capturing Intentions and Hidden Meaning

Loughran and McDonald (2011) introduced word lists specific to finance to capture both tone and behavioral aspects that investors care about. Besides positive or negative language, investment managers pay attention to the degree of confidence surrounding forward-looking statements to gain insights into the attitudes of more informed insiders.

Common word lists thus emphasize hints at obfuscation or deception (such as the overuse of favorable terms) or uncertainty (for example, via the possibly unintentional use of such "weak modal" words as "may" or "could," in earnings calls). Therefore, Loughran and McDonald added lists that flagged when the word choice strengthens or weakens material statements. **Exhibit 8** lists the five most common terms for the original seven lists, which have received minor updates since publication.

Loughran and McDonald further differentiated these lists by channel of communication to address additional bias. They also accounted for differences in the meaning of words in, for instance, regulatory filings, where the term "auditor" does not have the negative connotation typically perceived in business news.

Another text characteristic that investors frequently scrutinize is the readability of text, measured by such metrics as the number of words per sentence or the number of syllables per word. The rationale is that overly complex language may indicate an intent to mislead or distract the reader. Just as with sentiment analysis, the definition of

Exhibit 8. Most Common Terms in Select Word Lists

Negative	Positive	Uncertainty	Litigious	Strong_Modal	Weak_Modal	Constraining
LOSS	GAIN	MAY	SHALL	WILL	MAY	REQUIRED
LOSSES	GAINS	COULD	AMENDED	MUST	COULD	OBLIGATIONS
TERMINATION	ABLE	APPROXIMATELY	CONTRACTS	BEST	POSSIBLE	REQUIREMENTS
AGAINST	GOOD	RISK	HEREIN	HIGHEST	MIGHT	RESTRICTED
IMPAIRMENT	ADVANCES	RISKS	LAW	NEVER	DEPEND	IMPAIRMENT

Source: Loughran and McDonald (2011).

readability requires sensitivity to the context: The language in a financial report has a different baseline complexity than financial news, and the criteria and thresholds need to be adapted accordingly. Moreover, critics maintain that the complexity of language primarily reflects the size of an organization (Loughran and McDonald 2020).

From Sentiment Scores to Investment Decisions

Subsequently, vendors emerged that offered domain-specific word lists and ready-made sentiment scores. Document scores often become inputs to analysts' research process to compare their own values across a universe of competitors. Analysts also combine sentiment scores with the results of a topic model to quantify how differently alternative investment targets discuss similar themes.

Or, sentiment scores can feed into a model that aims to explain or predict returns. Academic evaluations of this approach tend to find a statistically significant yet economically small association between document sentiment and subsequent returns.

However, measuring text characteristics with dictionaries assembled by domain experts has several weaknesses:

1. Interpreting text by evaluating words in isolation ignores a lot of information.
2. Word lists are backward looking: Even if the domain expertise that maps terms to polarity scores successfully captures signal rather than noise, this relationship may break down at any time.
3. Moreover, if the communicators are aware of the word lists used by investors, they may adjust their word choice to influence the market favorably.

Word Lists in Practice

The Loughran–McDonald word lists are in the public domain, and the code example in **Exhibit 9** illustrates their use and predictive accuracy on the hand-labeled phrasebank dataset.

The traditional Loughran–McDonald word list approach achieves an accuracy of 66.03%. A defining characteristic of the methods described in this section is that the scoring or classification rules are typically handcrafted rather than learned by a machine from data. We now turn to a data-driven alternative.

Modern NLP: Learning to Predict Arbitrary Outcomes from Text Data

The evolution of sentiment analysis tracks the progress in NLP from rule-based to data-driven approaches outlined earlier in this chapter. The rapid adoption of state-of-the-art modeling techniques based on transfer learning are making sophisticated applications much more accessible. As in other industries, custom models that predict targets of interest are becoming commonplace beyond industry leaders.

These applications offer enormous flexibility because input data and target outcomes can be designed if training data are available. *Dataset curation* often poses the costliest hurdle: It requires the annotation of the input documents and other data with custom labels that reflect the historical realizations of the target outcome. Such outcomes may be price movements over a given horizon. However, they can also be more subtle, such as the appropriate confidence in management forecasts made during an earnings call, the adherence to some ESG standard, or compliance with specific regulations. If the targets are subsequent returns,

A Caveat: Campbell's Law

The last point in the preceding list illustrates a broader caveat to the analysis of human language: Humans adapt and modify their behavior to game the system. Campbell's law, also cited as Goodhart's law, originally formulated this phenomenon. Marylin Strathern (1997, p. 308) summarized it as follows: "When a measure becomes a target, it ceases to be a good measure."

Careful analysis of corporate communication after the release of the Loughran–McDonald word lists uncovers significant changes in word choice, particularly by companies most likely subjected to automated sentiment scoring (Cao et al. 2020).

Given the reality of executives' adaptation to automated sentiment analysis, it can be more effective to focus on how analysts ask questions because they do not have equally obvious incentives to pretend (Mannix 2022).

Exhibit 9. Sentiment Analysis Using Loughran–McDonald Word Lists

```python
def download_lm():
    """Source latest LM word-score dictionary"""
    url = 'https://drive.google.com/file/d/17CmUZM9hGUdGYjCXcjQLyybjTrcjrhik/view?usp=sharing'
    url = 'https://drive.google.com/uc?id=' + url.split('/')[-2]
    return pd.read_csv(url)

def lm_counter_by_theme():
    """Return list of terms associated with the seven LM themes"""
    df = download_lm()
    df = df.rename(columns=str.lower).assign(word=lambda x: x.word.str.lower())
    return {theme: Counter(df.loc[df[theme].gt(0), 'word'].tolist()) for theme in lm_sentiment}

def get_lm_sentiment(df):
    lm = lm_counter_by_theme()
    phrases['sentence_'] = phrases.sentence.str.lower().str.split().apply(Counter)
    for direction in ['positive', 'negative']:
        df[direction] = (df.sentence_.apply(lambda x: len(list((x &
lm[direction]).elements())))
                        .clip(lower=-1, upper=1))

    df = df.drop(['sentence_'], axis=1)
    df['lm'] = df.positive.sub(df.negative)
    df['delta'] = df.sentiment.sub(df.lm)
    return df.drop(['positive', 'negative'], axis=1)

labels = ['negative', 'neutral', 'positive']
phrases = read_phrase_bank()
phrases = get_lm_sentiment(phrases)

lm_cm = confusion_matrix(y_true=phrases.sentiment, y_pred=phrases.lm)
lm_cm = pd.DataFrame(lm_cm, columns=labels, index=labels)
lm_acc = accuracy_score(y_true=phrases.sentiment, y_pred=phrases.lm)

          negative   neutral   positive
negative    120        177        6
neutral      68       1284       39
positive     70        409       91
```

one can automate the annotation process. However, if they depend on domain expertise, labeling can turn into a time-intensive use of human capital.

Numerous vendors offer annotation services because this step is critical for state-of-the-art NLP projects across industries. These include solutions that themselves rely on AI, such as Scale AI, Snorkel AI, and Labelbox, startups valued over USD1 billion each.[1] There are also efficiency-enhancing software tools, such as Prodigy.[2]

Currently, NLP applications that rely on custom models based on transfer learning are beginning to proliferate outside the largest quantitative hedge funds with dedicated research teams. Proof-of-concept developments can today be put together by smaller teams so that R&D pilots are more common in mid-sized investment firms.

From Rule-Based to Data-Driven Approaches

Over the past few years, substantial advances in deep learning have moved the frontier for state-of-the-art applications from rule-based to data-driven approaches. Here, machines learn directly from data how to interpret

---

[1]For more information, go to the companies' respective websites: https://scale.com/; https://snorkel.ai/; https://labelbox.com/.

[2]Go to https://prodi.gy/.

language and predict sentiment scores or other outcomes of interest, such as subsequent asset returns or ESG scores, more accurately. In other words, cutting-edge applications eschew handcrafted lists and rely on ML models to identify patterns relevant to the predictive target.

Approaches range from white-box models that learn transparent word lists from data (Ke, Kelly, and Xiu 2019) to large language models that are pretrained on the generic text and fine-tuned to domain-specific documents (Araci 2019; Huang, Wang, and Yang, forthcoming).

As with a rule-based approach, a downstream model that aims to predict returns can combine sentiment scores produced by a language model with other inputs. Alternatively, models can be designed and trained in an end-to-end fashion.

The benefits include exploiting much richer semantic input than word lists and the flexibility to train a model to learn outcomes directly relevant to the investment strategy. However, the custom approach requires curated, labeled data: Each training document requires annotation with the corresponding ground truth outcome.

Risks include overfitting to noise in the training sample and limited ability to transfer the model's learning from the pretraining inputs to the domain-specific documents. Fortunately, these risks can be managed and measured before using the resulting model in a production setting.

Modern NLP and Transfer Learning in Practice with Hugging Face and FinBERT-Tone

Hugging Face is an NLP startup based in New York City with USD160 million in funding and a USD2 billion valuation that offers state-of-the-art custom solutions. It also hosts many pretrained and fine-tuned language models and allows for free downloads.

One of the models is FinBERT, a large-scale BERT model based on the transformer architecture with almost 1 million downloads per month. It trained on SEC reports, earnings call transcripts, and analyst reports containing close to 5 billion tokens, with further fine-tuning on the hand-labeled phrasebank documents.

The code in **Exhibit 10** illustrates how to access the fine-tuned model and evaluate its predictive performance relative to the Loughran–McDonald word lists.[3]

FinBERT achieves 91.7% accuracy, a 39% improvement over the Loughran–McDonald approach.

The sample sentence we used for Exhibit 10 to illustrate basic NLP techniques shows why the language model outperforms: "Finnish metal products company Componenta Oyj (HEL: CTH1V) said today its net loss narrowed to EUR500,000 (USD680,000) in the last quarter of 2010 from EUR 5.3 million for the same period a year earlier."

The phrase "net loss narrowed" requires taking at least some context into account, which simple word lists cannot do.

From the Research Frontier: Multimodal Models Integrate Text and Tone

Speech recognition is key to the analysis of companies' periodic earnings calls. Given the tight controls of the textual content and adaptation to popular sentiment scoring approaches, it can be informative to incorporate the speaker's style and tone into the analysis.

Recent so-called multimodal learning models jointly process different modalities, such as text and speech or video data, and learn how to interpret these complementary signals considering the target outcome. Such applications will likely become more common as more appropriately labeled data become available in house or from vendors.

Early results already suggest these applications can reveal what analysts ask about and how they do so, including which tone they use (and how company representatives respond). A quantified profile of the speakers' behavior is a valuable complement to textual analysis of the actual content and can be used to inform either human research or downstream models.

Summary and Conclusion

NLP applications have become much more widespread over the past 5–10 years because the greater amount of data increased demand and improved performance. At the same time, high-quality open-source software has become available and popular, reducing the cost of customized applications, developed either in house or through third-party vendors.

Many investment firms that rely on research driven by textual input use some form of automated text processing or scoring to manage the data explosion and human productivity while potentially improving results through the efficient discovery of hidden insights.

Applications that quantify text content regarding relevant metrics, such as sentiment or ESG scores, have become

---

[3]The comparison is not entirely fair because FinBERT has been trained on these documents. However, the comparison demonstrates how a language model overcomes the word list limitations mentioned previously.

Exhibit 10. Sentiment Analysis Using a Fine-Tuned Transformer Model

```
from transformers import BertTokenizer, BertForSequenceClassification
def get_finbert_sentiment(df):
    finbert = BertForSequenceClassification.from_pretrained('yiyanghkust/finbert-tone', num_labels=3)
    tokenizer = BertTokenizer.from_pretrained('yiyanghkust/finbert-tone')

    sentiment = []
    for sents in chunks(df.sentence.tolist(), n=50):
        inputs = tokenizer(sents, return_tensors="pt", padding=True)
        outputs = finbert(**inputs)[0]
        sentiment.extend(list(np.argmax(outputs.detach().numpy(), axis=1)))

    df['finbert'] = sentiment
    df.finbert = df.finbert.apply(lambda x: -1 if x == 2 else x)
    return df

phrases = get_finbert_sentiment(phrases)

fin_cm = confusion_matrix(y_true=phrases.sentiment,
                         y_pred=phrases.finbert)
          negative  neutral  positive
negative     120      177       6
neutral       68     1284      39
positive      70      409      91
```

very common. Most importantly, the unprecedented breakthroughs in deep learning for language and transfer learning have boosted the accuracy of such measures, especially when tailored to the specific use case relevant to an investor.

Progress will almost certainly continue in the direction of large language models that learn to understand domain-specific language well in cost-effective ways. The challenges will consist of harnessing these new technologies to automate existing processes and identifying predictive targets that add value to the investment process.

References

Araci, D. 2019. "FinBERT: Financial Sentiment Analysis with Pre-Trained Language Models." Cornell University, arXiv:1908.10063 (27 August).

Blei, D. M., A. Y. Ng, and M. I. Jordan. 2003. "Latent Dirichlet Allocation." *Journal of Machine Learning Research* 3: 993–1022.

Bommasani, R., Drew A. Hudson, Ehsan Adeli, Russ Altman, Simran Arora, Sydney von Arx, Michael S. Bernstein, Jeannette Bohg, Antoine Bosselut, Emma Brunskill, et al. 2021. "On the Opportunities and Risks of Foundation Models." Cornell University, arXiv:2108.07258 (16 August).

Bybee, L., B. T. Kelly, A. Manela, and D. Xiu. 2021. "Business News and Business Cycles." NBER Working Paper 29344 (October).

Cao, S., W. Jiang, B. Yang, and A. L. Zhang. 2020. "How to Talk When a Machine Is Listening?: Corporate Disclosure in the Age of AI." NBER Working Paper 27950 (October).

Cowles, A. 1933. "Can Stock Market Forecasters Forecast?" *Econometrica* 1 (3): 309–24.

Chuang, J., Christopher D. Manning, and Jeffrey Heer. 2012. "Termite: Visualization Techniques for Assessing Textual Topic Models." In *International Working Conference on Advanced Visual Interfaces (AVI)*, 74–77.

Firth, J. R. 1957. "Applications of General Linguistics." *Transactions of the Philological Society* 56 (1): 1–14.

Harbert, T. 2021. "Tapping the Power of Unstructured Data." MIT Sloan (1 February). https://mitsloan.mit.edu/ideas-made-to-matter/tapping-power-unstructured-data.

Huang, Allen, Hui Wang, and Yi Yang. Forthcoming. "FinBERT: A Large Language Model for Extracting Information from Financial Text." *Contemporary Accounting Research*.

Ke, Z. T., B. T. Kelly, and D. Xiu. 2019. "Predicting Returns with Text Data." NBER Working Paper 26186 (August).

Lewington, D., and L. Sartenaer. 2021. "NLP in Financial Services." LSEG Labs.

Loughran, T., and B. McDonald. 2011. "When Is a Liability Not a Liability? Textual Analysis, Dictionaries, and 10-Ks." *Journal of Finance* 66 (1): 35–65.

Loughran, T., and B. McDonald. 2020. "Textual Analysis in Finance." *Annual Review of Financial Economics* 12: 357–75.

Mannix, R. 2022. "Analysts Reveal More than Company Execs on Earnings Calls—AB." Risk.net (23 February). www.risk.net/node/7932076.

Marinov, S. 2019. "Natural Language Processing In Finance: Shakespeare without the Monkeys." Man Institute (July).

Mikolov, T., I. Sutskever, K. Chen, G. Corrado, and J. Dean. 2013. "Distributed Representations of Words and Phrases and Their Compositionality." *Proceedings of the 26th International Conference on Neural Information Processing Systems* 2: 3111–19.

Pollack, A. 1983. "Technology; The Computer as Translator." *New York Times* (28 April). www.nytimes.com/1983/04/28/business/technology-the-computer-as-translator.html.

Polu, S., and I. Sutskever. 2020. "Generative Language Modeling for Automated Theorem Proving." Cornell University, arXiv:2009.03393 (7 September).

Popel, M., M. Tomkova, J. Tomek, Ł. Kaiser, J. Uszkoreit, O. Bojar, and Z. Žabokrtský. 2020. "Transforming Machine Translation: A Deep Learning System Reaches News Translation Quality Comparable to Human Professionals." *Nature Communications* 11.

Saret, J. N., and S. Mitra. 2016. "An AI Approach to Fed Watching." Two Sigma. www.twosigma.com/articles/an-ai-approach-to-fed-watching/.

Sievert, Carson, and Kenneth Shirley. 2014. "LDAvis: A Method for Visualizing and Interpreting Topics." In *Proceedings of the Workshop on Interactive Language Learning, Visualization, and Interfaces*, 63–70. Baltimore: Association for Computational Linguistics.

Srivastava, A., A. Rastogi, A. Rao, A. A. M. Shoeb, A. Abid, A. Fisch, A. R. Brown, A. Santoro, A. Gupta, A. Garriga-Alonso, et al. 2022. "Beyond the Imitation Game: Quantifying and Extrapolating the Capabilities of Language Models." Cornell University, arXiv:2206.04615 (10 June).

Strathern, Marilyn. 1997. "'Improving Ratings': Audit in the British University System." *European Review* 5 (3): 305–21.

Vaswani, A., N. Shazeer, N. Parmar, J. Uszkoreit, L. Jones, A. N. Gomez, Ł. Kaiser, and I. Polosukhin. 2017. "Attention Is All You Need." In *Advances in Neural Information Processing Systems 30*, edited by I. Guyon, U. V. Luxburg, S. Bengio, H. Wallach, R. Fergus, S. Vishwanathan, and R. Garnett, 5998–6008.

Wang, A., Y. Pruksachatkun, N. Nangia, A. Singh, J. Michael, F. Hill, O. Levy, and S. R. Bowman. 2019. "SuperGLUE: A Stickier Benchmark for General-Purpose Language Understanding Systems." Cornell University, arXiv:1905.00537 (2 May).

6. EXTRACTING TEXT-BASED ESG INSIGHTS: A HANDS-ON GUIDE

Tal Sansani, CFA
Founder, Off-Script Systems, and Co-Founder, CultureLine.ai

Mikhail Samonov, CFA
Founder, Two Centuries Investments, and Co-Founder, CultureLine.ai

Introduction

This chapter presents several increasingly prevalent and effective applications of natural language processing (NLP) techniques in environmental, social, and governance (ESG) investing. Our guide simultaneously progresses down two tracks: the recent history of quantum leaps in NLP modeling and applying those advances to the present-day, high-stakes challenges of ESG investing. Modern NLP thrives in a vibrant, open-source environment, allowing investment practitioners to stand on the shoulders of AI giants by leveraging immense cumulative knowledge and computational processing power toward customized investment solutions. The key features of NLP—seamless customization and dynamic adaptability—are uniquely suited for the rapidly evolving language and standards in the ESG ecosystem.

With approximately USD17 trillion in equity capital invested in ESG-oriented funds (US SIF Foundation 2020), NLP-based insights and signals already underpin a variety of ESG datasets, widely used ratings and scores, alternative data offerings, and proprietary buy-side investment tools. These relatively new tools are helping address many of the most-cited challenges faced by institutional ESG investors—a lack of standardized data from third-party providers, limited disclosures from companies, and subjectivity of metrics (Cerulli Associates 2022).

This chapter covers a selection of foundational and state-of-the-art NLP advances, from word embeddings (word2vec, originating in 2013) to large language models (BERT, originating in 2018) to machine inference (zero-shot classifiers, originating in 2020). To support a learning journey, the text introduces NLP techniques in progressive layers, applying models that detect and connect *who* is mentioned, *what* topic is discussed, and *how* that topic is described in terms of tone and sentiment.

The simultaneous paths of this chapter are "hands-on" experiences with numerous examples, plain English explanations, and illustrations of how advanced NLP techniques can help identify ESG themes at the broad market level, the sector level, the individual company level, and even in the context of the more nuanced topic of "greenwashing." By showcasing recent NLP innovations, this chapter seeks to empower and ultimately inspire readers to apply NLP solutions to ESG problems.

ESG Investing: The Need for Adaptive Tools

As the concept of ESG has become part of investment vernacular (IFC 2004), the volume of data associated with related topics has grown exponentially. An entire subindustry of rating providers, index creators, gatekeepers, and industry coalitions has emerged to make sense of these growing inputs. Consequently, regulatory scrutiny has intensified, leading to the formation of various rules, guidelines, and proposals.

However, the dynamic nature of ESG metrics continues to pose challenges to the formation of industry standards. In just the last two years, investors have endured supply chain risks from COVID-19, diversity and inclusion initiatives resulting from racial justice protests, energy security concerns in the wake of the war in Ukraine, and climate risk related to carbon emissions. The fast pace and market volatility of these major global events demonstrate the need for flexible and adaptive tools for analysis and risk management. This chapter highlights how NLP can dynamically and objectively distill this complex landscape at scale.

ESG covers a multitude of valuation-relevant, intangibles-related topics missing from financial statements, such as product quality, supply chain resilience, human capital, and management quality, as well as other metrics traditionally associated with fundamental investment frameworks. The breadth of topics makes standardization challenging, which provides an opportunity for active investment research. ESG investing is yet another example of how market participants can gain an investment edge with novel and dynamic information that goes beyond traditional metrics.

NLP: Applying Human Insights at Scale

Natural language processing, which seeks to create statistical models that understand text and spoken words, is a rapidly growing branch of artificial intelligence (AI). In a short time, NLP models have gone from counting words in text to accurately inferring tone and meaning, a job that has historically been reserved for analysts. In a world awash in digital content, deciphering the trustworthiness, quality, context, and biases in language requires the collaboration of machines.

The nexus of ESG and NLP creates a scalable and customized way to extract timely insights from volumes of unstructured datasets, such as news (broad, curated, and widely consumed information), company and product review sites (crowdsourced information), company earnings calls, corporate social responsibility (CSR) reports, industry journals (information from practitioners and experts), and countless other sources. Whereas Deep Blue seeks to best humans at chess (machine over human), the most useful applications of AI in investment management put people and machines to work collaboratively, emphasizing each other's strengths in the hope of the sum being greater than the parts. In the investment context, ESG and fundamental analysts can apply their knowledge with NLP tools by creatively collaborating with in-house technical experts or consultants—teamwork that requires stepping out of traditional silos.

In the sections that follow, we demonstrate how NLP solutions are applied to some of the pressing questions surrounding ESG:

- Which issues matter most on a broad market level?
- What ESG issues are most prominent for a given sector or a particular company?
- Is the sentiment around a company's performance on sustainability variables worsening or improving?
- Is management spinning a story that is met with skepticism in the financial press?
- Which companies might have rising reputational and regulatory risk regarding "greenwashing"?

Extracting Text-Based ESG Insights

This chapter highlights ways to explore new ESG research or prototype new products by stacking relatively contemporary approaches on top of foundational NLP techniques.

These techniques can be learned and developed by layering on each technological advancement. To illustrate this progression, the framework in **Exhibit 1** combines three core approaches to extracting insights from text along with a guide to the initial structuring and sourcing of the information: *who* the text is about (publicly traded company), *what* the text is about (ESG topics), and *how* the topic is described (tone and sentiment).

Exhibit 1. Process Diagram: The Who, the What, and the How of NLP

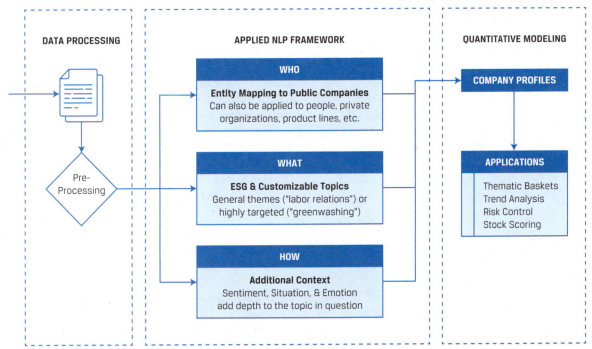

Corpus Creation: Financial News and Earnings Calls

Machine-driven insight is only as good as its data inputs. For this study, two complementary yet contrasting data sources—quarterly earnings transcripts and financial news—cover company developments across a variety of ESG issues from significantly different perspectives. The cost and time involved with fetching, cleaning, and organizing unstructured data typically represent a large first step; however, strong demand for text-based information sets (Henry and Krishna 2021) has led many data vendors to provide structured feeds of news[4] and earnings call transcripts[5] for NLP modeling, backtesting, and production processes.

Data evaluation

Preparing and aggregating data for analytical purposes are contextual and informed by how biases in the data could affect the model's output. In this study, earnings calls and financial news have three primary contrasting features: *timeliness* (calls are quarterly; news flow is periodic), *distribution of text* (earnings calls are done for virtually all publicly traded companies, while news is heavily skewed toward large companies), and *author's perspective* (calls are primary-source, first-person information originating from company executives, while news is third-party information).

Looking at the distribution and frequency of information flow in **Exhibit 2**, financial news is heavily biased toward large companies and coverage rises around earnings season. To correct for the large-company bias, metrics are aggregated at the company level and equally weighted to determine sector- and market-level trends (as opposed to weighting them by market capitalization or information share). For example, the thousands of articles discussing ESG issues important to Tesla are all mapped to Tesla, whereas the small number of articles covering ESG issues for Newmont Corporation are mapped to the mining company. When those companies are rolled up into one group for analysis, their ESG issues roll up with equal emphasis, meaning the ESG trends revealed will not be biased toward the largest companies that generate the most news.

Organizing the data: Entity mapping (the who)

Entity mapping is the process of connecting fragments of text (from sentences to full documents) to various entities (people, places, organizations, events, or specific product lines). Entity mapping answers the first important question: Who is this document or sentence about?

Mapping thousands of articles from multiple news outlets and earnings calls back to their entity (who) across thousands of companies is a challenging task, but the integrity of entity mapping drives the trustworthiness of subsequent insights. For example, references to "Meta," "Facebook," and "FB" need to map back to one entity, even though the references have changed over time. Other important questions arise in this process: Was the company mentioned in passing, or was it the focus of an in-depth, "long-read" article about the company? In addition to these details, online news outlets have different layouts, formats, advertisements, pop-ups, and other obstacles to systematically structuring text data for reliable downstream analysis.

Leveraging third-party technology

Although entity mapping is a daunting technical undertaking, sourcing and structuring vast quantities of new information from the internet has never been easier. For example, financial data vendors offer a wide range of off-the-shelf solutions, including structured, entity-mapped news feeds, so AI-driven insights are unencumbered by the difficulties of gathering and organizing data.

The example in **Exhibit 3** illustrates the simplicity, effectiveness, and scale of modern third-party solutions. Diffbot's query language (DQL) allows its users to query the web like any other database.

Five simple lines of code generate over 1,000 news articles in machine-readable form (e.g., CSV or JSON), each containing the article's text and title and the original article URL, augmented with rich metadata, such as the article's sentiment and the people, places, and general topics being discussed. While this example illustrates a single query, this paper draws on thousands of such queries, codified to collect English news articles for companies in the Russell 1000 Index, across 13 of the most popular financial news sources.[6] Modern, NLP-driven application programming

---

[4]Over 30 news analytics vendors are listed at the AlternativeData.org database of data providers: https://alternativedata.org/data-providers//search,news.

[5]Earnings call transcripts are sold and distributed by a handful of large data vendors, such as FactSet, S&P Global, and Refinitiv. They are also publicly available at https://seekingalpha.com and www.fool.com.

[6]www.bloomberg.com, www.wsj.com, www.reuters.com, www.barrons.com, www.nytimes.com, www.cnbc.com, www.marketwatch.com, www.ft.com, https://finance.yahoo.com, https://apnews.com, www.cnn.com, www.foxnews.com, www.foxbusiness.com.

Exhibit 2. Information Flow by Company Size and Time of Year

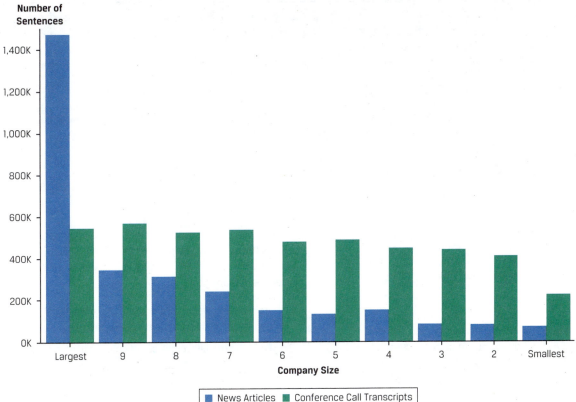

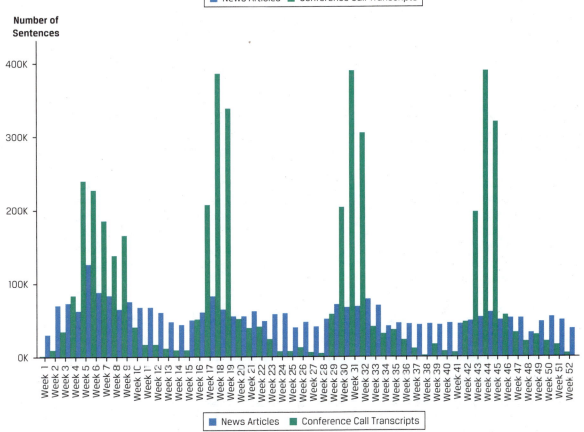

Note: Data are for 1 January 2019 to 31 December 2021.

Exhibit 3. Example Usage of Diffbot Query Language

Plain English Request	I want to see every news article about Nike or Adidas, written in English, published by Reuters, Yahoo! Finance, or Bloomberg, and published between the years of 2016 and 2021.

Diffbot Query Language (DQL)	`type:Article`
	`OR(tags.uri:"EnpdllhyQM-SckYV3z0i1Dw",tags.uri:"EikhmjkE8MlSihDC4RKNRWg")`
	`language:"en"`
	`OR(pageUrl:"reuters.com",pageUrl:"finance.yahoo.com",pageUrl:"bloomberg.com")`
	`date>="2016-01-31" date<="2021-12-31"`

interfaces (APIs) remove the barriers of collecting, cleaning, and structuring data, so the analyst can remain focused on investment insights.

A Robo-Analyst's First Steps: Word Embeddings and Text-Based Analytics

Having defined the "who" with entity mapping, the next step is identifying "what" topics are being discussed in a document, paragraph, or sentence. Counting the frequency of specific words in a body of text is a simple way to start, but doing so necessitates determining all the possible words and combinations of words related to each topic. Determining synonyms by committee can be very time consuming and requires deep subject matter expertise. For example, research on terms related to "greenhouse gas" would include "GHG," "chlorofluorocarbon," "carbon emissions," individual greenhouse gases, such as "methane" and "carbon dioxide," and so on.

To solve this problem of synonyms and tangentially related terms, word embeddings, a foundational NLP concept, can find relevant keywords associated with a given topic. Once trained on a corpus of text, word-embedding models can generate a family of semantically similar phrases for any given seed word (the technical name for the word the researcher inputs to find related terms). With these topic definitions, commonly referred to as "dictionaries," the researcher can begin to comb volumes of text in a comprehensive, consistent, and scalable manner.

Process overview: Identifying ESG topics in text

The process for connecting specific topics to companies follows the sequence below (see **Exhibit 4**), which was informed by research from the academic community and investment managers:[7]

1. Train a word2vec (word-embedding) model on earnings call transcripts and news articles.

2. Feed the model a small set of seed words for which the researcher is seeking synonyms and related words. The Sustainability Accounting Standards Board (SASB), a pioneer in determining ESG standards, has defined 26 ESG categories.[8] This study uses roughly two- to three-word summaries for each of the 26 categories as seed phrases for the word-embedding model, which then created 26 phrase lists (dictionaries), resulting in approximately 2,500 phrases across all dictionaries.

3. Match words in the ESG category–specific dictionaries with instances of those phrases in the corpus (news articles and earnings calls).

4. Finally, the number of matches with terms in the dictionary needs to be rolled up to numerically define the original seed word. To do so, the researcher calculates the weighted sum of the phrase frequencies for each SASB issue. The weights are a combination of the term frequency–inverse document frequency (TF–IDF)[9] of a given phrase multiplied by its similarity to the seed phrase.

---

[7]This process is motivated by the creative work of Li, Mai, Shen, and Yan (2020) and Wu (2021).

[8]Seed words were manually extracted from issue-level descriptions available at the SASB's "Materiality Finder" website: www.sasb.org/standards/materiality-finder/?lang=en-us.

[9]TF–IDF is a numerical statistic that is intended to reflect how important a word is to a document in a collection or corpus. The TF–IDF value increases proportionally with the number of times a word appears in the document and is offset by the number of documents in the corpus that contain the word, which helps adjust for the fact that some words appear more frequently in general.

Exhibit 4. Process Diagram: Applying Word-Embeddings to ESG

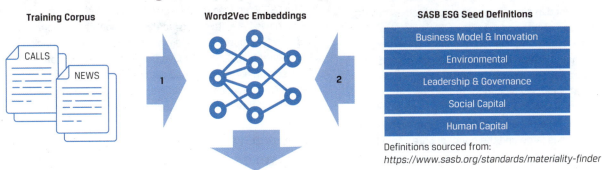
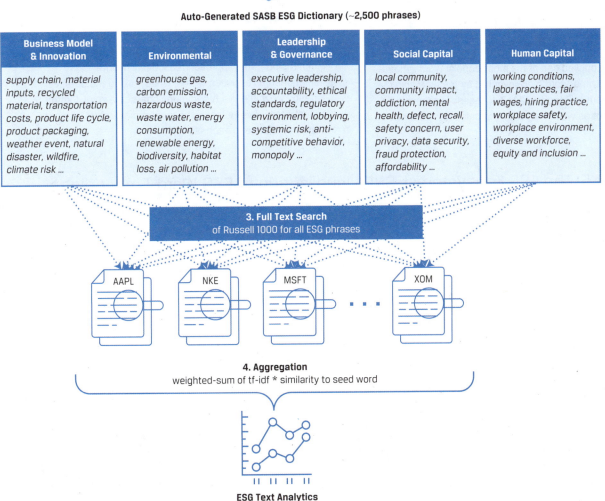

This dataset now has a variety of use cases, including evaluating market trends and shifts in materiality for a given sector and monitoring company-specific news across a large swath of ESG issues. Also, the process itself is fully customizable to any set of seed words, allowing industry practitioners to update or adjust the original SASB taxonomy or create an entirely new taxonomy based on customized organizing principles.

ESG word embeddings

In 1957, a leading English linguist named John Rupert Firth (1957) noted that "you shall know a word by the company it keeps." Firth's prescient words have stood the test of time; neural networks can derive meaning by piecing together relationships between various combinations of different words in multiple contexts.

In word-embedding models, each word is represented by a numeric vector based on the usage of words and their co-occurrences over a large set of documents. As such, words used in similar ways are captured as having similar representations and meanings. For example, if the words that surround "carbon" are often related to the words that surround "emissions," the geometric distance between these word vectors will be small, inferring that "carbon" is closely related to "emissions." At the other extreme, if the context surrounding "carbon" is quite different from the context surrounding "hiring," the vector distance is large and the concepts are considered less related.

Training word2vec on earnings calls and news

This study applied one of the most popular word-embedding algorithms, word2vec, invented by Tomas Mikolov and his team at Google in 2013. A decade in technology years might as well be a century in calendar years, yet word2vec's simplicity and effectiveness are still useful to researchers 10 years later.

The ESG word2vec model was trained on the earnings call and news data. Training a word2vec model can be done via a variety of open-source programming languages,[10] including Python, R, C, C#, and Java/Scala. The implementation presented here was carried out by using Python (the most popular language for implementing machine learning and NLP algorithms) within the topic-modeling library Gensim.[11]

The ecosystem of ESG topics, issues, and words

A common technique for visualizing and exploring similarities of words in a word2vec model is *t*-SNE,[12] which collapses multidimensional word vectors down to two dimensions. This approach reasonably maintains the relationships between words, while making the dataset neatly viewable in a two-dimensional scatterplot. **Exhibit 5** illustrates where each of the most prominent SASB words appear relative to each other.

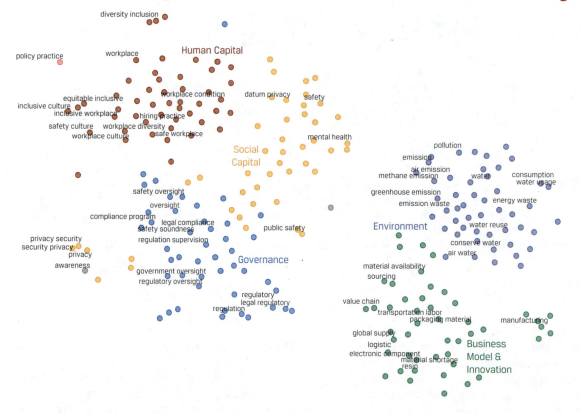

Exhibit 5. The ESG Ecosystem: t-SNE Visualization of ESG Word-Embeddings

---

[10]See Wikipedia's article on word2vec: https://en.wikipedia.org/wiki/Word2vec.

[11]Gensim is an open-source library for unsupervised topic modeling, document indexing, retrieval by similarity, and other NLP functionalities.

[12]*t*-Distributed stochastic neighbor embedding (*t*-SNE) is a method for visualizing high-dimensional data by giving each datapoint a location in a two- or three-dimensional map and doing so in such a way that similar objects are modeled by nearby points and dissimilar ones by distant points.

The output in Exhibit 5 demonstrates intuitive relationships between SASB's five major ESG topics. For example, human capital and social capital are displayed near one another, meaning their underlying word embeddings often share similar contexts and themes within the financial corpus. Similarly, governance has overlapping language with social and human capital. Looking at the subtopics in black font, some governance issues, such as "safety," tend to relate to employees, customers, and public perceptions, but terms tied to industry standards, such as "regulation" and "oversight," are more distant from human and social capital.

Even a less experienced ESG analyst could replicate the overlap and interrelationships of ESG terminology in an approximately similar way. However, in this example, a machine with no prior information learned these relationships in about two hours of computation time. This trained word-embedding model is repeatable and consistent and provides a foundation for unleashing endlessly scalable "machine knowledge" onto a wide variety of contexts and information sources.

Text-based investment insights

The word embeddings illustrated in Exhibit 5 provide an intuitive map of individual words to ESG. These terms, which are collected into dictionaries for each ESG theme, are then detected and tabulated across millions of news articles and earnings calls. ESG themes (the "what") can now be tied to individual companies (the "who"). The output of this process can be considered a metric for the ESG concept of materiality, which measures the significance of a given ESG topic to a sector or company.

Guided by large teams of sustainability experts, materiality mapping is primarily qualitative and relatively static in standardized ESG frameworks. By contrast, the text-based model in this study systematically and dynamically connects companies to their most relevant ESG issues over time. This is particularly relevant for keeping up with shifts in corporate strategy. For example, Amazon's ESG materiality evolved as the company transitioned from selling books online to cloud computing, food distribution, and health care. Mergers and acquisitions can also abruptly shift materiality.

These dynamic, company-level ESG exposures can then be rolled up and applied to a variety of investment use cases, including evaluating market trends, identifying shifts in materiality for a given sector, creating thematic baskets of stocks focused on certain ESG issues, and monitoring company-specific news across a large swath of ESG risks and opportunities.

Trend analysis

Applying this framework at the highest level, **Exhibit 6** illustrates what mattered most in ESG for the Russell 1000 from 2019 to 2022, highlighting ESG issues that created the most chatter in the financial press and company earnings calls.

Exhibit 6. Trend Analysis of ESG Issues

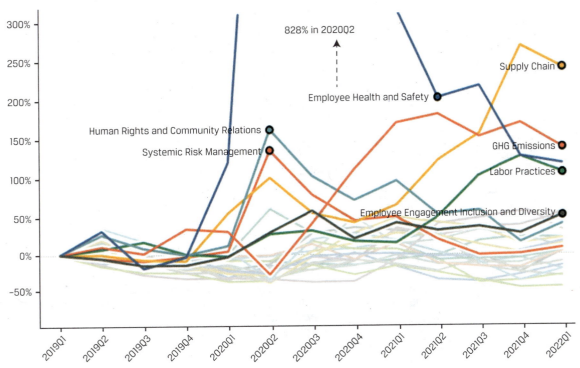

Interpreting the output in Exhibit 6, employee health concerns immediately spiked at the onset of the pandemic, well ahead of the imposition of public health restrictions in early 2020 (AJMC 2021). Shortly thereafter, systemic risk management rose in frequency. Thereafter, the NLP-based materiality measure detected widespread supply chain issues due to abrupt shifts in supply and demand. Exhibit 6 also shows a 50% increase in references to labor practices in 2021. This increase was later confirmed by the National Labor Relations Board (NLRB), which reported a 58% increase in the number of union representation petitions over that same year (NLRB 2022). With no a priori knowledge beyond basic seed words, this aggregate market perspective of ESG topics detected several significant market drivers in real time, unlike traditional ESG reporting outlets.

Dynamic materiality

Company-level ESG mappings can be rolled up for sector analysis in much the same way that company valuations, such as the price-to-earnings ratio (P/E), can be rolled up into sector valuations. In other words, this machine-driven process yields a materiality map (**Exhibit 7**) that is dynamic, consistent, and customizable, which connects sectors to their most prominent ESG issues over time.

The NLP process generated an intuitive and compelling materiality map. Among other insights, environmental topics are mapped to energy-intensive sectors, such as energy, materials, and utilities, while consumer-facing industries (staples and discretionary) are mapped to human and social capital.

Company-level alerts and profiles

The same NLP framework allows analysts to build ESG profiles for individual companies to identify, highlight, and monitor the most relevant company-specific ESG trends.

In **Exhibit 8**, the bars represent the aggregate frequency of a given ESG issue across thousands of news articles, broken out by year. This dashboard is intended to highlight company trends. If overlayed with a user interface, analysts could click on each individual bar to investigate specific statements from the underlying news articles and earnings calls.

As Exhibit 6 showed, labor issues are rising from an aggregate market-level perspective and tied closely to consumer-facing sectors via materiality mapping (Exhibit 7). Connecting those big-picture themes to the

Exhibit 7. Text-Based ESG Materiality Map

	Most Material	2nd Most	3rd Most	4th Most	5th Most
Energy	GHG Emissions (ENV)	Air Quality (ENV)	Water & Wastewater Mgmt. (ENV)	Ecological Impacts (ENV)	Critical Incident Risk Mgmt. (GOV)
Materials	Material Sourcing & Efficiency (BM&I)	Product Design and Life-Cycle Mgmt. (BM&I)	Water & Wastewater Mgmt. (ENV)	Air Quality (ENV)	Supply Chain (BM&I)
Industrials	Labor Practices (HC)	Waste & Hazardous Materials Mgmt. (ENV)	Material Sourcing & Efficiency (BM&I)	Air Quality (ENV)	Supply Chain (BM&I)
Utilities	Energy Management (ENV)	GHG Emissions (ENV)	Physical Impacts of Climate Change (BM&I)	Mgmt. of Legal and Regulatory Env. (BM&I)	Air Quality (ENV)
Real Estate	Ecological Impacts (ENV)	Business Ethics (GOV)	Access & Affordability (SOC)	Labor Practices (HC)	Systemic Risk Mgmt. (GOV)
Financials	Systemic Risk Mgmt. (GOV)	Critical Incident Risk Mgmt. (GOV)	Mgmt. of Legal and Regulatory Env. (GOV)	Physical Impacts of Climate Change (BM&I)	Business Ethics (GOV)
Consumer Staples	Labor Practices (HC)	Supply Chain (BM&I)	Material Sourcing & Efficiency (BM&I)	Ecological Impacts (ENV)	Product Design & Life-Cycle Mgmt. (BM&I)

(continued)

Exhibit 7. Text-Based ESG Materiality Map (*continued*)

	Most Material	2nd Most	3rd Most	4th Most	5th Most
Consumer Discretionary	Access & Affordability (SOC)	Labor Practices (HC)	Supply Chain (BM&I)	Employee Health & Safety (HC)	Selling Practices & Product Labeling (SOC)
Information Technology	Data Security (SOC)	Customer Privacy (SOC)	Supply Chain (BM&I)	Selling Practices & Product Labeling (SOC)	Product Design & Life-Cycle Mgmt. (BM&I)
Communication	Customer Privacy (SOC)	Competitive Behavior (BM&I)	Human Rights & Community Relations (SOC)	Employee Engagement Inclusion & Diversity (HC)	Selling Practices & Product Labeling (SOC)
Health Care	Product Quality & Safety (SOC)	Customer Welfare (SOC)	Selling Practices & Product Labeling (SOC)	Access & Affordability (SOC)	Competitive Behavior (GOV)

Note: The SASB legend is environmental = (ENV), leadership & governance = (GOV), business model & innovation = (BM&I), human capital = (HC), and social capital = (SOC).

Exhibit 8. Company-Level ESG Profiles: McDonalds vs. Starbucks

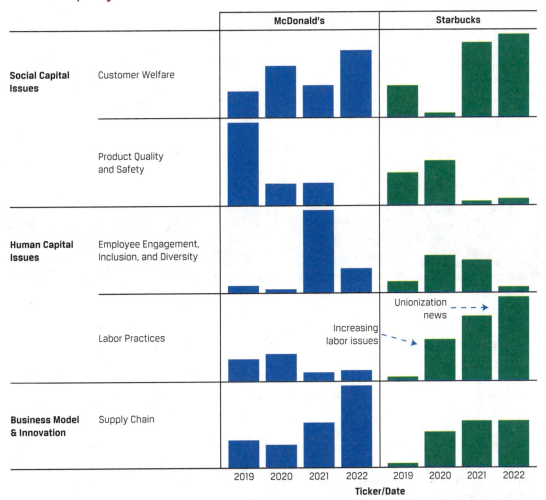

company level, two of the largest public-facing brands in the world, Starbucks and McDonald's, can be scrutinized along a handful of their most material ESG issues.[13]

Starbucks' labor practices received additional attention at the onset of COVID-19 when many companies faced staff shortages and wage pressure. Exhibit 8 indicates that labor issues were already brewing in 2020, culminating in the announcement of a large minimum wage increase in 2021 and a coordinated push for unionization in May 2022. By contrast, McDonald's faced less scrutiny on labor practices; however, supply chain durability issues, another hidden risk that arose from the economic disruption of COVID-19 (Exhibit 6), appeared to generate more attention given the company's supply chain challenges in 2022.

Training Techniques: Language Models and NLP Tasks

The process described in the subsection titled "Process overview: Identifying ESG topics in text" dynamically and systematically captures fast-moving, real-time shifts in ESG events at the market, sector, and company levels. For best results, however, the underlying word-embedding model needs to be monitored and periodically retrained to capture broader shifts in the English language. This section provides real-world examples highlighting this point, while also clarifying key differences between domain-specific training (e.g., word embeddings derived from financial text) and task-specific training (topic classification of ESG issues). This distinction helps frame more advanced NLP models discussed in subsequent sections of this chapter.

Retraining Models for the Changing Linguistic and Cultural Landscape

As the world changes, so too do the words used to describe it. Word-embedding models learn from the language they are trained on. Therefore, as the language shifts, models trained on older versions of text will lose efficacy when applied to current issues.

Language shifts can be illustrated by analyzing the topic of "telecommuting" across similar word-embedding models that were trained at different times. Telecommuting, an SASB Human Capital topic focusing on workplace standards and employee well-being, underwent a monumental cultural shift during the pandemic. **Exhibit 9** compares how three word-embedding models—Google (created in 2013), Facebook (created in 2017), and the custom model built for this paper (in 2022)—determine which phrases are most closely related to "telecommuting."

Looking closer at the actual terms related to telecommuting, the older models from Google and Meta reflect a different lexicon with more emphasis on ways to maximize office time and minimize commuting time, whereas this study's model, which is trained on language from the last few years, relates telecommuting to only remote-work concepts and picks up the pandemic-driven paradigm shift toward working from home. While pretrained, open-source models are effective for exploring new ideas and deploying minimally viable products, outdated language models, no matter how accurate at the time of training, will fail to identify significant shifts in meaning.

Exhibit 9. Top 5 Phrases Most Similar to "Telecommuting"

Source	Google	Meta	This Study
Year	2013	2017	2022
Model	word2vec-google-news-300	fasttext-wiki-news-subwords-300	word2vec-newscalls-cfa
1	Teleworking	Teleworking	Remote work
2	Flextime	Commuting	Work from home
3	Compressed workweeks	Flextime	Teleworking
4	Flextime schedules	Job sharing	Shift to remote
5	Carpooling	Work at home	Work remotely

---

[13]Starbucks' material issues can be found at the SASB's Materiality Finder webpage: www.sasb.org/standards/materiality-finder/find/?company[]=US8552441094&lang=en-us. Those for McDonald's can be found at www.sasb.org/standards/materiality-finder/find/?company[]=US5801351017&lang=en-us.

Domain-Specific Training versus Task-Specific Training

There are two key steps for training a model to accomplish a specific NLP task. First, it needs to learn the language of a specific domain (financial text). Second, it needs to apply that learned knowledge to accomplish a specific task (identify what a sentence is about or how a topic is described).

In the subsection titled "Process overview: Identifying ESG topics in text," the word-embedding model (word2vec) trained itself on text from financial news and earnings calls, allowing it to better understand language in the financial domain. This training step was an example of unsupervised learning, meaning the algorithm learned patterns and associations directly from the text by itself without any need for human input.

Even if a model understands the language of a given domain, it still needs the requisite knowledge to solve specific tasks. The next step in the process—creating dictionaries from seed words—was an example of semi-supervised learning because the human researcher defined seed words to describe SASB's ESG categories that the machine then used to create phrase dictionaries of synonyms and related words, which were used to find topic matches in financial articles and earnings calls. While lacking sophisticated machine knowledge, this semi-supervised approach is perfect for effectively and efficiently exploring any theme (ESG or otherwise).

For more narrowly defined classification tasks, researchers often apply supervised learning, which requires humans to manually label many thousands of sentences with pre-defined classes, or categories. The machine then learns from these labels, detecting underlying patterns and relationships, and applies that knowledge to classify entirely new sentences that it has never seen before. While supervised learning is more time consuming and labor intensive, classification outputs tend to be more targeted and precise than unsupervised models with no human input.

The next two sections—a case study from Robeco and a section on sentiment classification with large language models—illustrate how this two-step process can be applied to real-world ESG problems: first by establishing requisite domain-specific knowledge via unsupervised learning and then by applying supervised learning to solve specific classification tasks learned from the intelligence of human labels.

NLP at Robeco: An Industry Case Study

Mike Chen and the Alternative Alpha Research Team at Robeco authored the research discussed in this section, which demonstrates the power of word embeddings and machine learning (ML) for NLP tasks, weaving the United Nations Sustainable Development Goals (SDGs) into ESG analysis.

NLP can be used for sustainability and alpha purposes, such as detecting employee sentiment from comments in online forums or determining traits of corporate culture emphasized by senior management. In this example, Chen, Mussalli, Amel-Zadeh, and Weinberg (2022) demonstrate how NLP can be used to measure corporate alignment with the 17 SDGs.

In recent years, the SDGs have emerged as a framework that impact-minded investors can use to align their investment portfolios with sustainability. The SDGs are defined qualitatively, which raises questions as to how company products and operations can be quantitatively measured in alignment with each of the goals. NLP is one way to translate qualitative descriptions into quantitative scores. Chen et al. (2022) described a combination NLP and ML framework to do so, illustrated in **Exhibit 10**.

In this framework, the authors outline a two-step approach whereby the initial inputs into the NLP model are various company CSR reports. These are vectorized in Step 1 via word embedding, which allows the model to understand individual words and the context in which the words appear, thereby obtaining deeper insight into the written text.

In Step 2, the output vectors are passed into the ML portion of the framework, which has been fed labels showing company alignment with the specific SDGs. The vectors, in conjunction with the SDG alignment labels, allow ML to ascertain how vectorized descriptions of business models and products map to the various SDGs (an example of supervised learning). This two-step framework provides significant flexibility, because each component (the corpus, the labeling inputs, and the NLP and ML algorithms) can be substituted as newer technologies are developed and better or more appropriate corpus or alignment data become available.

A key challenge when classifying SDG alignment using ML is that few companies are aligned with any given SDG. This data imbalance can present a problem for ML algorithms because the naive approach of classifying all samples to the majority case (in our example, the majority case is non-alignment to any SDG) can result in reasonably high accuracy. To address this issue, the authors used the synthetic minority oversampling technique (SMOTE) to artificially create training samples to allow the ML algorithm to learn on a balanced training set.

Since the data sample is imbalanced, the authors also used recall, precision, and F1 score to measure and compare the performance of various permutations of the NLP–ML framework. The authors found the best results are achieved using a combination of the doc2vec embedding technique for the NLP portion and support vector machine (SVM) for the ML part of the framework. The results obtained are shown in **Exhibit 11**. Under this combination, the F1 scores for alignment to the various SDGs range from a low of 69% to a high of 83%.

This case study demonstrates how NLP and ML can be combined to improve the investment decision-making process while maintaining alignment with clients' unique sustainability interests.

Exhibit 10. NLP–ML Framework Used to Assess a Company's Alignment with UN SDGs

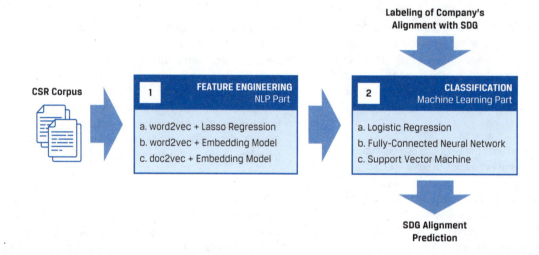

Exhibit 11. Classifier Accuracy Measures

	Balanced Test Acc.	F1 Score	Recall	Precision
SDG1	0.87	0.70	0.81	0.62
SDG2	0.83	0.70	0.67	0.73
SDG3	0.79	0.80	0.74	0.86
SDG4	0.65	0.73	0.61	0.90
SDG5	0.67	0.76	0.66	0.89
SDG6	0.79	0.78	0.83	0.74
SDG7	0.78	0.79	0.76	0.82
SDG8	0.76	0.76	0.66	0.89
SDG9	0.81	0.81	0.83	0.79
SDG10	0.64	0.72	0.67	0.78
SDG11	0.88	0.73	0.82	0.66
SDG12	0.77	0.83	0.76	0.90
SDG13	0.79	0.77	0.67	0.92
SDG14	0.86	0.81	0.78	0.85
SDG15	0.76	0.79	0.71	0.89
SDG16	0.87	0.69	0.84	0.59

Context Is King: Large Language Models and Sentiment Analysis

Having covered "who" is being discussed (entity mapping) and "what" (insights from matching words in the corpus with automatically generated ESG dictionaries), the next step addresses "how" a given topic is discussed in the text. The company-specific dashboard in Exhibit 8 highlighted how often company-specific ESG issues were mentioned in the news for McDonald's and Starbucks. While helpful, the tone of the articles was absent from that analysis. Were events and topics recounted in a positive or negative light? Is the company doing better or worse on a specific ESG topic? Sentiment analysis offers answers to these questions by measuring the magnitude of an ESG event, as well as the tone and shifts in tone over time.

Beyond Word Embeddings

While word2vec models serve a wide variety of applications, they have a critical limitation: context awareness. In word2vec, each word is represented by a single vector, resulting in a single meaning. For example, the following two sentences use the word "freeze" in different contexts that change the underlying meaning:

- With demand slowing, the firm is undergoing a hiring *freeze*.
- An unseasonable mid-spring *freeze* impaired the coffee harvest.

Using a word2vec-based approach, the word "freeze" will maintain the same vector representation despite the obvious differences in context. The model's inability to capture these differences in meaning will have a negative impact on the accuracy of downstream classification tasks.

BERT and the leap from words to sentences

In 2018, the AI language team at Google created Bidirectional Encoder Representations from Transformers (BERT), which was a clear inflection point in NLP. The large language model (LLM), which learned much of the nuanced meaning of the English language from Wikipedia (approximately 2.5 billion words) and Google's Book Corpus (approximately 800 million words), vastly improved the accuracy of NLP models by enhancing contextualization.[14]

LLMs, such as BERT, allow for multiple representations of each word, depending on the other words in a sentence and the order in which they appear. Operating on sentences as inputs instead of individual words or phrases, these new models brought machines one step closer to understanding text in a nuanced, human-like way (see, for example, **Exhibit 12**).

Portable intelligence with transfer learning

A massive dataset of 3.3 billion words contributed to BERT's vast knowledge of the English language, but this immense scale also limited its adoption beyond an exclusive set of AI superlabs with enormous computational resources. Retraining LLMs for every new task was impractical, expensive, and completely out of reach for everyone else.

Around the same time, practitioners began combining LLMs with transfer learning, a complex mathematical technique that enables the vast knowledge inherent in such models to be transferred to a new classification task. With this new ML architecture, a general purpose model, such as BERT, could be pretrained, packaged, and reused as a starting point for fine-tuning domain-specific tasks, such as sentiment classification of financial text. This advancement allowed research teams of all sizes to inherit and apply existing knowledge, ultimately leading to rapid innovation.

Exhibit 12. Limitations of Word-Matching in Sentiment Analysis

	Sentiment via Word Matching	Actual Sentiment
"As far as we can tell, the company has yet to make any *progress* in this direction."	Positive	Negative
"In total, a lower nickel price eases some of our *concerns* about ATI and its metal (stainless/nickel alloys) exposures."	Negative	Positive

---

[14]Before BERT, a number of models improved accuracy across a battery of language tasks, including sentiment analysis. A few notable models include GloVe (in 2013), fastText (in 2016), CoVe (in 2017), ULMFiT (in 2018), ELMo (in 2018), and GPT-1 (in 2018).

Additionally, the training of LLMs requires roughly five times the carbon emissions compared with owning a car in the United States for one person's entire lifetime (Hao 2019). Transfer learning architecture boasts an improved environmental footprint by reducing the energy usage necessary for applying LLMs[15] (see **Exhibit 13**).

Democratizing NLP: Hugging Face transformers, PyTorch, and TensorFlow

Open source is the final ingredient necessary for the broad application of NLP. Hugging Face is at the forefront of an increasingly democratized NLP movement with its intuitively designed API that abstracts powerful deep learning libraries, such as PyTorch and TensorFlow,[16] thereby streamlining and simplifying ML workflows. The Hugging Face Hub, also known as "the GitHub of machine learning," allows its community members (from hobbyists to AI superlabs) to share their work with the world, hosting over 50,000 models, 5,000 datasets, and 5,000 demos.

Combining Topic and Tone

The three advancements described in the prior subsections (large language models, transfer learning, and Hugging Face transformers) can now be directly leveraged to create more nuanced ESG models that understand both the topic being discussed (the "what") and the tone (the "how").

The next step of this study builds on work from researchers at Hong Kong University of Science and Technology (HKUST), who pre-trained the original BERT model on financial text using 10Ks and 10Qs (2.5 billion tokens), earnings calls (1.3 billion tokens), and analyst reports (1.1 billion tokens; Huang, Wang, and Yang, forthcoming). In other words, via Hugging Face's implementation of transformers, they were able to refine BERT (trained to the English language) to understand relevant financial language.

Huang et al. (forthcoming) also share two fine-tuned (task-specific) models: FinBERT-ESG and FinBERT-tone.[17] Both models were trained using supervised learning, with researchers manually labeling thousands of statements as "E," "S," or "G," (for FinBERT-ESG) and "positive," "negative," or "neutral" (for FinBERT-tone). This entire process, detailed in **Exhibit 14**, offers researchers an expedient way to combine topics with tone. Note, however, that while borrowing models is great for exploratory analysis, experimentation, and illustrative guides, for production, it is imperative to fully evaluate the labels and test overall efficacy for a specific NLP task.

Company-level alerting

To combine topic and tone, this study parses every sentence in the news dataset using the FinBERT-ESG classifier of Huang et al. for each sentence (E, S, G, or none) and then analyzes the same sentence using the FinBERT-tone classifier (positive, negative, or neutral). By aggregating the

Exhibit 13. Common Carbon Footprint Benchmarks (in pounds of CO_2 equivalent)

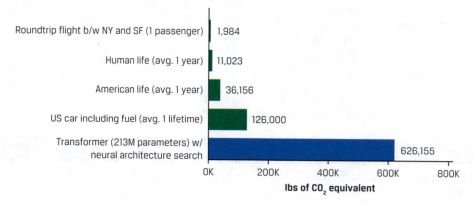

Sources: Hao (2019); data are from Strubell, Ganesh, and McCallum (2019).

---

[15] See Hugging Face's "How Do Transformers Work?" webpage at https://huggingface.co/course/chapter1/4.

[16] PyTorch and TensorFlow are free open-source ML and AI frameworks used most often for applications in NLP and computer vision. PyTorch was developed by Meta AI, and TensorFlow by Google.

[17] See the models' webpages at, respectively, https://huggingface.co/yiyanghkust/finbert-esg and https://huggingface.co/yiyanghkust/finbert-tone.

Exhibit 14. Process Diagram: Classifying ESG Topic and Tone with BERT

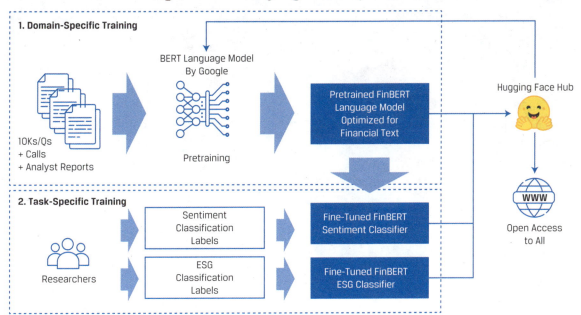

outputs of these two classifiers for each company, shifts in tone from 2021 to 2022 for a given ESG topic are visible, thereby offering a real-time system for detecting rising ESG risk for all the companies in a given equity universe.

Exhibit 15 displays the sentiment shift relating to environmental practices for individual companies. Companies in the upper-left corner represent sharply deteriorating sentiment from 2021 to 2022, which indicates rising risk related to perceptions about their environmental stewardship. In this example, NextEra Energy (NEE), PepsiCo (PEP), Lockheed Martin Corporation (LMT), and Uber (UBER) all received increasingly negative attention across a swath of environmental issues.

Deeper analysis into this methodology reveals the challenges of desensitizing models to pervasive events, such as severe market crashes, pandemics, and wars, because economic shocks can add noise and false positives to the results. For example, Uber's negative news was related to the increased cost of gas and its effect on the bottom line for its ridesharing services, which was only tangentially related to environmental practices, whereas the other companies received more scrutiny that directly targeted their environmental practices.

Applications in investment management

The following list provides examples of how this technology is being applied in investment management.

1. **Interactive dashboards:** Analysts tracking specific companies can create continually refreshed dashboards (as illustrated in Exhibit 15) and click on dots that link directly to relevant reports for further analysis.

2. **Risk alerts:** Risk alerting is a more automated and comprehensive approach to informing portfolio management decisions in real time by setting thresholds that send notifications to teams or combining real-time alerts with other measures, such as the application of an exclusionary stock screen.

3. **Quantitative analysis:** While the focus of this study is SASB-defined ESG issues, this framework is fully customizable to any company dimension (company culture scores, exposures to world events, etc.) covered in public data sources. Text-based signals are used across the industry as differentiating sources of alpha and for event-based risk control. This type of analysis is available in third-party applications, such as Alexandria Technologies, RavenPack (2022), RepRisk, and Truvalue, among many others.[18]

ESG Success: It Depends on Who You Ask

Comparing differences in tone between companies' earnings calls and their coverage in the financial press reveals notable if unsurprising results: Companies' descriptions

---

[18]For more information, go to www.alexandriatechnology.com/esg (Alexandria Technology); www.reprisk.com/ (RepRisk); and https://developer.truvaluelabs.com/catalog (Truvalue).

Exhibit 15. Text-Based ESG Alerting

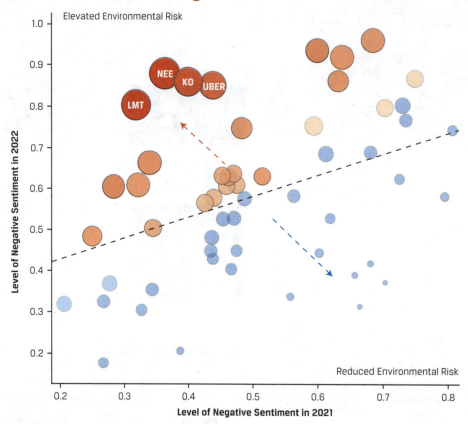

of their ESG performance tend to be far more glowing than how the news characterizes their performance.

Exhibit 16 shows that management is far more likely to speak positively about the big three ESG categories than about non-ESG issues. The "exaggeration" or "spin" is most pronounced when management is discussing governance issues. Specifically, management's tone is nearly three times *more positive* when talking about governance (9.5 positive-to-negative ratio) than when discussing non-ESG issues (3.8 positive-to-negative ratio). News coverage offers the opposite perspective with similar magnitude: Governance issues are discussed three times *more negatively* compared to statements about non-ESG issues (0.5 versus 1.3, respectively).

Drawing Inference: Zero-Shot Classification and Greenwashing

Sugar coating company performance in earnings calls is a well-known phenomenon to fundamental analysts and quants alike. A case study titled "Dissecting Earnings Conference Calls with AI and Big Data: American Century" in the report "AI Pioneers in Investment Management"

(CFA Institute 2019, pp. 26–27) empirically demonstrates that NLP can identify signs of management spin, manipulation, and even obfuscation in earnings calls. In the context of ESG, there's a specific term for this phenomenon: greenwashing.

Greenwashing is an increasingly important topic in the investment community and society at large. It describes the activity of misleading the public about an entity's commitment and performance with respect to ESG topics. In fact, the negative implications of greenwashing might be the only common ground that exists between ESG investing's advocates and its skeptics. While most standardized ESG frameworks include more broadly defined issues, such as selling practices and product labeling, the narrow topic of greenwashing has yet to be explicitly measured, which presents an exciting opportunity to use NLP to supplement standardized ESG frameworks with metrics for greenwashing risk. Greenwashing increasingly carries heightened reputational and legal risk, so identifying early signals of this concept has substantial economic value.

Designing a Greenwashing Classifier

The goal of this section is to provide simple and effective techniques to identify sentences that contain content

Exhibit 16. Comparison of Tone between Conference Calls and News across Varying ESG Topics

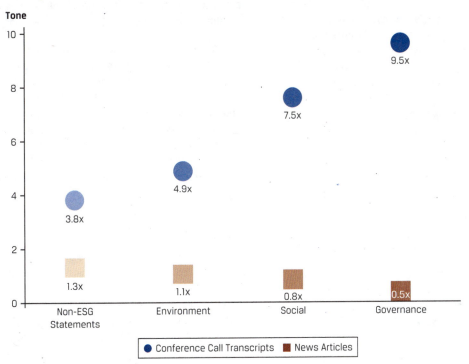

Note: Tone = Ratio of positive-to-negative sentences.

related to greenwashing. A word search–based process—one that simply looks for the word "greenwashing" in text—is a reasonable place to start and would suffice for many use cases. But the model can be further refined with techniques that can classify sentences that are about greenwashing without explicit mention of the term in the text.

In this study, sentences flagged for greenwashing simply indicate that the content of a sentence is about greenwashing. This does not indicate that the company in question is greenwashing. Like the risk-alerting applications presented previously, classification techniques provide critical first steps for dynamically and systematically tracking high-stakes ESG issues in tandem with analyst oversight.

When a word has no synonyms

Eskimos have 50 words for "snow" because thriving over millennia in the frigid climate required a nuanced understanding of snow. By contrast, the ESG ecosystem that investors inhabit is so new that there is only one word that is typically used to describe greenwashing.

Applying the word2vec model to other business words with more history and nuanced meaning, such phrases as "data breach," yield a rich family of associated words, such as "hacked" and "security compromised." In contrast, the term "greenwashing" returns no dictionary of similar phrases because greenwashing is a relatively new term that combines a few concepts into one word with a meaning that can be roughly deconstructed as follows: greenwashing = company + misleading + sustainability.

To broaden the machine's understanding of greenwashing, one could apply a supervised learning approach wherein a group of researchers would label sentences ("about greenwashing" versus "not about greenwashing"), while attempting to address common label-quality issues related to ambiguity and differences in reviewer opinions. However, this would be an enormous task, especially considering that different sectors have entirely different materiality to ESG topics. The next section addresses the challenge of using unlabeled data and advances a foundational objective of AI research: maintaining or increasing model accuracy while reducing human input.

Introducing Zero-Shot Classification

Zero-shot classification is a relatively new NLP task that answers the question, *what is this sentence about?* Unlike fine-tuned classifiers, it does so without previously seeing a sentence or a label (hence the name "zero shot"). Hugging Face researchers found that zero-shot classifiers are surprisingly accurate when deployed on LLMs (Davison 2020), albeit not quite as accurate as classifiers explicitly trained on the same topic via thousands of human labels.

Powered by natural language inference

Zero-shot classifiers were popularized by Yin, Hay, and Roth (2019) and rely on natural language inference (NLI), an NLP task that compares two sentences—a premise and a hypothesis—and determines whether the hypothesis aligns with the premise (entailment), contradicts it (contradiction), or does neither (neutral). Our study applies the hypothesis "This is about greenwashing" to a series of sentences using Meta's *bart-large-mnli* model, the most popular zero-shot classifier on the Hugging Face Hub.[19] The model responds with its assessment of whether the hypothesis is true, false, or neutral for each sentence. The output ranges between 0% (not at all related to greenwashing) to 100% (entirely related to greenwashing).

Test driving the zero-shot classifier

Zero-shot classifiers can understand multiple dimensions about a sentence—namely, topic, emotion, and situation (as described by Yin et al. 2019). This is especially appropriate for such a relatively novel and complex topic as "greenwashing." **Exhibit 17** illustrates the model's intuition and sensitivity to subtle changes in language. The zero-shot model intuitively adjusts its output (ranging from 0% to 100%) to the hypothesis "This sentence is about greenwashing" according to changes in the same sentence (relating to tone, emotion, situation, and negation).

Exhibit 17 demonstrates how the model handles nuanced meaning by substituting words in each sentence. For example, the sentence "The firm overstated its commitment to *debt*" (topic = debt) has a 16% chance of being about greenwashing, whereas the sentence "The firm overstated its commitment to *reducing emissions*" (topic = emissions) has a 95% chance of being related to greenwashing. This example-driven analysis highlights the model's ability to understand language and infer meaning in the context of ESG.

Preliminary analysis

Exhibit 17 helps illustrate how the model "thinks." The next step, detailed in **Exhibit 18**, examines *how well* it thinks by manually labeling 200 sentences and evaluating its ability to distinguish between three different types of sentences: sentences that contain the words "greenwash," "greenwashed," or "greenwashing" (15 sentences); sentences

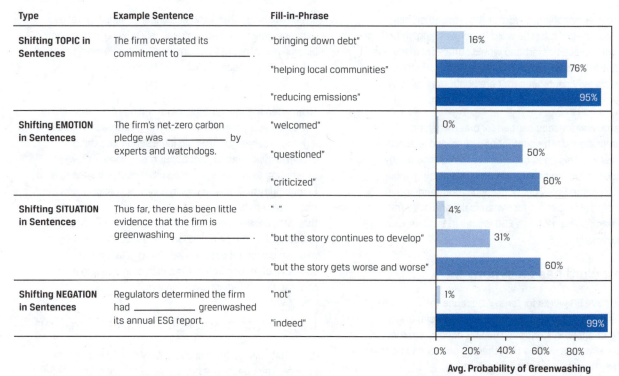

Exhibit 17. Test-Driving the Zero-Shot Classifier

Type	Example Sentence	Fill-in-Phrase	Avg. Probability of Greenwashing
Shifting TOPIC in Sentences	The firm overstated its commitment to _____ .	"bringing down debt"	16%
		"helping local communities"	76%
		"reducing emissions"	95%
Shifting EMOTION in Sentences	The firm's net-zero carbon pledge was _____ by experts and watchdogs.	"welcomed"	0%
		"questioned"	50%
		"criticized"	60%
Shifting SITUATION in Sentences	Thus far, there has been little evidence that the firm is greenwashing _____ .	" "	4%
		"but the story continues to develop"	31%
		"but the story gets worse and worse"	60%
Shifting NEGATION in Sentences	Regulators determined the firm had _____ greenwashed its annual ESG report.	"not"	1%
		"indeed"	99%

---

[19]Go to https://huggingface.co/facebook/bart-large-mnli. The model was developed by Meta Platforms, downloaded roughly 1.5 million times per month in 2022, and trained on 433,000 hypothesis/premise pairs.

Exhibit 18. Preliminary Accuracy Measures for Zero-Shot Classification of "Greenwashing"

	Confusion Matrix 1￼Matching Word "Greenwash(ed/ing)"		Confusion Matrix 2￼Zero-Shot Classifier for "Greenwashing"	
200 Total Sentences	Predicted: Sentences Related to Greenwashing	Predicted: Sentences Unrelated to Greenwashing	Predicted: Sentences Related to Greenwashing	Predicted: Sentences Unrelated to Greenwashing
Actual: Sentences Related to Greenwashing 50 Sentences	15 (True Positive)	35 (False Negative)	30 (True Positive)	20 (False Negative)
Actual: Sentences Unrelated to Greenwashing 150 sentences	0 (False Positive)	150 (True Negative)	0 (False Positive)	150 (True Negative)
	Precision = 100%; Recall = 30%; F1 Score = 46%		Precision = 100%; Recall = 60%; F1 Score = 75%	

that describe greenwashing without mentioning the term (35 sentences); and sentences completely unrelated to greenwashing (150 sentences). These 200 sentences were run through the zero-shot classifier using a 50% threshold; that is, if the classifier output is more than 50%, the sentence gets classified as relating to greenwashing. While this test is run on a small sample, it takes a critical first step in understanding the model's effectiveness.

The confusion matrices in Exhibit 18 detail reasonably encouraging results. The rudimentary word-matching model is incapable of picking up on sentences that did not explicitly contain the terms "greenwash," "greenwashed," and "greenwashing." By contrast, the zero-shot classifier powered by *bart-large-mnli* correctly identified the 15 sentences containing those words, in addition to 15 additional sentences that merely alluded to greenwashing, all without generating any false positives. In other words, the zero-shot classifier captures twice the number of sentences that relate to greenwashing without making any additional mistakes.

Next steps

Running the same zero-shot classifier on a larger set of unlabeled data (approximately 5 million sentences from news) was fruitful but exposed the pain points of imbalanced classes (greenwashing is an extremely small fraction of broader market discussions), which requires further refinement of the original 50% threshold. There are also easily correctable blind spots in the classifier, such as the word "green" leading to false positives. These early insights provide a path forward for improving the model.

Tackling the subject of greenwashing head on with more scrutiny and analysis will ultimately benefit the public and improve on what constitutes adhering to ESG principles. Meanwhile, language models are advancing at an incredible pace, reducing the amount of human input required to achieve the same results. Improving accuracy while reducing costs is a powerful accelerator for additional research in this rich intersection of ESG and NLP.

Conclusion

The customizable and dynamic nature of NLP makes it an ideal match for the rapidly evolving data and definitions and the significant challenges of ESG analytics. The investment community's application of the techniques outlined in this chapter will further refine their usefulness, while the combination of humans and machines is fast becoming the new frontier in investment insight. There has never been a better time to collect, process, and draw meaning from text, and the innovations are only poised to continue.

Whether building AI tools from the ground up, sourcing solutions from third-party data providers, or effectively interpreting model outputs, the foundations detailed in this chapter can entirely reframe how problems are solved and redefine the questions that can be asked of data. Quite simply, NLP can move the investment industry beyond its current limitations of data, time, resources, and imagination and, in tandem with ESG, create meaningful and high-performing contributions to active investing.

We would like to thank Matt Spain, Rebecca Jackson, Vinod Chandrashekaran, Jonathan Berkow, Mike Chen, and Mike Tung.

References

AJMC. 2021. "A Timeline of COVID-19 Developments in 2020." (1 January). www.ajmc.com/view/a-timeline-of-covid19-developments-in-2020.

Cerulli Associates. 2022. "ESG Issue." The Cerulli Edge—US Institutional Edition (First Quarter).

CFA Institute. 2019. "AI Pioneers in Investment Management." www.cfainstitute.org/-/media/documents/survey/AI-Pioneers-in-Investment-Management.pdf.

Chen, M., G. Mussalli, A. Amel-Zadeh, and M. Weinberg. 2022. "NLP for SDGs: Measuring Corporate Alignment with the Sustainable Development Goals." *Journal of Impact and ESG Investing* 2 (3): 61–81.

Davison, Joe. 2020. "Zero-Shot Learning in Modern NLP." *Joe Davison Blog* (29 May). https://joeddav.github.io/blog/2020/05/29/ZSL.html.

Firth, J. 1957. "A Synopsis of Linguistic Theory, 1930–55." In *Studies in Linguistic Analysis*, 1–31. Oxford, UK: Blackwell.

Hao, Karen. 2019. "Training a Single AI Model Can Emit as Much Carbon as Five Cars in Their Lifetimes." *MIT Technology Review* (6 June). www.technologyreview.com/2019/06/06/239031/training-a-single-ai-model-can-emit-as-much-carbon-as-five-cars-in-their-lifetimes/.

Henry, P., and D. Krishna. 2021. "Making the Investment Decision Process More Naturally Intelligent." Deloitte Insights (2 March). www2.deloitte.com/us/en/insights/industry/financial-services/natural-language-processing-investment-management.html.

Huang, Allen, Hui Wang, and Yi Yang. Forthcoming. "FinBERT: A Large Language Model for Extracting Information from Financial Text." *Contemporary Accounting Research*.

IFC. 2004. "Who Cares Wins—Connecting Financial Markets to a Changing World" (June). www.ifc.org/wps/wcm/connect/topics_ext_content/ifc_external_corporate_site/sustainability-at-ifc/publications/publications_report_who-careswins__wci__1319579355342.

Li, Kai, Feng Mai, Rui Shen, and Xinyan Yan. 2020. "Measuring Corporate Culture Using Machine Learning." Working paper (29 June). https://papers.ssrn.com/sol3/papers.cfm?abstract_id=3256608.

NLRB. 2022. "Correction: First Three Quarters' Union Election Petitions up 58%, Exceeding All FY21 Petitions Filed." Office of Public Affairs (15 July). www.nlrb.gov/news-outreach/news-story/correction-first-three-quarters-union-election-petitions-up-58-exceeding.

RavenPack. 2022. "ESG Controversies: March 2022" (5 April). www.ravenpack.com/blog/esg-controversy-detection-march-2022.

Strubell, Emma, Ananya Ganesh, and Andrew McCallum. 2019. "Energy and Policy Considerations for Deep Learning in NLP." Cornell University, arXiv:1906.02243 (5 June). https://arxiv.org/abs/1906.02243.

US SIF Foundation. 2020. "2020 Report on US Sustainable and Impact Investing Trends." www.ussif.org/files/Trends/2020_Trends_Highlights_OnePager.pdf.

Wu, Kai. 2021. "Measuring Culture." Sparkline Capital (24 August). www.sparklinecapital.com/post/measuring-culture.

Yin, Wenpeng, Jamaal Hay, and Dan Roth. 2019. "Benchmarking Zero-Shot Text Classification: Datasets, Evaluation and Entailment Approach." Cornell University, arXiv:1909.00161 (31 August). https://arxiv.org/abs/1909.00161.

HANDBOOK OF ARTIFICIAL INTELLIGENCE
AND BIG DATA APPLICATIONS IN
INVESTMENTS

III. TRADING WITH MACHINE LEARNING AND BIG DATA

This book can be found at cfainstitute.org/ai-and-big-data

7. MACHINE LEARNING AND BIG DATA TRADE EXECUTION SUPPORT

Erin Stanton

Global Head of Analytics Client Support, Virtu Financial

Introduction

As a result of recent advances in computing power, data abundance, and cloud services, asset managers are increasingly eager to use artificial intelligence (AI) and machine learning (ML) solutions to unearth meaningful insights from their data. However, despite their willingness and investment, many buy-side firms are struggling to establish an efficient and programmatic way to do ML-based analytics at scale. Why are these efforts failing to meet expectations?

Making Sense of the Data

As asset managers push their competitive edge into the digital sphere, AI/ML solutions are growing out of the necessity for better and faster processes, calculated decisions, and data-driven insights. In the TRADE's October 2020 article "Buy-Side Lags behind Sell-Side in Adoption of Machine Learning and Artificial Intelligence," a Refinitiv study found that only 28% of buy-side firms were leveraging ML and AI (Smith 2020). This lag was recently confirmed by a Q1 2022 Quant Strats survey of 100 hedge funds, asset managers, and investment banks across the United States and Canada that pegged regular use of machine learning in decision making at 22% (Finadium 2022). Anecdotally, a different picture is emerging, one fueled by significant buy-side interest and active ML skill building and development.

Like the chicken and egg paradox, the buy side needs advanced technology and established efficient processes to capture and store data in sufficient granularity and requires ML expertise to help sift through the reams of structured and unstructured data. Though buy-side traders still consider sourcing liquidity their biggest challenge—one that statistical algorithms cannot easily solve—they recognize the advantages of ML-assisted approaches. Based on our observations, data delay and capture capabilities are improving and there is enthusiasm for putting existing data to work. ML's abilities to uncover patterns in large datasets and surface correlations that humans cannot detect have buy-side traders and portfolio managers learning about and turning to open-source ML libraries, such as scikit-learn, tools similar to those used by traditional data scientists. In turn, these budding quasi-data scientists are developing such ML-based solutions as trigger algorithms that can help inform a direction to take when unforeseeable events occur or ML-powered solutions that overcome limitations by using data gathered from other industries.

In this chapter, five use cases detail real-life examples of ML's application in the analytics and trading spaces, while noting both the effective combination of data and ML-based techniques used to enrich the decision-support processes and some of the current barriers facing buy-side firms as the technology matures. Here is a synopsis:

- **Use Case 1: Feature Importance.** Designed to reduce the number of inputs a trader needs to consider when selecting the optimal trading strategy, feature importance calculates a score or rank for each input in a model. It is common for trading blotters to contain dozens, if not hundreds, of different security and market metrics, so using an ML-based approach can help traders focus on the most meaningful factors.

- **Use Cases 2 and 3: Transaction Cost Analysis (TCA).** Portfolio managers and traders use TCA to learn from post-trade data and to improve future performance. In searching for trends about which strategies work, data are typically broken down by components, such as the size of the order or the market cap of the stock. In Use Cases 2 and 3, different ML-based approaches help extract additional insights from existing trade data to further enhance TCA analysis.

- **Use Case 4: Normalized and Unbiased Algo Trading.** The automated, randomized testing performed by algo wheels helps traders find the best trading algorithm across a variety of brokers; it is like the A/B testing an e-commerce site would run to find the best product. Just like a retailer needs to ensure consistency of service for its customers, a data analyst must be aware that, aside from the testing component itself, all testers receive the same experience. In comparing algo wheel orders, a trader must account for the different order characteristics and market characteristics that each broker receives. Traditional market impact models are built statistically, but now, based on the size and scope of available data, it is possible to handicap brokers using ML-based models.

- **Use Case 5: Trading Strategy Recommendation Model.** In Use Cases 1–4, traders had to select the optimal trading strategy. In Use Case 5, an ML-based trading strategy recommendation model is offered with an option to override should the recommendation not align with the trader's human intuition and experience. Incidentally, when a trader chooses to override, this too is captured and can be analyzed to better enhance the model.

Not All Data Are Created Equal

Computers cannot make decisions as humans do. Human decisions are based on heuristics and cognitive biases against a broad field of attention to fully comprehend an event. The use of ML-based models depends heavily on data, and more specifically on granular data, as well as on the humans that build them. It is important to acknowledge that all ML analyses begin with data, but not all data are created equal. In addition to the variance in data quality, humans also add variability via the multiple decisions they make throughout the ML model construction process.

Advanced models, such as neural networks, make such firms as Google successful, but they are like black boxes; it is hard to explain why they come up with the results they do. In trading, this approach is not optimal. In accordance with data science best practices, model builders should consider the following questions carefully during and after model construction. As a matter of transparency, their responses should also be included for every model submitted into production.

- What data were included versus excluded, and why?
- Assuming the data were available, what would improve the model?
- What consistency checks and quality assurances were performed on the input datasets?
- What features were included and excluded, and why?
- What model was chosen, and why?

Use Case 1: The Role of Feature Importance in TCA for Auto-Order Routing

Each ML-based model created is an experiment since they fail as often as they succeed. Sometimes, one may be able to make a model operational, but the predictive accuracy is low or the model does not work owing to a technical problem. Nevertheless, ML techniques are evolving, reducing the amount of time spent on manual analysis.

The feature importance approach is often where most buy-side firms start their ML implementation journeys. When evaluating the performance of a portfolio, a portfolio manager typically performs an attribution analysis to determine which stocks contributed positively and negatively. The output information can be used to explain performance to an end client and/or to predict the viability of future investment decisions.

The process of TCA is a data-driven way traders and portfolio managers can benefit by reviewing past results. Historically, TCA has primarily been observational, dissecting the changes in trading costs into factors, such as liquidity, volatility, and spread. Ideally, the trader may leverage the enhanced post-trade information when execution planning and when demonstrating or confirming execution quality/best execution.

Although observational TCA is less statistical, it has proven to be an invaluable tool for bridging the consumer trust gap. Experience has made clear that it is essential to prove to your end audience how well their data and processes are understood before they can be convinced to adopt emerging technologies, such as AI and ML; TCA has been an effective catalyst toward ML-based analytics. Usually, once a client gains confidence in traditional TCA capabilities, their thinking leads them to ask whether anything is missing. For Harris Associates, their search led them to the feature importance approach for auto-routing execution, according to Jason Siegendorf, the firm's head of trading analytics:

> Harris Associates had previously set up a workflow within our execution management system to auto-route or send a subset of trades directly to a pre-defined algorithmic trading strategy, bypassing the trading desk. This enabled cash flows and other low risk orders to be traded very consistently and without trader bias in broker selection and allowed our traders to focus on the orders that they can have the most impact on by sourcing liquidity and deciding on the optimal execution strategy. We know that order size is an important consideration when deciding if an order is auto-routing eligible, but we also wondered if there might be other contributing factors we were missing out on. Applying the feature importance function confirmed our intuition and helped spotlight other meaningful order characteristics we typically pay less attention to.[1]

Typically, a human trader's execution decision making involves the synthesis and weighing of dozens of inputs to make instant decisions regarding how to best execute an order. However, brain processing studies show that interactions are limited to three, sometimes four, inputs (Cowan 2001). The feature importance approach assists human traders by statistically confirming observational

---

[1]Jason Siegendorf, personal communication with author.

TCA and human intuition by explaining subtle post-trade transaction cost patterns that may have otherwise gone undetected. It can also be used as a guide for pre-trade and auto-routing strategies.

The recommended ML-based approach for this use case was a supervised random forest model[2] (feature importance is built in natively); however, some buy-side clients may prefer the straightforward linear regression[3] approach. Most traders are already familiar with the linear regression coefficients, which can be used to determine the direction and impact of a specific feature.

The following steps taken in this use case can be implemented for any ML-based model.

- **Step 1: Cleansing and Normalizing Data**

    Any ML-based process must first identify the right data for the intended objective and determine whether any data normalization is required. Although not explored in this article, most of a model builder's time is spent on the data—data cleansing, normalizing, and removing outliers and blank values—in addition to selecting and normalizing features before they can be passed into the model.

- **Step 2: Chunking (Breaking Down) Data into Subsets for Easier Interpretation**

    The following examples illustrate how chunking (breaking down) data into smaller subsets enhances understanding:

    - **Have the drivers of trading costs changed over time?** Ideally, the data should be broken down into time periods (e.g., month, quarter) and a separate model should be run for each. When completed, the model builder can compare the feature importance for each distinct period and determine whether drivers of costs have shifted or stayed the same.

    - **What are the cost drivers between two types of order flow?** A trader may want to know the difference in transaction costs between single-stock versus program trading flow, so the data would be chunked into two respective datasets and modeled separately.

    - **Do transaction costs differ by fund type?** To understand the cost impacts on small-cap cap growth and large-cap cap value, for instance, a trader would need to segment the data into relevant attribute datasets and then run a model for each attribute to pinpoint the most important drivers of the transaction costs.

- **Step 3: Data Labeling and Testing and Training Datasets**

    As inputs, labeled datasets are required for the supervised model. Following the selection of which labeled dataset(s) to use, it is necessary to further separate the data into training and testing subsets. Model builders must reserve a portion of the data for testing to determine how well the model predicts with data it has not previously interacted with, also known as generalization.

- **Step 4: Selecting the Model's Features**

    When selecting the model's inputs, avoid using a 'kitchen sink' approach that includes every possible driver of transaction costs since this type of model does not perform well with highly correlated inputs. Several techniques exist to identify and remove the highly correlated features; it is a step in the process.

- **Step 5: Selecting the ML Model's Library and Training a Supervised Model**

    Among the open-source ML libraries, scikit-learn is a popular option, and since the use case involved predicting continuous trading costs rather than discrete ones, the RandomForestRegressor was chosen. Despite spending less time tweaking the model to improve accuracy, its predictive power remains a significant factor when analyzing the feature importance.

- **Step 6: Selecting a Feature Importance Approach**

    Finally, the model builder must identify the most influential inputs for model prediction. Here are a few techniques:

    - **Default scikit-learn's feature importance.** Informally looks at how much each feature is used in each tree within the training forest. **Exhibit 1** shows an example output from the scikit-learn feature importance module.
        - *Pros*: Single command to retrieve and fast
        - *Cons*: Can be biased to continuous features and high-cardinality categorical features; can only be run on the user's training dataset

    - **Permutation feature importance.** Shuffles a feature to see how much the model changes its prediction accuracy.
        - *Pros*: Can be run on both testing and training datasets
        - *Cons*: More computationally expensive and can overestimate the importance of correlated features

---

[2]A random forest grows multiple decision trees that are merged for more accurate predictions. The reasoning behind these models is that multiple uncorrelated models (i.e., individual decision trees) achieve much better performance as a group than individually.

[3]The simple linear regression forecasting method can be used to plot a trend line based on relationships between dependent and independent variables. In linear regression analysis, changes in a dependent variable are shown on the *y*-axis and changes in the explanatory variable are shown on the *x*-axis.

Exhibit 1. Selecting Feature Importance

Weight	Feature	
0.2904 ± 0.0302	tradeHorizon	
01733 ± 0.0100	tradedValue	**Expected Results Sample**
0.1663 ± 0.0131	historicalVolatility	The trading horizon is the most important factor influencing transaction costs, followed by traded value and historic volatility. Traders can use this to explain transaction costs post-trade and to inform them of the costs before placing an order in the market (pre-trade).
0.1217 ± 0.0137	participationRate	
0.0560 ± 0.0111	percentMDV	
0.0523 ± 0.0094	spread	
0.0310 ± 0.0042	marketCap	
0.0230 ± 0.0041	sector	
0.0064 ± 0.0053	securityType	
0.0022 ± 0.0013	side	
0 ± 0.0000	country	

Source: Virtu Analytics.

- **Drop column feature importance.** Manually drop one feature and examine model prediction accuracy.
  - *Pros*: Highly intuitive and accurate
  - *Cons*: Need to retrain the model each time, which can be resource-intensive
- **Feature importance computed with Shapley additive explanation (SHAP) values.** Uses the SHAP values from game theory to estimate how each feature contributes to the prediction.
  - *Pros*: Provides more information through decision and dependence plots and impact directionality
  - *Cons*: Can be computationally expensive and requires a separate library

Use Case 2: Semisupervised Learning to Cluster Similar Orders Where Clear Tags Are Missing

The lack of clear and consistent data tags is one of the biggest hurdles ML must overcome. Currently, vast amounts of data are either untagged, in free-form text, or hard to integrate into the core dataset. In this use case, unsupervised and semisupervised approaches are explored for populating tags where data are missing, and in the next use case, I examine these approaches for parsing free-form text.

The objective for this use case is to determine the type of commission rate when the data populating the commission-type tag are missing. The example is useful because it illustrates that model builders might have to get creative in how to use the data they have—solving the problem using a different tack.

ML-based techniques can be applied more broadly to identify segments of orders that are similarly structured across a range of partially or fully untagged attributes. Examples include the following:

- *In cases where the fund is not consistently tagged*, details such as the number of stocks, average market cap, average momentum, and volatility can be used to extrapolate the style of investment strategy.
- *In cases where a trading desk discretionary tag is not consistently tagged*, details around the order horizon, the type of algorithm used, the observed transaction costs, and the existence of a limit price can be used to extrapolate whether the buy-side trading desk had full discretion over the trading strategy of the order.

In contrast with the first use case, Use Case 2 has only a small segment of clearly labeled data, so model builders

Illustrative Example of Using Semisupervised Learning to Solve a Long-Running Data Tagging Issue

Any time data are sourced from multiple systems, such as from multiple trading systems, data tagging can become an issue. An example is that while some trading platforms easily capture the type of commission rate paid with a trade, many do not. Buy-side traders want to be able to compare their commission rates to a large peer-based database to get a sense of how much relative commission they are paying.

While not easily solvable with traditional observation-based analytics, semisupervised learning allows for the training of a model that can learn off clearly tagged examples and then predict the commission type for trades that do not have clear tagging. The buy-side trader can now compare her execution-only rate on an apples-to-apples basis to other investment managers.

could choose to implement an unsupervised or semisupervised approach.[4]

As previously noted, ML model construction requires significant data preparation, and in Use Case 2, this involved the parsing of the client–broker code as an extrapolated model feature. While the broker tag itself differs from firm to firm, many broker destinations indicate the category of commission paid—for instance, *brokerA_HT* and *brokerA_LT*—data that were parsed and tagged as inputs for the model (**Exhibit 2**).

If an unsupervised clustering approach is taken, then a model needs to be selected that allows for both continuous numerical information, such as the average commission rate paid, and discrete categorical information, such as the country the client traded in. Using a *k*-means algorithm for the model's purely numerical input and a *k*-modes algorithm for the model's purely categorical input is recommended. The model builder may also opt for Zhexue Huang's *k*-prototype clustering algorithm that combines both approaches into one (Huang 1998).

When the model is complete, the model builder will have an output cluster number that, in this example (**Exhibit 3**), indicates whether the record represents an execution-only or a non-execution-only commission rate.

The output cluster number can be used to report the execution-only commission rate; the use case goal was achieved. Nevertheless, good data science practices require model builders to review not only results but also the components of the model. In so doing, the modeler found that the dataset contained more labeled data than expected and re-ran the model, this time using a semisupervised approach (some labeled data and some unlabeled data).

In the semisupervised model approach, a small set of data labels was used to train a supervised classification model, and once trained, the model could be used to predict the

Exhibit 2. Broker Code Commission Parsed and Data Tagged

Client ID (categorical)	Country (categorical)	Turnover (numerical)	Avg. Commission Rate (cps) (numerical)	Broker Destination Code (categorical)	Parsed Broker Code Tag (categorical)
1	USA	$1,000,000	1	brokerA_LT	Execution Only
1	USA	$2,000,000	4	brokerA_HT	Not Execution Only
2	USA	$1,000,000	1.5	brokerabcd	Unknown

Source: Virtu Analytics.

---

[4]Semisupervised model learning involves a learning problem, as well as the algorithms created for the problem, that pertains to a small amount of labeled examples and numerous unlabeled examples from which the model learns and makes predictions on new examples.

Exhibit 3. Model Cluster Output Number Using Parsed and Data Tagged Broker Commission Code

Client ID (categorical)	Country (categorical)	Turnover (numerical)	Avg. Commission Rate (cps) (numerical)	Broker Destination Code (categorical)	Parsed Broker Code Tag (categorical)	Model Output Cluster #
1	USA	$1,000,000	1	brokerA_LT	Execution Only	1
1	USA	$2,000,000	4	brokerA_HT	Not Execution Only	2
2	USA	$1,000,000	1.5	brokerabcd	Unknown	1

Source: Virtu Analytics.

unlabeled portion of the dataset. Even though the model builder ultimately opted to use the semisupervised method, the fully unsupervised and semisupervised approaches yielded similar average execution-only rates. In ML-based data analysis, reproducibility is an important aspect of confirming that techniques and approaches are working as intended.

Use Case 3: Natural Language Processing to Parse Free-Form Text Fields into Data Tags

Frequently, the parsing of inputs is from free-form text, such as a portfolio manager's note to a buy-side trader that might include trading instructions and constraints that can impact a trade's outcome. The following are some examples:

- Target this order for the close
- Part of a prog, trade cash neutral
- Avoid impact, trade in line with volume

A human reader can easily parse this text into a few simple tags; however, to programmatically extract information from free-form text fields, model builders must be familiar with natural language processing (NLP). The goal in Use Case 3 is to automate what a human can understand on a more systematic and consistent basis, as follows:

- Close
- Program trade
- Go along

Useful in post-trade learning, parsed tags can provide a data-driven perspective on how the portfolio manager's instruction may have affected trading costs, and in execution planning, they can help the trader better understand what strategies work best based on the instructions received. NLP can be used against any free-form text field to help parse out additional information, even though our examination in this use case focuses on the portfolio manager's instructions.

Google's Bidirectional Encoder Representations from Transformers (BERT) model was chosen because it has the capability of enhanced context understanding because of its process of evaluating text in both left-to-right and right-to-left directions. As with other models, BERT is open source and has the advantage of being pretrained on an enormous dataset. Since its initial launch, BERT has been adapted into sub-language versions, such as FinBERT, which handles financial documents, and LEGAL-BERT, which handles legal documents. The Virtu Analytics team performs most of its NLP work on an internal JupyterHub, where they have installed the necessary libraries and built their codebase; however, AWS SageMaker and Comprehend can be much quicker to set up. BERT also offers the advantage of being fine-tuned using a relatively small number of labeled examples, which, due to the size requirements, can be labeled by humans manually.

At this point, BERT runs like any other supervised method, producing tagged predictions alongside probability.

Use Case 4: Transaction Cost/Market Impact Prediction

Leveraging market impact models, TCA determines the quality of the execution versus the expected cost. Currently, various transaction cost outcome prediction approaches are based on a combination of order characteristics, stock-level market data inputs, and a model calibration process that incorporates the results of realized trades.

Exhibit 4. Precleansed Data Noise in a Typical Dataset

Training Example	Ticker	Trade Time	Shares	Volatility	Spread	Observed Transaction Cost Outcome (implementation shortfall)
1	AAPL	3/1/2022 10:00 a.m.	1,000	9 bps	10 bps	5 bps
2	AAPL	3/1/2022 10:05 a.m.	1,100	8 bps	9 bps	20 bps

Source: Virtu Analytics.

Building an ML-based model off observed transaction costs can be challenging because of the data noise in a typical dataset and the lack of data labeling that hampers the parsing of text. **Exhibit 4** illustrates the problem with data noise in the use case's dataset.

The training example in Exhibit 4 shows different observed transaction cost labels despite nearly identical inputs for ticker, trade time, shares, volatility, and spread, which can result in model confusion. Data analysts are advised that there may be other factors not captured in traditional TCA analysis that can affect a trade, which can similarly confuse a model. Attempts to estimate market impact using Virtu's Global Peer database in its entirety were unsuccessful; however, when filtering off more homogeneous order flows, such as those from the algo wheel, useful estimates were obtained.

An algo wheel provides automated, randomized routing to brokers according to user-defined allocations. When using an algo wheel, the trader selects the desired algo strategy and sends the order. Then, the algo wheel's broker-allocation engine routes the order to a user-defined set of normalized algo strategies. Post-trade data are accumulated over time (on average, 300 orders per broker represent a useful dataset) to assess performance and guide future broker allocations.

An ML-based market impact prediction model can be applied to cross-firm flows (giving insight into how brokers perform relative to each other) or to firm-specific flows to account for specific nuances in their proprietary investment processes. Enrico Cacciatore, senior quantitative trader and head of market structure and trading analytics at Voya Financial, explains why this capability matters: "Performance is what determines which brokers receive more flow on our algo wheel, and we need to account for differences in order difficulty across the flow that each of our counterparties receives. The Machine Learning Market Impact model we subscribe to allows us to handicap our brokers while at the same time giving us a sense of what transaction costs competing firms are achieving."[5]

The random forest model was chosen to accomplish the use case goal for market impact prediction. Several other model types were tested, including forest-related variations, such as gradient-boosted trees, but a simple random forest implementation performed the best in this case. We have found that random forest models provide high accuracy for our use cases and off our specific dataset, which includes both numeric and categorical data, and the results are also quite easy to explain and troubleshoot.

Every model builder is advised to incorporate a third-party review as an integral step in the construction process. Non-model builders with knowledge of the dataset, ML, and subject matter should review the approach with the model builder(s)—with all participants being strongly encouraged to challenge the model based on the data, features, and model type selected.

Use case in point, during our Transaction Cost Impact Algo Wheel Model peer review, someone raised a potential endogeneity issue related to a few features that included order horizons. Even though the order horizon greatly improved the model's prediction accuracy, it is directly controlled by the broker. The purpose of a peer review is for users to have a common understanding of the model's objective so they can assess whether it performed as intended. In this use case, the peer review team agreed that the broker had too much control over the order horizon and the feature was removed from the model.

Use Case 5: Trading Strategy Recommendation

In Use Cases 1–4, ML-based approaches provided data-driven trade information but left optimal trading strategy selection to the buy-side trader. In this use case, the review closes with an ML-based trading strategy recommendation model. Even though this example invokes greater risk—a suboptimal trading strategy can result in a higher-cost trade—the reader should now have a better understanding of ML-based alternative approaches to

---

[5]Enrico Cacciatore, personal communication with author.

segment order flow when data tags are unclear, how to parse free-form text from an ML perspective, and how market impact estimates can be constructed solely from observed trades.

This use case's data represented all algorithmic trades captured across all brokers from Virtu's execution management system. Leveraging the model at a firm-specific level is possible; however, data requirements are more stringent as accuracy is emphasized when a recommendation is being submitted.

The feature importance approach was applied to identify the key data inputs for the model, which include the following:

- *Order attributes*, such as the ticker, side, sector, size, and market cap
- *Stock clustering and NLP techniques*, used to fill in the gaps, such as whether a limit price was set and whether an urgency setting was used for the algo trade
- *Real-time market condition metrics*, such as relative volume, volatility, and spread compared with historical distributions

Random forest models were then trained using historical data for each of the algorithm trading styles available to a buy-side trader, including implementation shortfall, VWAP, liquidity seeking, and dark.

Finally, the buy-side trader receives a prediction of the transaction cost outcome based on all available algorithms. Though it is possible to display only the winning, low-cost strategy, it is also useful to show the cost and variability of outputs across all strategies as part of the trader's implementation display. Separately, some trades will be marked as not-low-touch-eligible because of the high strategy estimates provided across all models.

Conclusion

Although the use cases presented in this chapter are successful, many experiments do not perform as expected. To provide some balance, an example of a failed experiment would be the effort to build a stock clustering model that could inform a trading strategy. Though the experiment was successful in clustering stocks by characteristics, it could not tie them to a model that consistently informed how to trade them.

ML-based model building can sometimes be creative, should be collaborative, and is always iterative.

References

Cowan, Nelson. 2001. "The Magical Number 4 in Short-Term Memory: A Reconsideration of Mental Storage Capacity." *Behavioral and Brain Sciences* 24 (1): 87–114. www.researchgate.net/publication/11830840_The_Magical_Number_4_in_Short-Term_Memory_A_Reconsideration_of_Mental_Storage_Capacity.

Finadium. 2022. "Quant Strats Survey Shows ML Adoption Lagging, Third Party Spend Drops, Quantum Computing Tops Future Tech" (17 March). https://finadium.com/quant-strats-survey-shows-ml-adoption-lagging-third-party-spend-drops-quantum-computing-tops-future-tech.

Huang, Zhexue. 1998. "Extensions to the *k*-Means Algorithm for Clustering Large Data Sets with Categorical Values." *Data Mining and Knowledge Discovery* 2: 283–304. http://citeseerx.ist.psu.edu/viewdoc/download?doi=10.1.1.15.4028&rep=rep1&type=pdf.

Smith, Annabel. 2020. "Buy-Side Lags behind Sell-Side in Adoption of Machine Learning and Artificial Intelligence." *The TRADE* (27 October). www.thetradenews.com/buy-side-lags-behind-sell-side-in-adoption-of-machine-learning-and-artificial-intelligence/.

Effects of Training with Biased Data

While not discussed previously, if the datasets used to train machine learning models contain biased data, then the model predictions will most likely be biased as well. If most of the training data for the volume-weighted average price (VWAP) strategy represented large-cap stocks, which inherently have lower transaction costs, this strategy could look incorrectly cheap when compared to other models that have a more representative training sample. There are several ways to deal with bias, and it is an important consideration for any model that is used directly in the trading space.

8. MACHINE LEARNING FOR MICROSTRUCTURE DATA-DRIVEN EXECUTION ALGORITHMS

Peer Nagy
ML Intern, Man Group
DPhil Student, Oxford-Man Institute, University of Oxford

James Powrie, PhD
Principal Quant, Man Group

Stefan Zohren, PhD
Principal Quant, Man Group
Faculty Member, Oxford-Man Institute, University of Oxford

Introduction

A central task in implementing any trading strategy is executing the trades required to reach a desired portfolio position. Typically, larger trades are required to change positions for funds with higher assets under management, and the larger a trade is, the more impact it tends to have on market prices. This impact can be measured as slippage (i.e., the difference between a reference price before the start of the trade and the prices at which trades are executed). To minimize this slippage cost, which can lead to a significant performance degradation over time, machine learning (ML) methods can be deployed to improve execution algorithms in various ways.

An execution problem is usually framed as follows. The execution algorithm is presented with a block of shares to buy or sell within a required time frame, which typically ranges from seconds to hours. To minimize the adverse impact of trades on the market price, this large order is split into smaller slices that are then executed over the available time horizon. The role of the algorithm is to choose an execution schedule that reduces the slippage bill as much as possible. If the order was not split up this way and distributed over time but instead was executed as a market order at the moment the trade instruction was presented, then large buy orders would push prices up, sell orders would push them down, or there might simply not be enough liquidity in the market at the time to complete the trade, leading to a less favorable slippage cost or an incomplete execution.

In any execution problem, there is a trade-off between the price impact and the risk of the price moving unfavorably over the execution horizon. If we are risk neutral and have no information on the direction the price is likely to move or on future trading activity, the optimal execution schedule involves partitioning all trades into smaller slices spaced evenly over the execution horizon. This strategy is referred to as TWAP (time-weighted average price) execution, which serves as a benchmark for more advanced execution algorithms to surpass. Using methods from stochastic optimal control, TWAP can even formally be shown to be optimal under these assumptions, so it constitutes a valid baseline (Almgren and Chriss 2000).

However, it might appear obvious that we can further improve execution if we have useful predictions of where prices might move in the short term. Another commonly used execution strategy makes use of information on trading volume, or market turnover, because a higher volume allows larger trades to be executed for the same amount of price impact. This type of strategy targets execution of a block of shares at the volume-weighted average price (VWAP) by splitting up execution over time proportionately to the expected volume profile. While expected volume is inherently a forward-looking variable, it shows patterns depending on the time of day and can be predicted reasonably accurately using ML models. The mathematical finance literature also shows that VWAP is an optimal execution strategy when volume information is available under the assumptions of risk neutrality and permanent market impact (Kato 2015; Cartea and Jaimungal 2016). In practice, we can enhance our execution performance in contrast to TWAP by adjusting trade sizes proportionately to expected volume. Estimating trading volume can be as simple as observing a volume profile by time of day or as complex as using deep learning models with a plethora of market features.

One role for ML algorithms in execution is therefore to compute forecasts of short-term price movements and expected volume that an execution algorithm can use to front- or back-load the execution schedule—in effect, locally speeding up or slowing down trading activity. For example, given a signal forecasting decreasing prices over the next few seconds, the algorithm would place a sell trade now rather than wait for the price to fall. This supervised learning—or more specifically, regression problem—has been approached using a variety of methods, ranging from statistical modeling to deep learning. It is possible to apply advanced ML techniques, such as

Jamuna deep learning, only because of the abundance of high-frequency data, which are essential for their training.

Predicting price movements directly is only one task of the many that ML can be applied to. For example, ML can also be used to forecast other relevant variables for optimizing the execution problem, such as market spreads, available future liquidity in the market, or volatility of the returns. Indeed, one can even have reinforcement learning algorithms directly choose concrete execution actions, such as sizing, timing, and pricing of slices, to solve the execution problem.

Microstructure Data and Analysis

Most electronic exchanges involved in the trading of cash equities, futures, or options use limit order books (LOBs) to match buy and sell orders using a price–time priority matching mechanism. In this prioritization scheme, orders are first matched by their price levels, with orders at the same price on a first-come, first-served basis. Every limit order to buy with a price lower than any sell order in the LOB is added to the bid side of the LOB, where levels are ordered from best (highest price and earliest arrival) to worst (lowest price and latest arrival). Similarly, if an order to sell is posted at a price higher than any order to buy in the LOB, it is added to the ask side of the LOB. Together, the bid and ask levels of the LOB constitute the visible supply and demand for any instrument and any moment in time (see **Exhibit 1**). The bid level with the highest price is called the best bid, and the ask level with the lowest price is called the best ask. The difference in price between the best ask and best bid is called the spread. If a market order is placed to buy (sell), it is first executed against the best price level of the ask (bid) side, then executed in order of arrival time of the corresponding limit order, and finally executed against the next level if the order is larger than the number of shares available at the best price. Rather than market orders, practitioners often use limit orders that are targeted against the best bid or ask. A refinement of this tactic is to use immediate-or-cancel (IOC) orders, which are automatically canceled if they cannot be filled at the limit price.

Given this order matching mechanism, LOBs are often described as double-sided continuous auctions, since a continuous order flow changes the book dynamically over time. Limit orders that cannot be matched immediately at the time of arrival, because either the bid is too low for a buy order or the ask is too high for a sell order, enter the book and provide liquidity to the market. Market orders, IOCs, or executable limit orders—buy (sell) limit orders with prices higher (lower) than the best ask (bid)—however, take away liquidity from the market, do not enter the LOB, and are executed immediately. In the case of executable limit orders, we can also have a situation where part of the limit order is executed, which thus removes liquidity, while a remainder stays on the book and provides liquidity.

To train ML models for execution tasks, LOB data are required in some form. These data can be represented at different levels of granularity. For most tasks in this space, a univariate price time series is insufficient, and at the least, a dataset with best bid and ask prices and volumes over time is required to learn useful relationships. Some ML models even train on data including multiple or all levels of the LOB to forecast variables of interest. Such datasets can be represented either as a stream of individual orders—so-called market-by-order (MBO) data—or as a sequence of snapshots of the state of the LOB over time. MBO data contain different order types (limit, market, cancel, and modify), which allow a dynamic reconstruction of the LOB in full fidelity. For modeling purposes, however, time series of features of the LOB state are usually more amenable to be used as model inputs.

As mentioned in the previous section, supervised ML techniques can be fruitfully applied to several prediction targets in the execution domain. Models that can predict future values of these variables over even part of the execution horizon can help reduce slippage. One such target is the market spread, because lower spreads imply more favorable execution prices for marketable orders crossing the spread. Similarly, high trading volume makes it more likely that a passively placed limit order will be executed at each time step. Conversely, forecasting return volatility can be useful for gauging the risk of large price moves over the execution horizon. In periods of high volatility, for example, it might pay to front-load the execution schedule to limit exposure to the downside risk of adverse price shocks.

Exhibit 1. Illustration of an LOB with Five Bid and Ask Levels

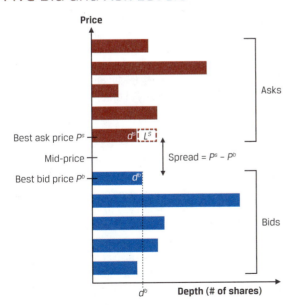

Note: The arrival of a new limit sell order of size L^s at the best ask is added to the book by increasing the depth at that level.

Over the short term, one of the best indicators of immediate price moves in the LOB is the *order flow imbalance* (Cont, Kukanov, and Stoikov 2014). The definition of the order flow imbalance (OFI) is the order flow on the buy side: incoming limit buy orders at the best bid, L^b, net of order cancellations, C^b, and market orders, M^b, minus the opposing sell-side flow, within a period of time:

$$OFI = (L^b - C^b - M^s) - (L^s - C^s - M^b).$$

This measure captures an imbalance between demand and supply in the market, which is an essential determinant of the market price. A high positive order flow imbalance indicates excessive buy pressure at current prices, thereby making it more likely that prices will rise imminently. Cont et al. (2014) describe an empirical linear relationship between OFI and price changes.

A related LOB-derived measure of supply–demand imbalance, which can be used as a predictive signal of short-term price changes, is the *order book imbalance* (OBI):

$$OBI = \frac{d^b - d^s}{d^b + d^s}.$$

Here, d^b and d^s are the depths of the best bid and best ask, respectively (see Exhibit 1). The OBI calculates the normalized difference between the depth (number of available shares) on the buy side at the best bid, d^b, and the number of shares posted on the sell side at the best ask, d^s. This measure is limited between –1 and 1, ranging from a strong downward price pressure to a strong upward price pressure.

The order book imbalance is also often used by practitioners to calculate a *micro-price*, p^{micro}, which more closely reflects the microstructure effects than the mid-price. The micro-price simply weighs the bid and ask prices, p^b and p^s, respectively, by the imbalance, I:

$$P^{micro} = IP^s + (1-I)P^b,$$

where

$$I = \frac{d^b}{d^b + d^s} = \frac{OBI + 1}{2}.$$

ML-Based Predictive Signals for Execution Algorithms

A classical approach in statistical modeling is to start out with simple, perhaps linear, models and a small set of variables, or features, that are likely to have some predictive power for the quantity of interest. Over the modeling process, model complexity is gradually increased and features are further engineered and refined to extract more information from the raw data. Driven by the domination of the ML literature by deep learning and artificial neural network (ANN) models, most recent approaches, however, have moved away from handcrafted feature engineering and instead approached prediction problems using raw data directly. This trend has also taken hold in financial ML and quantitative trading.

A recent exception to this rule is the deep order flow imbalance model (Kolm, Turiel, and Westray 2021), which uses order flow imbalance, as described in the previous section, to predict a vector of returns over multiple short-term horizons. The authors show that extracting order flow features from the top 10 levels of the order book is sufficient to achieve state-of-the-art predictive performance with relatively simple conventional neural network models, such as LSTM (long short-term memory) networks, or combinations of LSTMs with multilayer perceptrons (MLPs). This implies that practitioners might be able to get away with simpler models in some cases by performing an input data transformation from raw data to order flows. These results contrast with those of the same simple neural network models that instead use raw order book features, which cannot achieve any predictive power on the same task, implying that the data transformation is essential. However, another result of this study is that linear models and simple MLP feed-forward networks alone are not useful for forecasting such short-term alpha signals.

Notwithstanding deep order flow imbalance models, the trend in the current ML literature on forecasting short-term price signals points in the direction of using raw order book states directly, using more advanced ANN architectures to automatically extract feature representations amenable to forward return regression or classification tasks. One such model is DeepLOB (Zhang, Zohren, and Roberts 2019a), which uses a deep neural network architecture with convolutional layers and an inception module (Szegedy, Liu, Jia, Sermanet, Reed, Anguelov, Erhan, Vanhoucke, and Rabinovich 2015) also based on convolutional layers. Convolutional neural networks (CNNs) were originally developed for visual classification tasks, such as handwritten digit recognition or classifying images based on their content. The start of the current popularity of CNNs came with AlexNet (Krizhevsky, Sutskever, and Hinton 2012) and its superior performance on the ImageNet challenge, a classification problem of a large database of images with more than 1,000 prediction classes. Convolutional layers act as local filters on an image, aggregating local information in every special region. During learning, the weights of many such filters are updated as the overall system learns to recognize distinct features in the data, such as horizontal or vertical lines, corners, and regions of similar contrast. LOBs can be likened to images because they also contain local information; for example, price and volume information at each level of the book can be combined with adjacent levels to automatically extract new features using convolutional layers. Similarly, CNNs can learn local temporal information by convolving order book states over the time dimension.

Building on this analogy between images and LOBs, the state-of-the-art deep learning model DeepLOB (Zhang et al. 2019a), which uses raw order book states directly as inputs to the network, constitutes a new tool in the execution toolbox. This type of model currently provides the most accurate short-term price signals, which can be used to improve execution trajectories. To improve the robustness of forecasts, DeepLOB can also be extended to perform quantile regression on the forward return distribution (Zhang, Zohren, and Roberts 2019b). To do this, the final LSTM layer of the network is split into multiple separate parallel parts for as many quantiles as should be forecast, and each network branch uses a corresponding quantile loss function. Quantile predictions can then be combined to compute more robust point estimates and add a measure of uncertainty and risk for the practitioner. Training separate models for the bid and ask sides has the additional advantage of producing estimates of the market spread, which can help in deciding the prices at which the order should be placed and whether the spread should be crossed.

To improve the planning of an execution schedule, a point-in-time price forecast can be useful; ultimately, however, a price path over the execution horizon would be more beneficial for concrete planning. Using ideas from natural language processing and machine translation, a sequence-to-sequence model with an attention mechanism can be used to achieve such multihorizon return forecasts using LOB data (Zhang and Zohren 2021). To translate written text from one language to another, the idea of the sequence-to-sequence model (Sutskever, Vinyals, and Le 2014) is to use an LSTM encoder to learn a representation of a sentence as a fixed-length vector and then use a separate LSTM-based decoder to again translate this vector representation into the target language. Adapting this idea to predict return trajectories, the model in Zhang and Zohren (2021) uses the DeepLOB network (Zhang et al. 2019a) as an encoder, while an *attention mechanism* (Vaswani, Shazeer, Parmar, Uszkoreit, Jones, Gomez, Kaiser, and Polosukhin 2017) allows using selected hidden states of the encoder layers in the decoding step, producing the forecast time series. This way, the model drastically improves forecasting performance over longer time horizons as forecasts sequentially build on each other in an autoregressive fashion.

Because deep learning models benefit from large amounts of data, in the extreme case, models could even be trained on market-by-order messages directly. Given that deep order flow imbalance models already showed the advantage of this more stationary data source, using all the raw data in a deep learning framework is a logical next step.

From Integrating Predictive Signals into Execution Algorithms to Automatically Learning Policies Using Reinforcement Learning

An execution strategy in an LOB market can be viewed as essentially two dimensional. One dimension is how very large order volumes are sliced up over time, while the other dimension describes the prices at which slices are placed in the order book. A simple TWAP strategy might, for instance, split a large order uniformly over time and always place marketable limit orders by crossing the spread (see **Exhibit 2**). This would imply, however, that half the spread is lost with every trade relative to the mid-price, incurring slippage costs even if the mid-price stays constant over the entire execution time. In contrast, placing trades passively by using limit orders at the near touch (i.e., without crossing the spread) has the opposite effect of earning half a spread whenever a marketable order is placed in the opposing direction. The downside of passive orders is that execution is uncertain and depends on other market participants' order flow and future price moves. Thus, if one had a directional signal of future prices, it would be sensible to deviate from the simple TWAP strategy. For example, if the execution task is to sell a block of shares, a favorable price signal might indicate that the mid-price is expected to rise; hence, a slice of the order could be placed more passively deeper in the book (at a higher price), anticipating that a price swing

Exhibit 2. Simple TWAP Strategy

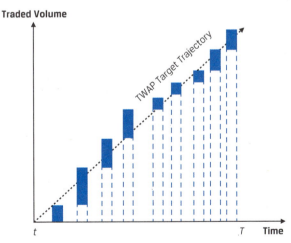

Note: This exhibit shows an illustration of an execution schedule with a linear TWAP target trajectory and executed discrete slices as blocks over time around the target trajectory.

could complete the trade. If price forecasts point downward, however, a market order could still make use of the higher price by executing a slice before the move happens.

Using a combination of ML models, we can thus engineer a complete execution strategy. An example algorithm might work as follows. Volatility forecasts, obtained using any method from historical averaging over generalized autoregressive conditional heteroskedasticity (GARCH) models to deep learning, can be used to schedule either the time allowed for an execution ticket or the amount of front-loading over a fixed time horizon by controlling how execution slice sizes decrease over time. Using ML forecasts of trade volume, we can further modulate execution schedules by proportionately changing future slice sizes with expected volume forecasts. Predicted price paths can then be used to fine-tune the strategy by varying placement levels (prices) dynamically. Should we expect a favorable price move, we would place a passive limit order in the book at the first level—or even deeper into the book if the expected price move is sufficiently large. Such a strategy could be refined in various ways—for example, by using a probabilistic level placement to increase the probability of passive placements with more favorable price moves and wider spread forecasts. A probabilistic strategy also has the benefit of being less predictable by other market participants, who might want to exploit the effect that large orders have in moving the market.

Another ML approach encompassing the execution problem uses reinforcement learning (RL) algorithms to plan the execution trajectory. RL—and especially deep RL using deep neural networks—has been tremendously successful in solving complex problems, from learning to play games (Mnih, Kavukcuoglu, Silver, Graves, Antonoglou, Wierstra, and Riedmiller 2013) to predicting three-dimensional protein structures from genomic data (Jumper, Evans, Pritzel, Green, Figurnov, Ronneberger, Tunyasuvunakool, Bates, Žídek, Potapenko, et al. 2021). In the execution context, Ning, Lin, and Jaimungal (2021) describe a good example using deep RL for optimal execution problems using double Q-learning (Hasselt 2010), employing a modern algorithm previously used to train autonomous agents to play Atari games at a superhuman level from raw pixel input.

On a theoretical level, the execution problem can be framed as a partially observable Markov decision process (POMDP), which can be amenable to being solved using RL algorithms. The RL learning paradigm works analogously to biological learning processes in animals and humans. The agent, our execution algorithm, interacts with a market environment in state s, which describes all information necessary to characterize the current state of the market, by performing an action, a, thereby transitioning the state to $s' = T(s,a)$. The environment state is further assumed to satisfy the Markov property, which means that past states do not add any further relevant information for the future. The agent, however, perceives not the entire state of the world but only an observation, $o' = obs(s')$, and hence does usually not know the underlying state exactly. In addition to the new observation o' at each step, the learner also receives a reward signal, r. Based on the reward signal, the RL algorithm learns over time which sequence of actions leads to the highest expected cumulative rewards.

Observational features for the RL algorithm might include various data from the LOB, including such handcrafted features as order flow imbalance and order book imbalance, or even specific model predictions, such as future price paths, spreads, or volatility. In the extreme case, using deep RL can help one even learn policies directly from raw order book data. Rewards in this scenario are usually based on incurred slippage during training.

A difficulty in real-world RL applications is that training the algorithm necessarily must be done in a simulated environment. The most basic kind of "simulator" simply uses historical market prices. This approach limits the action space to timing market orders, because past prices alone cannot determine whether a limit order would have been executed or not. Another shortcoming of relying solely on historical prices for simulation is that trades do not generate any market impact, because neither do they take away liquidity in the book nor can they cause any other market participant to react to the trade. To alleviate the latter problem, simulation environments are sometimes enhanced with stochastic models of price impact to represent more realistic costs of aggressive trading. Another approach to help with the former problem of handling limit orders is to model the environment as a complete market replay using market-by-order data. This way, new market or even limit orders can be injected into the historical order flow. This approach accurately handles how the order would have been executed at the time.

However, this alone does not solve the problem of counterfactual behavior by other agents. For example, if one of our orders *is* executed, it might imply that someone else's order was *not* executed. They then might have placed another order at a different price; however, this is not represented in the historical data. One approach to handle these counterfactual scenarios is agent-based modeling, which represents individual traders explicitly in a simulation. These simulated agents follow their own trading strategies and can react to changes in the market caused by our execution algorithm, as well as to actions and reactions of other agents. Capturing realistic trading behavior remains a challenging task, and building realistic LOB models is the subject of active research.

Conclusion

How large trades are optimally executed depends on the details of a market's microstructure environment. We have described price–time priority LOB markets, because this is the most common market design at major exchanges trading cash equities, futures, and options. Limit order books thus provide a wealth of high-frequency data that can be used for developing data-driven execution algorithms using ML methods. LOB data can be used to engineer informative features for the prediction of a range of relevant variables: spreads, trade volume, volatility, and even short-term price movements (fast alpha signals). Separate ML models, each predicting a different variable, can then be combined into a sophisticated execution algorithm that plans an execution trajectory in both the volume and placement level (price) dimension.

The trend in ML research more generally points in the direction of using growing computer resources to further automate feature extraction from raw data instead of relying on handcrafted features. The DeepLOB model from Zhang et al. (2019a) and further models building on it are good examples demonstrating that this trend also holds in finance and particularly for trade execution. Given expansive LOB datasets and current computer power, deep learning models are already outperforming simpler models in many tasks, such as generating fast alpha signals. Taking trade automation a step further, RL offers an appealing framework to reduce slippage costs by letting an execution algorithm learn to take optimal actions directly. Actions can be defined on varying levels of abstraction—from choosing parameters in an existing execution algorithm dynamically to placing trades outright. The research outlook in ML for execution shows a path toward more complete end-to-end execution systems using more advanced deep learning and (deep) RL algorithms and architectures, improving predictive performance while maintaining critical issues, such as model robustness.

References

Almgren, Robert, and Neil Chriss. 2000. "Optimal Execution of Portfolio Transactions." *Journal of Risk* 3 (2): 5–39.

Cartea, Álvaro, and Sebastian Jaimungal. 2016. "A Closed-Form Execution Strategy to Target Volume Weighted Average Price." *SIAM Journal on Financial Mathematics* 7 (1): 760–85.

Cont, Rama, Arseniy Kukanov, and Sasha Stoikov. 2014. "The Price Impact of Order Book Events." *Journal of Financial Econometrics* 12 (1): 47–88.

Hasselt, Hado. 2010. "Double Q-Learning." In *Advances in Neural Information Processing Systems 23 (NIPS 2010)*, edited by J. Lafferty, C. Williams, J. Shawe-Taylor, R. Zemel, and A. Culotta. https://papers.nips.cc/paper/2010/hash/091d584fced301b442654dd8c23b3fc9-Abstract.html.

Jumper, J., R. Evans, A. Pritzel, T. Green, M. Figurnov, O. Ronneberger, K. Tunyasuvunakool, R. Bates, A. Žídek, A. Potapenko, et al. 2021. "Highly Accurate Protein Structure Prediction with AlphaFold." *Nature* 596: 583–89.

Kato, Takashi. 2015. "VWAP Execution as an Optimal Strategy." *JSIAM Letters* 7: 33–36.

Kolm, Petter, Jeremy Turiel, and Nicholas Westray. 2021. "Deep Order Flow Imbalance: Extracting Alpha at Multiple Horizons from the Limit Order Book." Working paper (5 August). Available at https://papers.ssrn.com/sol3/papers.cfm?abstract_id=3900141.

Krizhevsky, A., I. Sutskever, and G. E. Hinton. 2012. "ImageNet Classification with Deep Convolutional Neural Networks." *Advances in Neural Information Processing Systems 25 (NIPS 2012)*, edited by F. Pereira, C. J. Burges, L. Bottou, and K. Q. Weinberger. https://papers.nips.cc/paper/2012/hash/c399862d3b9d6b-76c8436e924a68c45b-Abstract.html.

Mnih, V., K. Kavukcuoglu, D. Silver, A. Graves, I. Antonoglou, D. Wierstra, and M. Riedmiller. 2013. "Playing Atari with Deep Reinforcement Learning." NIPS Deep Learning Workshop 2013. Cornell University, arXiv:1312.5602 (19 December). https://arxiv.org/abs/1312.5602.

Ning, Brian, Franco Ho Ting Lin, and Sebastian Jaimungal. 2021. "Double Deep Q-Learning for Optimal Execution." *Applied Mathematical Finance* 28 (4): 361–80.

Sutskever, Ilya, Oriol Vinyals, and Quoc V. Le. 2014. "Sequence to Sequence Learning with Neural Networks." *Advances in Neural Information Processing Systems 27 (NIPS 2014)*, edited by Z. Ghahramani, M. Welling, C. Cortes, N. Lawrence, and K.Q. Weinberger. https://papers.nips.cc/paper/2014/hash/a14ac55a4f27472c5d894ec-1c3c743d2-Abstract.html.

Szegedy, C., W. Liu, Y. Jia, P. Sermanet, S. Reed, D. Anguelov, D. Erhan, V. Vanhoucke, and A. Rabinovich. 2015. "Going Deeper with Convolutions." *Proceedings of the 2015 IEEE Conference on Computer Vision and Pattern Recognition*.

Vaswani, A., N. Shazeer, N. Parmar, J. Uszkoreit, L. Jones, A. N. Gomez, Ł. Kaiser, and I. Polosukhin. 2017. "Attention Is All You Need." *Advances in Neural Information Processing Systems 30 (NIPS 2017)*, edited by I. Guyon, U. Von Luxburg, S. Bengio, H. Wallach, R. Fergus, S. Vishwanathan, and R. Garnett. https://papers.nips.cc/paper/2017/hash/3f5ee243547dee91fbd053c1c4a845aa-Abstract.html.

Zhang, Zihao, Stefan Zohren, and Stephen Roberts. 2019a. "DeepLOB: Deep Convolutional Neural Networks for Limit Order Books." *IEEE Transactions on Signal Processing* 67 (11): 3001–12.

Zhang, Zihao, Stefan Zohren, and Stephen Roberts. 2019b. "Extending Deep Learning Models for Limit Order Books to Quantile Regression." Time Series Workshop of the 36th International Conference on Machine Learning. Cornell University, arXiv:1906.04404 (11 June). https://arxiv.org/abs/1906.04404.

Zhang, Zihao, and Stefan Zohren. 2021. "Multi-Horizon Forecasting for Limit Order Books: Novel Deep Learning Approaches and Hardware Acceleration Using Intelligent Processing Units." Cornell University, arXiv:2105.10430 (27 August). https://arxiv.org/abs/2105.10430.

HANDBOOK OF ARTIFICIAL INTELLIGENCE
AND BIG DATA APPLICATIONS IN
INVESTMENTS

IV. CHATBOT, KNOWLEDGE GRAPHS, AND AI INFRASTRUCTURE

This book can be found at cfainstitute.org/ai-and-big-data

9. INTELLIGENT CUSTOMER SERVICE IN FINANCE

Xu Liang, PhD
Chief Engineer, Ping An OneConnect

Development of AI-Enabled Intelligent Customer Service in the Financial Industry

The ubiquitous penetration of internet and big data applications has led to tremendous changes in consumers' behavior patterns and lifestyles, raising the expectations and requirements for financial services while steering service channels and models toward greater personalization. However, the traditional IT plus human customer service model can barely cope with the expanding user scale and service needs that have become increasingly diversified and fragmented. This situation intensifies the conflict between the limited availability of human customer services and massive volumes of customer inquiries and service needs. Financial institutions continue to add customer service positions, but the customer service function frequently falls into the operational trap of sharp increases in labor costs, fragmentation of user needs, and lower service satisfaction (Liping 2018). There is a pressing need for financial institutions to convert their customer service systems into intelligent digital systems to improve customer service responsiveness, optimize service experience, and at the same time, reduce costs and boost efficiency.

With the development of a new generation of intelligent technologies, intelligent customer service systems powered by artificial intelligence (AI) technologies, such as big data analysis, knowledge engineering, machine learning (ML), and intelligent voice, can build the bridge to interact with those using media, such as text, voice, and images, as well as to assist in human conversations, quality inspection, and business processing and, in turn, to lower the manpower costs for financial institutions and improve their service response efficiency. Compared with traditional customer service systems, AI-driven intelligent customer service offers significant advantages in various dimensions—such as channels, efficiency, and data—driving customer service centers to shift to a digital operation model powered by AI (Yuan 2021). Besides addressing the pain points of traditional customer service, AI-based intelligent customer service also helps financial institutions build closed-loop data value chains that enable the monetization of data and accelerate their transition to become smarter digital enterprises.[1]

On the one hand, the intelligent and digital transformation of customer service will significantly improve companies' operational efficiency and reduce costs to enhance cost efficiency. Intelligent customer service empowers enterprises to better identify the true needs of customers, leading to a more efficient allocation of customer service resources that improves business processing efficiency and reduces manpower costs. In addition, companies can upgrade their products and services according to customer requirements obtained from customer insights to boost a company's profitability.

On the other hand, intelligent customer service will offer better user experience, enhance a company's reputation, increase user satisfaction, and create a differentiated brand image in its role to reinforce positive incentives in both directions. Intelligent customer service can support omni-channel services, satisfy customer inquiries anytime and anywhere, offer customers a personalized service experience, and improve customer satisfaction. Moreover, an increase in user recommendations generated from improvements in digital service capabilities will help build the brand image and strengthen the brand's competitiveness. According to a McKinsey survey conducted in 2019 (Breuer, Fanderl, Hedwig, and Meuer 2020), user recommendations of banks increased significantly with improvements in the banks' digital service capabilities. Companies in the financial industry that have improved their digital service capabilities are more likely to receive a higher level of user recommendations when compared to other industries (see **Exhibit 1**).

The COVID-19 pandemic has further spurred the transformation of financial services to a new online and contactless service mode. This creates an unprecedented development opportunity for intelligent customer service centers, and the outlook for the global intelligent customer service market is rosy. The market size of global intelligent contact centers was USD1.07 billion in 2019 and is expected to grow at a compound annual growth rate (CAGR) of 36.45% from 2023 to 2028).[2]

---

[1]This information came from DBS Bank's Marketplace website: www.dbs.com.sg/personal/marketplace/ (accessed 15 June 2020).

[2]For more information, see the Mordor Intelligence report titled "Intelligent Virtual Assistant (IVA) Market—Growth, Trends, COVID-19 Impact, and Forecasts (2023–2028)": www.mordorintelligence.com/industry-reports/intelligent-virtual-assistant-market?gclid=EAIaIQobChMI9Ki1i-nf_QIVuxCtBh1ZdARcEAAYASAAEgJGovD_BwE.

Exhibit 1. Relationship between Customers' Willingness to Recommend a Service Provider and Digital Service Capabilities in Various Industries

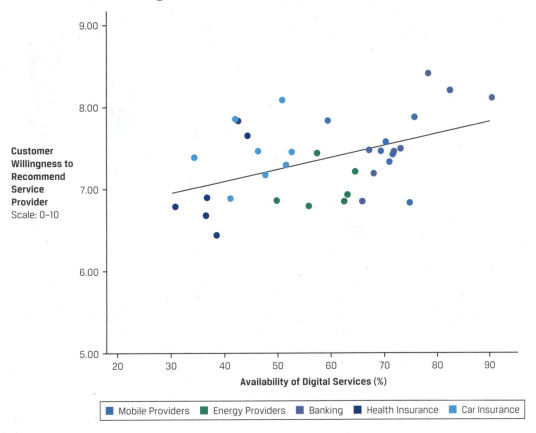

Source: Breuer et al. (2020).

The intelligent customer service industry and market in China are also booming. According to a survey by Frost & Sullivan China, the market size of China's intelligent customer service industry in 2020 was RMB3.01 billion, growing at an explosive rate of 88.1% year over year. As intelligence continues to make headway in the industry, the market size of China's intelligent customer service industry will proliferate in the next five years and is projected to reach RMB10.25 billion in 2025 (as shown in **Exhibit 2**), representing a projected CAGR of 35.8% from 2020 to 2025 (Yuan 2021).

The intelligent customer service industry is clearly experiencing a rapid growth with huge demand. Intelligent customer service systems will bring more value to financial institutions and strengthen their competitiveness. Currently, the industry is at the crossroads of divergence and reshuffling as giant players begin to emerge. Intelligent customer service is reshaping the value of the customer service center, transforming it from a cost driver to a value driver. The onset of the 5G era also brought new opportunities for the industry. Real-time interoperability, interconnection of all things, and innovative intelligent customer service application scenarios and formats combine to make real-time and intuitive interactive dialogue the goal and development direction for future R&D in intelligent customer service.

No matter where the financial institutions are in their digital transformation stage, the overall landscape of the financial industry has been fundamentally altered by the COVID-19 pandemic. In the future, financial institutions will have to compete and win in new ways.

The COVID-19 pandemic will have a far-reaching impact on future financial services in several aspects, including customer behavior, products and services, business operations (front-/middle-/back-office), operating models, external cooperation, and working methods.

- **As digital channels become the "basic offering," financial institutions must innovate to create unique customer service experiences.**

  As the COVID-19 pandemic accelerates the digitalization of front-office functions, customer experience differentiation in such areas as online account opening and login, one-click loan underwriting, and remote claim settlement will form the new fundamental requirements for customer service. Investment in

Exhibit 2. China's Intelligent Customer Service Market Size, 2019–2025E

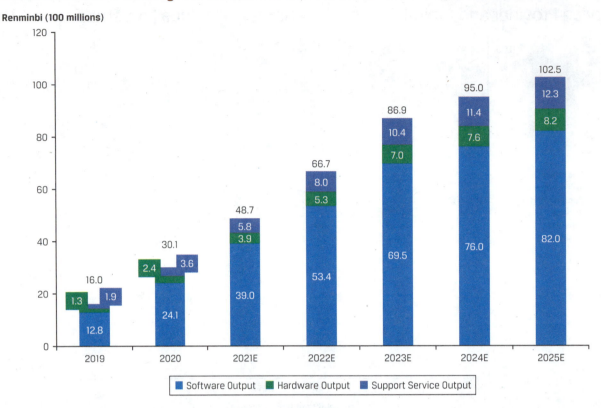

Source: Yuan (2021).

these areas may be the key for financial institutions to attract and retain their customers. To establish a differentiated value proposition, financial institutions can further explore products and services that meet customers' non-financial needs. In the case of banks in Asia, DBS Bank's Marketplace platform allows customers to search for, buy, and sell properties and cars; book their trips; and even compare and switch their payment plans for utilities (water and electricity).[3] These trends are apparent in both retail and corporate financial services, and financial institutions have to adjust their value proposition accordingly.

Likewise, the "last mile" of digital services may be the next arena as financial institutions strive to offer more personal and human digital interactions. To this end, financial institutions need to use more data to better understand their customers in order to deliver products that meet customer needs via the right channel at the right time.

Furthermore, even as financial institutions directly assign more control to customers with digital capabilities and self-service capabilities, there is still a need to maintain the human experience with branch offices and call centers. Once viewed as a traditional solution, call centers are now becoming more important. In addition, financial institutions should speed up the transformation of their branches to achieve a balance between supply and demand. New concepts and automatic teller machines (ATMs) with more autonomy offering the suite of legacy services and functions that was previously exclusive to branches may emerge, business outlets may be further integrated, and full-service branches may be reorganized to become specialized consulting centers.

- **A focus on service costs will be key to adapting to the new industrial economy and surviving difficult times.**

The recent market contractions are likely to continue. With additional pressure on profits, digital transformation may become an important means to improve efficiency and optimize costs. According to recent surveys by the European Central Bank (ECB), the average cost-to-income ratio for digital-only banks is 47%, well below the average for smaller banks (73%). Although digital-only banks are in the early stages of development, the difference in this ratio also highlights the

---

[3]For more information, go to the platform's website: www.dbs.com.sg/personal/marketplace/.

many cost advantages that full digitalization can bring (Deloitte 2020).

For traditional financial institutions, bridging the technology gap aggressively will significantly improve long-term operational efficiency and accelerate industry modernization and digitization (such as public cloud and AI). Technology investments may be more challenging in the macro business and economic environment, but in the long run, the elimination of structural costs through comprehensive digital transformation will be important for traditional financial institutions as they compete with digitally savvy newcomers. To achieve this outcome, traditional financial institutions have to look beyond conventional investment horizon preferences (i.e., more than three to five years).

To sum up, despite an unknown future fraught with uncertainty, the development trend of the financial services industry that will follow the end of the COVID-19 pandemic has already been set in motion. Over the next year, financial institutions will have the unique opportunity in the retail and small business spaces to build trust and loyalty among customers by being responsive to customer needs and providing quality services.

To this end, financial institutions have to align the services they offer with the current situation and accelerate their digital and intelligent development with a sense of urgency. Most importantly, however, they need to better adapt to customer needs. Customer trust and loyalty (and even willingness to share data) will come and go depending on how well the financial institutions build trust and loyalty.

Classification and Typical Application Scenarios of AI-Based Intelligent Customer Service in the Financial Industry

With the rapid development of fintech in China, the penetration rate of intelligent customer service in the financial industry continues to rise. The key role of intelligent customer service is to assist human operators and take over repetitive basic inquiries to free up manpower. However, problems related to specialized topics often require an intervention involving both intelligent and human customer services.

Classification

Based on the specific customer service duties, intelligent customer service can be divided into three types: service oriented, investment advisory, and outbound.

Service-oriented customer service

Service-oriented customer service applies natural language understanding formed from training with a large corpus and develops context models according to specific business scenarios to conduct a natural dialogue and question-and-answer session with users. It fulfills the service requirements for a natural dialogue and addresses the customer's service needs in general scenarios, such as account top-up and transfer, as well as business issues. The service is the most common basic application scenario of intelligent customer service in the banking industry. Currently, financial institutions in China have adopted such technology in PCs and mobile terminals. On the one hand, service-oriented customer service can automatically answer many repetitive basic inquiries to relieve the work pressure of human agents to a great extent. On the other hand, it can respond quickly to customer needs as soon as the user encounters a problem, making it convenient for customers to seek solutions, which promotes service satisfaction.

As AI technology progresses, service-oriented customer service will continue to improve in terms of recognition accuracy and diversity of responses to user inquiries and even provide different answers according to different services and scenarios. For example, the Ping An Pocket Bank app can provide targeted answers to inquiries based on the type of bank card held by the customer. This capability further bolsters service quality and user satisfaction.

Investment advisory customer service

As the Chinese economy has continued to develop, disposable income per capita has gradually increased, and beyond the expenses to fulfill basic daily living needs, the demand for asset appreciation has intensified. Investment advisory customer service has emerged to meet the investment and wealth management needs of financial customers. It can use algorithms and wealth management know-how to analyze users according to different risk preferences, expectations on returns, and investment directions and match users with various products offered by financial institutions. Users get investment recommendations on the type, scale, and timing of investment products, and the system also tracks the customer's investment returns to adjust such investment recommendations accordingly. Today, more and more financial institutions are deploying investment advisory customer services. Companies can use relevant codes developed on mobile terminals to allow investors to conveniently access investment advice and analysis reports on their mobile phones. As AI technology continues to advance, there will be further improvements in the capabilities of investment advisory customer service to offer a better service experience to financial customers.

Outbound customer service

Strong demand for telemarketing in the banking industry coupled with the need to curtail rising manpower and operating costs translate to increasing demand for outbound customer service. The conventional outbound customer service has to deal with not only manpower cost constraints but also extensive training for the agents, which drains a lot of resources. Moreover, data have demonstrated that the success rate of traditional telemarketing is relatively low. With technology advancements, the banking industry has initiated many studies on intelligent outbound customer service. The service can verify the user identity and, at the same time, provide users with simple feedback and guidance to complete the relevant sales and marketing process. Continuous technology optimization enables outbound customer service to gradually strengthen language skills, allowing it to offer the same dialogue capability and service experience as human agents and handle tasks that were originally performed by humans to save the related costs.

Typical Use Cases

Intelligent customer service is mainly applied in two scenarios: presales services and after-sales services. Presales services are mainly deployed in telemarketing scenarios and used to improve call efficiency, data security, and service quality control. After-sales services are mainly for customer consultation and service callbacks, and the key is to meet the accuracy requirements of outbound products.

By sector

Different sectors in the financial industry, such as insurance, banking, internet finance, and securities, have varying requirements for intelligent customer service due to their inherent business characteristics (see **Exhibit 3**).

Insurance

Insurance is a relatively complex business; every user has unique requirements from insurance purchase to claims. Therefore, the insurance industry has relatively high requirements on the intelligence level of the intelligent customer service, which has a direct impact on customer satisfaction, retention, and conversion.

Banking

The main banking applications are in handling highly repetitive queries, providing response services during peak periods, and providing intelligent collection services. Intelligent customer service mainly assists human customer service agents and frees up manpower during peak periods.

Fintech

Similar to banks, customer service in the fintech industry has to deal with a large volume of repetitive inquires, so intelligent customer service is mainly deployed to handle highly repetitive queries, with the intelligence focused on such areas as intelligent debt collection and smart marketing.

Securities

As with the banking industry, customer service in the securities industry also has to deal with a large volume of repetitive basic inquiries. Here, intelligent customer service is mainly used to address inquiries on basic problems in the securities sector, with the intelligence applied in smart stock selection and analysis, as well as smart push services.

Exhibit 3. Application and Business Scenarios of Intelligent Customer Service in Various Financial Sectors

Insurance
Enquiries on insurance-related issues such as insurance purchase are relatively complex, and the level of intelligent service will affect customer retention and conversion.

Banking
The main applications are in handling highly repetitive queries, providing response services during peak periods, and supplying intelligent collection services.

Internet Finance
Similar to banking, the main application is in handling highly repetitive inquiries. Intelligence is focused on intelligent collection and smart marketing.

Securities
It is mainly used to address inquiries on basic problems in the securities sector, with the intelligence applied in smart stock selection and analysis, as well as smart push services.

Within sectors

Within sectors (in banking, for example), the application scenarios of AI can be divided into the following six categories.

Robots in intelligent voice navigation and service scenarios

Application concept: To the extent that customers are receptive to robots, voice robots are used in navigation and service scenarios to improve service quality, reduce costs, and improve efficiency.

Today, applications using intelligent voice navigation robots have matured and are widely adopted by large banks. However, it is still possible to further expand the application of this technology. In terms of intelligent voice applications, due consideration should be taken to incorporate customer complaints, customer acceptance, and scene adaptability. Aggregate analysis based on the two dimensions of customer attributes and scene responsibility should be carried out to identify the most suitable business scenarios for robot applications and the type of customers who are most receptive to robots. Robots can be gradually introduced to eventually encompass all scenarios to reduce costs and improve efficiency. At the same time, customers' acceptance of robots has to be examined for service quality.

Smart identity verification with voiceprint

Application concept: Reduce costs and mitigate risks by using voiceprint to identify customers to reduce verification time, shorten the overall call duration, and retrieve historical recordings to identify counterfeit and fraudulent voiceprints.

Currently, the application scenarios and technical practice are still being developed for this technology. The recommended approach is to supplement the identity verification process with voiceprint technology when the service is being performed. With the permission of the customer, a customer voiceprint record is established that will be used together with other identification techniques to seamlessly verify the customer's identity for any incoming service request or inquiry from the customer. This will promptly identify incoming calls from parties impersonating the customer while reducing the time taken to verify the customer's identity to improve the customer experience.

Intelligent quality inspection

Application concept: Improve cost efficiency by substituting labor with quality inspection robots to perform objective and comprehensive inspections, reduce the need for manual and repeated playing of recordings, and pinpoint problems quickly.

Currently, this application technology and scenario have already matured, but there is still room for enhanced technology empowerment. An offline quality inspection system is suitable for service optimization. Once a customer problem is found, the offline quality inspection model can quickly locate similar problems in the database and determine the appropriate improvements. Real-time quality inspection is suitable for correcting customer service habits. It monitors the dialogue process between the customer service agents and customers, identifies the problems, and provides feedback promptly to correct mistakes by the customer service agents.

Intelligent human–machine collaboration

Application concept: Reduce costs and improve efficiency by analyzing the interaction linkages of the scenarios in the process flow and select business scenarios that can be substituted by robots.

The specifications for such applications are currently being developed. To engage customers using a mix of robot outbound call and human collaboration, start from the business operation process, subdivide the key interaction links of all scenarios in the end-to-end process, as well as the characteristics of customers who called, and match with the robot capabilities one by one to select the business scenarios and customer types that the robots can serve to improve customer satisfaction and business conversion rates.

Online service and sales

Application concept: Based on the text robot or chatbot, online service and sales use big data analysis and product configuration to recommend interactions for the center. It provides precise recommendations on touch points to complete service and offers sales and operations with better performance and precision—and thus manages to improve user experience and contributes to business indicators.

Customer centers and remote banks have higher requirements for text robots. The systems should be designed for flexibility to offer more diversity in service formats and facilitate operations and maintenance for greater convenience and speed. The goal is to achieve rapid coverage of service channels (such as WeChat, Weibo, and TikTok) and build capabilities to integrate services with marketing efforts.

Smart knowledge management

Application concept: Establish a knowledge management platform that supports all channels (agents, robots, customers), forming a centralized maintenance system to reduce repeated purchases and investments as well as to cut costs and improve efficiency.

Exhibit 4. Intelligent Customer Service Architecture for the Financial Domain

Customer service system composition	Functional module	Financial applications
Building a knowledge map	Multiple rounds of Q&A	Smart credit risk control
Knowledge map maintenance	Smart recommendation	Smart wealth management recommendation
Smart question answering system	H5 page display	Smart transaction processing
Back-office monitoring management	Knowledge map visualization	Smart scenario display
(Interaction module)	Self-service queries	Smart knowledge inquiry
	Smart replies	Smart pre-/mid-/after-sales
	……	……

The application should standardize the method used to organize the knowledge based on the service characteristics and scope, guiding each department to break down the knowledge systematically to implement the fragmentation, structuring, and labeling of scenario-based knowledge content.

Building a Financial Intelligent Customer Service Process

The development of financial intelligent customer service often requires the active participation of business analysts and implementation personnel in the early stage, online optimization of the customer service system, in-depth access to the businesses, and the organization of the business processes and user inquiry scenarios for a tight integration of the business and intelligent customer service functions with customizable configuration for the processes. The development of a financial intelligent customer service system can be divided into two parts: system construction and operation optimization.

System Construction

Before a financial institution builds an intelligent customer service system, first it needs to define the architecture of such a system by organizing the structure of the system and clarifying the composition, functional modules, and business applications that must be supported for the system. After which, it can carry out the work to implement the customer service system by technological means.

The intelligent customer service architecture for the financial domain is shown in **Exhibit 4**.

Currently, the intelligent customer service architecture for the Financial Domain consists of at least five components: interactions, graph construction, knowledge graph maintenance, intelligent Q&A, and back-office management. More functional modules can be derived from the interactions module, such as multiple rounds of Q&A, smart recommendation, H5 page display, knowledge graph visualization, self-service queries, and intelligent replies. Corresponding intelligent financial applications can be derived from a combination of various functions and embedded interactive formats, and these include applications for credit risk control, financial management advice, business processing, scenario display, knowledge search, presales, sales, and postsales.

The deployment modes for intelligent customer service include public cloud, hybrid cloud, and private deployment. The main differences between the three modes are reflected in such areas as data privacy, construction cost, and deployment cycles. Different modes meet the needs of different customers.

Of the three modes, deployment using the public cloud has the lowest construction cost and shortest deployment cycle, which is suitable for SMEs (small and midsize enterprises) that want to quickly build their intelligent customer service capabilities. On-premise deployment requires enterprises to establish their own technical teams; although the construction cost is high, such a deployment greatly enhances data privacy and security, which are suitable for large enterprises. A hybrid cloud deployment combines the characteristics of the previous two deployment methods. Although it uses the public cloud platform, the data are stored locally, and such a deployment may become the mainstream deployment mode for intelligent customer service in the future. Currently, on-premises deployment is still the market mainstream, but cloud deployment is increasingly favored by the market owing to its low cost, fast deployment, and agile iteration.

An excellent intelligent customer service system should have expertise in knowledge graph as its basis, supplemented by advanced speech semantic recognition and understanding technologies to deliver an outstanding interactive experience. At the same time, it can fulfill as many business functions as possible and enable access to the capabilities of many platforms and many channels so as to quickly deploy customer service capabilities in different business environments and support a variety of financial scenarios.

Operational Optimization

An intelligent customer service system is not built overnight. Many financial institutions are not able to achieve the business results that their intelligent customer service systems were projected to deliver after the systems were built or purchased. A major reason is that financial institutions' operational processes are generally not designed with intelligent customer service in mind and are not able to optimize and improve their services. A good intelligent customer service system is often the result of cooperation between products and business personnel.

The intelligent customer service product has to be supported by cumulative business expertise and experience in AI technology. Business operators need to listen to service voice recordings to understand recent user demands and be familiar with the business. They also need to be familiar with various channels, have an acute business sense, maintain communication with business departments, and understand the current business, the drivers behind the business, and the development trend of the business. They also need to acquire and constantly update their business knowledge and adjust the corpus in time to ensure that the customer service products can meet evolving business needs. At the same time, operators need to leverage business data to uncover existing problems in products or new demands in the industry and constantly iterate the intelligence level of the intelligent customer service system to improve the service capability to address inquiries.

A good vendor for intelligent customer service products, besides having advanced technologies, should also have extensive industry experience and a standard training and certification system to help financial institutions build an intelligent customer service system that consists of not just the hardware but also the soft power that can be derived from operating the intelligent customer service product, helping financial institutions gain a true understanding of AI so that they can leverage AI in intelligent customer service to achieve the twin goals of cost reduction and higher efficiency.

Financial AI Customer Service Case Studies

Financial institutions' diverse needs in serving their customers are increasingly met by a slew of AI-integrated applications merging voice products with AI technology.

Inbound Call Middle Office

Companies face many challenges in building their own AI products, such as repetitive development efforts, the pace of adoption not keeping up with business needs, and poor robot performance. Inbound call middle-office solutions can help enterprises build intelligent customer service systems faster and better by addressing these issues.

The middle-office solutions have proven effective in training new customer service agents and adapting existing AI solutions for new business. On the back end, these middle-office solutions can connect with and manage AI engines, such as natural language understanding (NLU) and voice recognition robots, from many vendors. Similarly, on the front end, they can accommodate inbound inquiries from multiple channels, such as phones or PCs. They also offer extensive business solution modules and allow clients to quickly build on their existing capabilities and adapt to changing business needs.

In one case, OneConnect's Gamma Mid-Office Voice Access helped a large Chinese bank simultaneously launch an intelligent assistant and an intelligent tutor within one month. The solution adopted the same underlying engine to offer two products with a one-time development effort. By resetting a variety of robot rules, the solution enabled the robots to fulfill new business scenario requirements, distinguish between scenarios, and accommodate the needs for both scenarios.

Intelligent Outbound Call

Traditional customer service has drawbacks, such as substantial manpower investment, long training duration, poor work efficiency, performance improvement challenges, and complex data analysis. There are three major customer service pain points in the industry. The first is business reminders. Financial institutions have a need for a lot of information synchronization and business reminders, such as credit card payment reminders and reminders about dues for financial products. Sending manual reminders will occupy 40% of the daily working hours of an operator and usually involves repetitive tasks that lead to low work enthusiasm and worsening customer experience. The second pain point is financial collection. Take the credit industry as an example. Every year, about 70% of overdue accounts could be attributed to account holders who forgot their repayments, and most of these amounts could be recovered after manual reminders and notifications are sent. However, manual collection is time consuming, with low work efficiency and poor time utilization. The third is active marketing, where sales personnel often have to filter through a massive number of leads for financial products, especially insurance products, which is a time-consuming and labor-intensive task that tends to undermine sales confidence. The inconsistent grading of customer intentions and the loss of high-quality customer leads are two problems that result in the low efficiency and high cost of active marketing.

The pain points in the previous scenarios call for an intelligent outbound call solution. With the call center system as the base, one such solution layers on a number of AI technologies, such as natural language processing (NLP), speech recognition, and speech synthesis, replacing manual calls with intelligent outbound robots to screen intended customers, target customers, and accurately classify different customers. By effectively reducing headcount, the product helps companies improve the customer experience and increase their marketing efficiency as it steers communications with customers toward greater professionalism, automation, and efficiency. In actual operations, the results are promising.

The specific process of an outbound robot is as follows:

1. First, the customers may call customer service, which is available 24/7. The efficiency is high, service availability is long, and incoming customer inquiries can be attended to at anytime and anywhere.

2. The customer service function will then respond intelligently, and supported by automated speech recognition (ASR), NLP, and text-to-speech (TTS) technologies, the robot can understand and respond to inquiries. In short, the intelligent customer service can identify the user's question, match the corresponding answer from the database, and provide the answer automatically.

3. The intelligent customer service then automatically classifies users according to the contents of the call, helping companies accurately target customers and acquire a better understanding of the customer's inquiry and pain points.

4. In addition, during this process, customer service will record the dialogue and store the complete recording and dialogue text, making it convenient to view and track the conversation. Furthermore, the complete dialogue recording is collected and trained by AI to further iterate and upgrade the AI products.

5. Customer service will conduct additional data analysis and clearly present several data indicators to help analyze the call performance and customers' behavior.

6. Lastly, customer service will automatically optimize itself, apply deep learning, and continuously add to the corpus to improve its Q&A performance.

In marketing, the system leverages big data to generate a 360-degree customer profile, locate target customer groups, and predict the customer's propensity with respect to loans, wealth management, and insurance products. When appropriate, the system can initiate conversations.

In risk management, the system collects user data for anti-fraud surveillance and to assess borrowers' willingness and ability to repay before the due date. Voice data are also collected to predict the repayment risk.

In investment advisory, the system automatically answers questions about loans and insurance, intelligently analyzes customer needs, assists in drafting optimal investment plans, and addresses after-sales questions.

For notifications, it provides timely payment reminders, personalized communication playbooks, multidimensional configuration logic trees, and intelligent external collection.

In internal and external customer service scenarios, the applications include external marketing to customers, collection, credit checks, internal employee inquiry hotlines, and outbound calls for surveys.

Such systems have proven to be highly valuable in production environments. As an example, a system developed by Ping An OneConnect significantly improved the response rate when used in promoting a new loan product that is part of Ping An's inclusive financial service offerings. Prior to the robot deployment, the outbound call capacity of the customer service center was about 150 calls per person per day, which did not meet customer demand during peak marketing periods. In terms of performance, the inquiry rate was only about 1% for customers in the first follow-up and about 5% by the fifth follow-up. The operating cost of the marketing outbound call center remained high, at RMB150 per customer after apportionment. After the robot was deployed, the call center achieved an average daily outbound call capacity of 1 million, with a 5% marketing response rate, while the outbound marketing cost for the same batch of customers was reduced to under RMB1 per customer. When used for loan collection, the robot can make about 900–1,000 calls a day to owners of overdue accounts, and it increased the repayment rate by 30% within a week.

Text Robots

In the past, AI customer service suffered from business pain points, such as low Q&A accuracy, support for only a single round of Q&A, inability to conduct business processing, and high knowledge base maintenance costs. The latest solutions use a more advanced NLP algorithm to gain deep semantic understanding and perform semantic analysis of the context, enabling robots to conduct multiple rounds of dialogue with users. These solutions may also adopt unsupervised ML and supervised ML to minimize maintenance costs and keep the knowledge base up to date.

Business process

- **Cloud/on-premises deployment:** The cloud version allows for quick access at a reasonable cost, allowing users to rapidly deploy intelligent Q&A, whereas the on-premises deployment offers better security and business privacy for the business environment.
- **Knowledge configuration/model training:** Data modules such as FAQ, dynamic menu, simple tasks, hot topics, and welcome messages are configured in the knowledge base, offering a set of rich content with diverse functions, while Q&A accuracy is validated by model training and running tests.
- **System use:** The system is used in intelligent robot Q&A, provision of various data reports for post-loan management, and optimization of the model for education quality inspection and marking.

Business functions

- **Powerful Q&A capabilities:** The text robot system can answer questions accurately, achieve accurate contextual understanding of speech, and easily handle complex interactive questions; in addition, one Q&A portal can support seamless switching between multiple knowledge bases. Human–machine cooperation can also be implemented to support two-way switching between robots and human agents.
- **Convenient back-office management:** The system will systematically carry out smart knowledge management, regularly perform quick model training and robot education for AI robot customer service, and support personalized configuration to satisfy the needs of different customers.
- **Efficient operation outcome:** Compared with human agents, advanced customer service solutions do not require training and can be launched quickly at an affordable cost. Moreover, the robot solutions can provide services around the clock and handle many customers at the same time. In terms of compliance, the text robot system is 100% controllable, stable, and standardized, requires no emotional care, and will not get tired of answering questions. At the same time, it can record full logs and various report data for business analysis.

Business characteristics

- **Full coverage of customer service marketing scenarios:** WeChat, official account, Weibo, H5, web, and other omni-channel coverage; Q&A scenarios involving presales, current selling processes, and after sales. The PaaS platform design facilitates business system connection, offering 24/7 high-quality service.
- **Leverage on Ping An Group's years of industry experience:** The system has a comprehensive knowledge base that includes knowledge about finance, banks, and smart cities, which empowers it to provide data support for algorithms and to quantify operational indicators.
- **Advanced technology:** 100% owned intellectual property rights with an average accuracy of 85% that offers outstanding performance and high availability and is scalable and secure.

Application scenario

The Xiaoyi text robot can answer such questions as service inquiries on how to proceed to complete the process, outlet information, product function introduction, and fees. For business processing, it supports credit card application, FX transaction, loan prepayment, and card replacement, among others. As for sales recommendation, it can offer product and fund recommendations for wealth management, as well as assist in loan processing, preliminary screening for loans, and other services.

The Xiaoyi text robot has been deployed in many banks, where it mainly handles three types of service: business inquiry, business process, and sales recommendations. To date, it has delivered excellent results. For example, the Ping An Bank app has an average monthly traffic of 13.2 million (customer inquiries), with a question recognition rate of up to 99.47%. The Lufax app has an average monthly traffic of 500,000, with a question recognition rate of up to 97.95%.

Risks and Challenges of Financial AI Intelligent Customer Service Application

In this section, I will discuss the risks and challenges involved in applying intelligent customer service in the financial industry.

Risks

AI intelligent customer service in the financial industry will facilitate the offering of products and services and save manpower costs. But owing to the constraints imposed by the current development state of related technologies, there are many potential risks in the intelligent customer service business.

Business risk from misinterpretation of intent

Intelligent customer service needs to be able to identify and answer the questions raised by customers. However, because the technology for NLU is still in its infancy, the AI solution may not fully understand the questions asked by customers the way the human agents do. Once the intention is misinterpreted, the system may not find a match in the knowledge base or may match a wrong answer. There is the risk of not being able to answer or providing the wrong answer and operating instructions, which may lead to customer dissatisfaction or even losses suffered by the customers, creating reputation risk for banks. As such, the usual solution is to deal only with questions recorded in the intelligent customer service database and hand over questions that cannot be identified or that are beyond the scope of the database to human agents. This solution reduces manpower wastage and improves the user experience.

Risk of declining customer satisfaction

Compared with AI intelligent customer service, human customer service can more accurately understand customer intentions, grasp customer emotions, and communicate with customers more patiently and humanely. Based on the current statistics on human customer service, the service satisfaction level for the majority of human customer service is above 90%. Constrained by inadequacies in current intelligence technology, in practice, the intelligent customer service solution is unable to provide services like an actual person can and cannot grasp the feelings of customers in time. When customers are forced to use intelligent customer service to relieve manpower pressure, it is likely to worsen the customer experience, increase the risk of declining customer satisfaction, and even lower customer stickiness, leading to losses for financial institutions. As such, financial institutions are taking a deep dive into applications involving deep learning networks so that intelligent customer service solutions can learn to handle customers' emotions to give users a more humanized experience. At the same time, financial institutions continue to hand over customers with emotional issues that cannot be handled by AI to human agents to ensure a more satisfactory user experience and to reduce manpower cost.

Business risks associated with outbound customer service

Although outbound customer service will improve operational efficiency and reduce costs, because the technology is immature, outbound customer service currently supports only simple interactions with customers in most cases, which may lead to misunderstandings by customers.

Owing to the unique nature of banking products, improper understanding may cause the client to lose assets and lead to unnecessary disputes between the client and the bank. As such, the intelligent outbound customer service also faces database limitations. If the user's question is not found in the AI database or cannot be identified by AI, the question will be automatically transferred to a human agent.

Risks from outsourcing of intelligent customer service products

AI technology is considered a cutting-edge technology that is developing rapidly, and the banking industry has not fully mastered its core content. Therefore, most customer service robot projects have to be outsourced to third-party institutions, which increases the dependency on third parties and uncontrollability for the banking industry. The bank relies on the source code of the outsourcing vendor for the transformation or project improvement, which weakens the bank's controllability. Meanwhile, because a large volume of data has to be provided to the third-party institutions for model training and user privacy is often embedded in such data, any disclosure may cause substantial risks.

Challenges

AI intelligent customer service is a comprehensive product solution that integrates industry knowledge, databases, speech recognition, NLP, and other technologies. Since there is still much room for improvement in intelligent technologies, such as NLP, and the sensitivity of financial industry data makes the industry knowledge graph less complete, there are challenges in deploying AI intelligent customer service in the financial industry.

AI technology is inadequate

A breakthrough is needed for better capability in interpreting intentions. AI customer service has low answer accuracy and poor customer satisfaction levels, supports only a single round of Q&A, and is not sufficiently responsive to questions raised in a continuous dialogue. It has simple functions, supports only dialogue inquiry, and is unable to handle business processes. In short, intelligent customer service answers lack a "human touch." As such, financial institutions should focus on the application of cutting-edge AI technology and ensure the rapid iterations of AI technology to satisfy the more demanding service requirements of users.

Stringent financial data security requirements and incomplete knowledge graph

The high costs of deployment and knowledge base maintenance lead to a relatively low cost performance presently. However, with further iterations and development of AI algorithms and the wider adoption of AI applications, the cost of intelligent customer service will gradually decrease, which will bring about better results.

Improving industry standards

With the gradual adoption of intelligent customer service, some problems have begun to surface. Intelligent customer service's ability to operate around the clock has created various social problems, such as harassment and privacy infringement, which are not conducive to the healthy development of the industry. As such, AI customer service leaders should jointly develop a single standard to ensure that all AI customer service products can fulfill the minimum industry requirements.

Development, Innovation, and Prospects of the Financial AI Intelligent Customer Service Industry

In this section, I elaborate on various aspects of the future of intelligent customer service in the financial industry and discuss its development, innovation, and prospects.

Development and Innovation

Financial AI intelligent customer service systems will continue to innovate in three aspects: technology, interaction, and business.

Technological innovation

The financial knowledge graph is in the building stage, and the potential linkages between knowledge units can be uncovered using such algorithms as knowledge reasoning, which can then be used to form a basis for potential customers' acquisition, new financial services development, and financial services promotion. AI technology is expected to continue to iterate rapidly, creating smarter and more capable knowledge applications and response mechanisms.

Interactive innovation

With the rapid development of rich media, the modes of information dissemination have become more diversified. Most of the knowledge in the financial industry is described in words or numbers; the format is simple, but with poor interpretability. By leveraging the intelligent customer service system in the rich media era, customer service products can enable various ways in which answers are presented, such as animations and short videos, to demonstrate the correct answers to users more clearly

and intuitively. It can build on the advantages of knowledge graph to enhance the fluency and compatibility of dialogue, improve the system's ability to identify customers' feelings and real intentions, and quickly gear up the capability to support multiple rounds of Q&A. Innovations in interaction will further elevate users' perception of the company and increase user stickiness.

Business innovation

With intelligent customer service, financial institutions can change the current practice of independently selling a single product. In the future, with further breakthroughs in such technologies as AI and big data, intelligent customer service will be able to grasp customer intentions more accurately and provide customers with more personalized business assistance and product portfolios, shifting the business model from a product-oriented approach to a user-oriented approach. In addition, AI customer service will be deployed in various businesses of the financial industry. It will adapt to the changing business characteristics and be able to deal with the pain points in the user's current business for efficient revenue generation.

Development Trends

There are three trends in the application of AI technology in banking customer service centers and remote banking: popularization, personalization, and diversification.

Popularization

As AI applications mature, their popularity will gradually spread to the whole industry and all fields. With escalating manpower costs, the staffing cost of call centers and remote banks will also increase over the years. Cost reduction and efficiency improvements have always been major goals of each call center and remote bank. By making use of applications based on AI, such as text robots, intelligent voice navigation, and intelligent quality inspection, customer service centers and remote banks can gain a major arsenal that they can adopt to reduce costs and boost efficiency.

Personalization

As users continue to fine-tune their needs, the increasingly demanding user requirements in terms of experience are driving the transformation of customer service centers and remote banking solutions toward greater personalization. With intelligent voiceprint recognition, online service/sales, human–machine collaboration, and other applications, we can gradually upgrade from the traditional human agent model to an intelligent customer service model for comprehensive, efficient, and intelligent operations and services, which will be key to user satisfaction.

Diversification

Relying on strong technical support and market demand, the interaction between traditional customer service centers and customers will transform from straight-line transactions to multichannel and multidimensional dialogue and exchanges. Various ways of communicating appear, including videos, gestures, and even virtual reality, in addition to traditional text and voice. Such communication methods are more natural and may be a real breakthrough beyond the existing service model, such as phone calls to provide customers with faster three-dimensional services using interactions from all media, bringing about a more diversified experience and creating more distinctively emotive services.

Future Prospects

In the era of AI and big data, an increasing number of financial institutions have begun to develop financial technology. As operating costs continue to increase, it becomes even more pressing to reduce manpower costs. Yet at the same time, the demand for personalized services for customers is gradually expanding. All these issues prompt financial institutions to have additional requirements for intelligent customer service. Looking ahead, AI intelligent customer service will become even more common in the financial industry. Upgrading of talents and technologies, continuous enrichment of industry applications, and continuous improvement of industry specifications will promote the healthy development of the intelligent customer service industry.

Strengthen talent pool and technology R&D

The intelligent customer service system relies on emerging and cutting-edge AI technologies, such as speech recognition and NLP. To better optimize and develop the technologies, businesses need to continuously strengthen the talent pool, adopt best practices at home and abroad, and groom talents with financial backgrounds and information technology expertise. This is the only way to achieve a higher level of intelligence, improve the accuracy of answers to customer inquiries, improve user experience, and increase satisfaction. Going forward, with support from neural networks and big data, such technologies as knowledge computing, multimodal fusion, and privacy computing are expected to form the basis for intelligent analysis and decision making at financial institutions and to make autonomous learning of financial market conditions a reality. Such systems will also be capable in trend projections and can even provide customers with intelligent suggestions for their decision making. An efficient and accurate trading system will provide the technological power to drive innovation and development in the financial industry.

Expand the applications of the intelligent customer service system

There is a need to focus on current technology R&D and promote comprehensive and all-around coverage of application scenarios by optimizing the basic functions for a large-scale intelligent customer service platform geared mainly to mobile terminals. In addition, the interactive mode can gradually evolve from traditional voice and text to video, augmented reality and holographic projection, and other formats by combining emerging media with traditional media.

Meanwhile, AI customer service should be deeply entrenched at several levels. In marketing, AI customer service is included to generate intelligent marketing scenario applications and personalized services for individual customers that can greatly improve the sales success rate for wealth management products and promote the development of inclusive financial services. In customer service, AI customer service will tap into more multiscenario applications, such as identity recognition, intelligent customer service, and intelligent claims settlement, to serve more customers during peak hours and fulfill demand in an effective and accurate manner that can improve customer satisfaction significantly.

Develop and refine relevant industry specifications

For this emerging industry system, regulatory authorities need to keep up with trends, draft corresponding regulatory plans and regulatory processes, avoid and prevent series of risks that emerging intelligent customer service systems may bring, promote the intelligent customer service systems, and optimize the development of smart finance. Building an intelligent customer service ecosystem with multiple parties will make it an important focal point in banking and financial services.

Conclusion

In view of the COVID-19 pandemic and the digital transformation wave, financial institutions need to reshape their business models and adapt their working methods to meet ever-changing customer and market demands quickly and nimbly. Looking ahead, financial institutions must take advantage of the cultural and behavioral changes brought about by the pandemic to accelerate their digital transformation process, even as they remain cautious to avoid overreliance on existing models once the pandemic is over. This move is critical for financial institutions to weather the storm and thrive in the emerging new normal.

Riding on the COVID-19 pandemic as a catalyst for digital transformation, financial institutions can also take this opportunity to reflect on their role in emerging ecosystems and how they can create value.

The intelligent customer service system enables the online transfer of human customer service workload by integrating current AI technology, NLU, and other emerging technologies. At the same time, with point-to-point communication with customers, it can improve customer experience and efficiency significantly. However, it is also necessary to fully understand the imperfections and dual characteristics of technology and to not blindly follow the trends in online services and intelligence. In certain banking scenarios, for example, intelligent customer service is still not able to replace human agents. It is important to recognize the possible risks of the intelligent customer service system to avoid the risks and plan rationally. However, there is an opportunity to leverage the power of technology to create a new model for the development of the banking industry that is more efficient, accurate, and convenient.

Within the supervision framework of the authorities, in-depth application of intelligent customer service can be used to develop innovative financial products, change business methods, and optimize business processes to ensure the safety of customers' assets, optimize financial investment experience, and reduce investment risks in this rapid transition to a modern digital financial system that is highly adaptable, competitive, and inclusive.

References

Breuer, Ralph, Harald Fanderl, Markus Hedwig, and Marcel Meuer. 2020. "Service Industries Can Fuel Growth by Making Digital Customer Experiences a Priority." McKinsey Digital (30 April). www.mckinsey.com/capabilities/mckinsey-digital/our-insights/service-industries-can-fuel-growth-by-making-digital-customer-experiences-a-priority.

Deloitte. 2020. "Realizing the Digital Promise: COVID-19 Catalyzes and Accelerates Transformation in Financial Services." www.deloitte.com/content/dam/assets-shared/legacy/docs/gx-fsi-realizing-the-digital-promise-covid-19-catalyzes-and-accelerates-transformation.pdf.

Liping, Xu. 2018. "AI-Driven Intelligent Customer Service." Shanghai Informatization.

Yuan, Xucong. 2021. "2021 China Intelligent Customer Service Industry Insight." LeadLeo Research Institute.

10. ACCELERATED AI AND USE CASES IN INVESTMENT MANAGEMENT

Jochen Papenbrock, Doctorate
Head of Financial Technology EMEA, NVIDIA

Introduction

A growing number of investment professionals are building up capabilities and resources to exploit artificial intelligence (AI) and big data in their investment processes systematically, using the most advanced technologies and infrastructures, like "factories" for AI and simulation. This trend results from the realization by many that AI and big data will give them access to diversified sources of alpha, more effective risk management, better client access, and customization opportunities. Embracing such technologies has become a clear differentiator.

In this chapter, I will take you behind the scenes, provide insight into the art of the possible, and discuss how to best make use of the most recent technologies, such as accelerated computing platforms in an implementation roadmap. I will also provide useful tools and describe their implementation in several real-world use cases, such as diversified portfolio construction and environmental, social, and governance (ESG) investing, using such techniques as natural language processing (NLP), Explainable AI (XAI), and Geospatial AI.

Learning how to implement AI technologies is highly relevant to investment companies that are aiming for an elevated level of ESG integration. These companies need to organize ESG scoring information, and they can have a motivation to generate their own ("shadow") ESG scores and to constantly monitor and audit ESG disclosure information—for example, to identify greenwashing and to close monitoring gaps. The scores are produced for ESG-integrating investment portfolios, such as by using cross-sectional systematic trading strategies to rank assets before portfolio construction. There is a constant tracking of trading portfolios, including AI-based detection of irregular transactions and behavior.

We are moving toward an evidence-based, data-driven, AI-powered ESG approach. If implemented correctly with the right data, data science approach, and IT/compute infrastructure, the improved analysis would be:

- neutral (in terms of no human bias), consistent, and less biased (in terms of unwanted bias);
- global, frequent, and available in a timely way;
- enabled in a bottom-up way; and
- comprehensive due to the coverage of undisclosed information.

Massive amounts of primary information such as text-based data (some of which are web-scraped) or alternative data from satellite imagery need to be collected, cleaned, streamed, and analyzed, activities that can be supported by machines very efficiently. On top of that are additional compute layers that help to trace back the processing steps and reasoning of the machines, which is important for human–machine interaction, such as providing validation, developing data narratives, and amplifying the subject matter experts. It would hardly be possible to reach those levels of reproducible and transparent information processing by manual analysis of those amounts of data.

Another example for innovative technologies that support the investment and risk management process is AI-fueled analytical capabilities, such as generating potential market scenarios that have never been observed before but can be viewed as realistic. In a second step, a machine learning (ML) program identifies links between properties of those market scenarios and the performance of a set of competing investment strategies. In the last step, a computationally intensive algorithm reveals the structures that the AI/ML system has learned in the training process. This step is particularly important because investment managers now have the option to understand the decision-making process of the AI/ML system using XAI to validate it and build a narrative for the choice of a certain investment strategy. This can be applied in many investment processes that seek to find the best way to diversify a given number of assets and aggregate them into a robust portfolio. In practice, this approach is applicable in a variety of investment companies, ranging from hedge funds to pension funds. The amount of computation involved is probably not feasible for a human being to execute manually in a lifetime.

Underrated Aspects of AI-Driven Investment Strategies

Successful investment firms of the future will be those that strategically plan to incorporate AI and big data techniques into their investment processes (Cao 2019). Besides the importance of advancements in mathematical modeling, several additional aspects of the AI strategy need to be addressed:

1. An appropriate infrastructure for AI training and inferencing, as well as for simulation for risk management, algorithmic trading, and back testing
2. A scalable enterprise-level workflow and process for developing and deploying AI models
3. Robust AI models that can be validated and explained, which removes barriers to AI adoption and builds confidence in these innovative technologies

All this is part of the skill set that investment companies can develop to make a difference and to use as a unique selling proposition.

A key technology to implement these three aspects is accelerated computing, which can be used for simulation, data manipulation, AI model building, and deployment/inferencing. Accelerated computing is widely available today, and it can increase developer team productivity, ROI (return on investment), model quality, and enterprise-level scalability while decreasing TOC (total cost of ownership), time to insight, energy consumption, and infrastructure complexity. It is all about building and using more effective models at higher speed and lower cost while keeping the models robust and explainable.

Data science and AI teams will be able to amplify their productivity using "AI and simulation factories." Using these is also a crucial factor in attracting talent that can do the "work of a lifetime" on such computing and accelerated data infrastructures.

The need for accelerated computing becomes noticeably clear when several data sources need to be acquired and combined. Several data sources are jointly aggregated, correlated, analyzed, and visualized in increasingly rapid ways. Technologies for accelerated data logistics and curation enable the gathering of datasets from dozens of sources—such as remote sensors, IoT (internet of things), social media, and satellite data. Iteration speed is increased by reducing analytical latency by seconds or even milliseconds. New forecasting techniques based on ML that use alternative, complex, unstructured datasets (such as satellite images) and new generative methods to create synthetic data are changing the way we produce and backtest strategies.

Investors around the world want to know more about the performance of individual companies before others do. They address leading indicators related to the impact of future financial results, sustainability, and environmental risk factors. Analysts need to effectively query and visually examine these vast datasets. Analytics software and AI/ML running on traditional CPU-based servers can be less capable of processing huge amounts of data required for advanced, multilayered, and multimodal analysis in a timely manner and might use more energy than graphics processing units (GPUs) do.

The Accelerated Computing Revolution and How It Enhances Investment Management

GPUs can be found in many compute clusters, ranging from supercomputing to public clouds and even enterprise data centers. They can accelerate the processing of huge amounts of structured and unstructured large datasets and execute large training and inferencing workloads. These ultra-fast processors are designed for massively accelerated training epochs, queries, complex image rendering, and interactive visualization. Combined with purpose-built analytics software, they deliver the kind of speed and zero-latency interactivity that professional investors need.

Investment companies of all shapes and sizes are taking advantage of this revolution in GPU analytics. GPU-accelerated platforms enable faster analytics to uncover more sophisticated investment and growth opportunities. GPU-powered models offer higher throughput with lower latency. As a result, more sophisticated models can be used for a given latency budget, leading to far more accurate results.

As the world generates increasingly new forms of data that provide meaningful signals for conclusions to be drawn about future business and market performance, accelerated computing platforms can become an increasingly valuable technology.

GPU-based acceleration technologies are universally applicable and help not only with data collection, preparation, and model building but also in the production phase, including model deployment, inferencing, and data visualization.

MLPerf[4] is a consortium of AI leaders from academia, research labs, and industry whose mission is to "build fair and useful benchmarks" that provide independent evaluations of training and inference performance for hardware, software, and services—all conducted under prescribed conditions. GPU-based systems shine in these benchmarks regularly, as can be seen in the MLPerf tables.

Equally important is the model validation step, where the model and data are made transparent and explainable to reconnect them to human intelligence, creativity, and

---

[4]For more information, go to the ML Commons webpage at https://mlcommons.org/en/#philosophy.

domain expertise—a step often forgotten or underrated. The explainability step can also be computationally demanding, which is the reason accelerated computing is a valuable resource, as it realizes significant speedups (Mitchell, Frank, and Holmes 2022).

To summarize, accelerated computing can build more model alternatives, with potentially higher accuracy and at the same time at lower cost and energy consumption and with greater flexibility. Such approaches as "fail fast, fail forward" can be implemented with accelerated computing, which can be viewed as a kind of "time machine" by speeding up the iterations required for model development.

Exhibit 1 shows some areas where GPU-accelerated computing supports investment (risk) managers, traders, and (AI/ML) quants.

Exhibit 1. Overview of GPU-Accelerated Domains plus Corresponding Tools and Software Packages for Implementation

Domains Enhanced by GPU-accelerated Computing	Descriptions of Useful Tools and Software Packages for Implementation
Loading and preprocessing enormous amounts of data in dataframe operations	• Open GPU Data Science with RAPIDS[a] suite of software libraries to execute end-to-end data science and analytics pipelines • Exposes GPU parallelism and high-bandwidth memory speed through Python interfaces • RAPIDS accelerator for Apache Spark supports the following steps: data acquisition, preprocessing, manipulation, data curation • RAPIDS library cuDF is related to Python library pandas
AI/ML/NLP and financial data science	• GPU-accelerated versions of PyTorch, TensorFlow, and other widely used deep learning frameworks • TAO: transfer learning based on optimized architectures and pretrained models • RAPIDS (as described before): end-to-end data science and analytics pipelines • RAPIDS cuML: GPU-accelerated versions of XGBoost and scikit-learn (like unsupervised learning, clustering decomposition, and dimensionality reduction); GPU-accelerated training for forest models, such as XGBoost, LightGBM, scikit-learn random forest • GPU-accelerated network analysis with RAPIDS cuGraph (linked to NetworkX) for community detection, link analysis/prediction, traversal, centrality, tree filtering, network visualization, Graph Neural Networks with Deep Graph Library (DGL), and PyTorch Geometric (PyG) • Dask[b] integrates with RAPIDS and can distribute data and computation over multiple GPUs, either in the same system or in a multinode cluster • MLOps (machine learning operations) tools, such as high-performance deep learning inference (such as a deep learning inference optimizer and runtime that deliver low latency and high throughput for inference applications) and inference server software (helps standardize model deployment and execution and delivers fast and scalable AI in production)[c] • Learning to rank (e.g., for constructing cross-sectional systematic strategies) • End-to-end frameworks for training and inferencing large language models (LLMs) with up to trillions of parameters[d] • Cloud-native suites of AI and data analytics software optimized for the development and deployment of AI, like an enterprise AI operating system for the accelerated AI platform[e]

(continued)

Exhibit 1. Overview of GPU-Accelerated Domains plus Corresponding Tools and Software Packages for Implementation (*continued*)

Domains Enhanced by GPU-accelerated Computing	Descriptions of Useful Tools and Software Packages for Implementation
Model risk management and human–machine interaction	• AI model validation and managing AI risk in the enterprise for AI models in production • Transparent, explainable, robust, auditable models for building trust techniques to test and improve robustness, explainability, fairness, and safety of the models, including large-scale visualization of data and model results with a usually considerable amount of compute • AI-generated synthetic data further enhance the model building process: Synthetic data improve model stability and explainability but can also generate stress-test scenarios that have never been observed but are realistic at the same time
High-performance computing (HPC) for derivative pricing, risk management, and portfolio allocation	• GPU-accelerated software development kits (SDKs) for Monte Carlo risk simulations for market risk applications (exotic derivative pricing, variable annuities, modeling underlying volatilities—e.g., Heston), counterparty risk (CVA, XVA, FVA, MVA valuation adjustments) and market generators/simulators • Relevant benchmark is STAC-A2[f] for risk models across throughput, performance, and scalability[g] • Advanced compilers, libraries, and software tools are available for real-world financial HPC applications, including American and exotic option pricing with multiple methods of writing GPU-accelerated algorithms, including the use of accelerated ISO (International Organization for Standardization) Standard C++ • Risk calculations with GPUs can be done 40 times faster, reducing costs by 80%. A Federal Reserve analysis showed speedups of over 250 times for GPUs vs. CPUs (central processing units) in running Monte Carlo simulations for European and American options pricing[h]
Algo trading, risk management, and backtesting	• Algorithm trading requires AI/ML workloads, filters, backtesting engines, bootstrapping scenarios, and optimization algorithms. Algorithm trading is a top use case with high growth rates and penetration. It makes use of HPC and GPU-accelerated deep learning for training and inference • GPU acceleration delivered more than 6,000 times speedup on the STAC-A3 benchmark algorithm for hedge funds[i]
Quantum computing with use cases in portfolio optimization, MC simulation, and ML	• GPU-powered speedup of quantum circuit simulations based on state vector and tensor network methods by orders of magnitude[j] • Hybrid quantum-classical computing involving QPU, GPU, CPU[k]

[a] www.nvidia.com/en-us/deep-learning-ai/software/rapids/.

[b] www.dask.org/.

[c] https://github.com/NVIDIA/TensorRT and https://github.com/triton-inference-server/server.

[d] https://github.com/NVIDIA/NeMo.

[e] www.nvidia.com/en-us/data-center/products/ai-enterprise/.

[f] www.stacresearch.com/a2.

[g] Some of the largest firms on Wall Street and the broader global financial industry rely on STAC-A2 as a key risk model benchmark to measure compute platform performance. "The STAC-A2 Benchmark suite is the industry standard for testing technology stacks used for compute-intensive analytic workloads involved in pricing and risk management" (www.stacresearch.com/a2). For example, it measures the time to complete the calculation of a set of Greek values for an option (which measure the sensitivity of the price of an option to changes, such as price of the underlying asset, volatility, or interest rates). Thus, Greeks—which should be recalculated as an option's price varies—provide a risk management tool for assessing market impacts on a portfolio of options.

[h] Scott (2018).

[i] Ashley (2019).

[j] https://github.com/NVIDIA/cuQuantum.

[k] https://developer.nvidia.com/cuda-quantum.

Further information can be found in Business Systems International's executive guide for the use of GPUs in data science and quantitative research in financial trading.[5]

Three Examples of Accelerated Computing in Real-World Investment Use Cases

This section demonstrates the GPU-accelerated tools and software package from the previous section in action. I describe three cases—two on ESG investing and one on diversified portfolio construction.

ESG and Risk Analysis Using NLP and Document Intelligence

NLP is one of the most prominent AI techniques that processes text information for many tasks. Among them are named entity recognition, topic modeling, intent identification, relation extraction, sentiment analysis, language translation, question answering, and text summarization.

Financial news and ESG disclosure reports exhibit complex formats along with images and tables, where document intelligence and AI are used to extract and digitize the relevant information (text, tables, pictures, etc.).

Sustainability reports need to comply with diverse taxonomies and reporting standards, which involves semantic understanding of various financial and nonfinancial disclosures. A central ESG and risk data repository can be built up to operationalize reporting and adapt to evolving regulatory requirements.

A real-time ESG analytics process drives ESG insights and scenario analysis with news and media screening. Adverse event monitoring further enables investors to stay in control of both reporting and assessment. Advanced NLP technologies monitor unstructured data in news and social media articles. The insights can be used in conjunction with the ESG scores from the rating agencies to provide a holistic view and thus improve decision making based on techniques.

Investors and fund managers use these assistive technologies to detect and mitigate ESG fraud, such as greenwashing. Fraud and anomaly detection platforms that monitor firm disclosures and are powered by a comprehensive greenwashing detection framework will drive investor confidence and flow of funds to truly green entities—one of the biggest challenges for ESG investors today.

NLP-based detection of fraudulent disclosures, news, and communications is the first line of defense against companies misrepresenting brown assets to solve their problem of stranded assets and loss of valuation. Quantitative and measurable data are needed to enable comparability. There can be real-time assessments of issuer operations.

In all these NLP-driven use cases, it becomes clear that large language models can be greatly beneficial from an engineering perspective because these models can be adapted to various tasks with a few shots with examples and prompt engineering (Gopani 2022).

Over the past few years, some leading software and solution companies have been established, making use of accelerated computing to be able to quickly process vast amounts of data. Some of them have developed no-code environments[6] and numerous AI-based services and data around NLP for ESG information.[7]

Earth Observation Data and Spatial Finance

Earth observation (EO) is the gathering of information about planet Earth's physical, chemical, and biological systems via remote sensing technologies, usually involving satellites carrying imaging devices, delivering reliable and repeat-coverage datasets.[8] EO is used to monitor and assess the status of and changes in the environment.

EO and remote sensing combined with ML have the potential to transform the availability of information in our financial system (Papenbrock, Ashley, and Schwendner 2021).

"Spatial finance" is the integration of geospatial data and analysis into financial services. It allows financial markets to better measure and manage climate-related and environmental risks, such as loss of biodiversity, threats to water quality, and deforestation. According to the EU Agency for the Space Programme (EUSPA 2022, p. 12), the insurance and finance segment will become the largest contributor to global EO revenues in 2031 (with EUR994 million and an 18.2% market share).

---

[5]https://media.bsi.uk.com/white-papers/Business_Systems_International_(BSI)_-_Nvidia_GPUs_in_Quantitative_Research_Executive_Guide.pdf.

[6]See, for example, https://accern.com/esg-investing and https://demo.softserveinc.com/esg-platform.

[7]See NVIDIA's on-demand webinar "How No-Code NLP Drives Fast and Accurate ESG Insights": https://info.nvidia.com/nlp-risk-management-esg-financial-services.html?ncid=so-link-135948-vt09&=&linkId=100000133473284&ondemandrgt=yes#cid=ix06_so-link_en-us.

[8]See the EU Science Hub's "Earth Observation" webpage: https://joint-research-centre.ec.europa.eu/scientific-activities-z/earth-observation_en#:~:text=Earth%20observation%20is%20the%20gathering,the%20natural%20and%20manmade%20environment.

EO and remote sensing data can be extremely complex to process. Processing massive amounts of EO data from multiple sources involves complex workflows and ETL (extract, transform, load) processes that first load and transform the data in several steps and then apply advanced AI models for computer vision and environmental monitoring. Typical steps are image formation, calibration and geospatial processing, data streaming, decompression, computer vision, model inference, scientific visualization, and (photorealistic, cinematic, 3D) rendering.

Also, the more granular and high-resolution the data, the more insight can be generated in finance and trading as individual assets can be observed and tracked. Sometimes the data need to be streamed or must be analyzed over time ("spatiotemporal"). The value creation for financial insights and trading sometimes also requires fusing multiple sensor sources to create a context. Imagery needs to be corrected, and features/patterns need to be extracted.

Accelerated computing can be a key technology in spatial finance to process EO and remote sensing data in a fast, reliable, cost-efficient, flexible, and energy-efficient way, and the models need to be of high quality and high resolution to build financial services, products, and signals for specific customers. Today it is possible to construct end-to-end (streaming) pipelines based on GPU acceleration, including processing of JPEG files, geolocation algorithms, spatial and trajectory computations, streaming, and computer vision, including clustering and graph analytics in RAPIDS.[9]

In the finance industry, the uptake of EO is becoming increasingly important in informing decision-making processes often before markets are affected. There are several concrete use cases in commodity trading where biodiversity and conservation across value chains can be analyzed. Trading of such products as metals, agricultural products, and energy (gas, oil, etc.) is being monitored and factored into value chains to make energy price predictions.

Investment managers are interested in identifying supply–demand balance changes. These are fed into trading models, such as in the oil market. Disruption of supply in hard and soft commodities by extreme weather, climate change, natural or other disasters/accidents, and pollution can be evaluated by processing EO data. Doing so usually includes an analysis of the history and assessment of the current physical situation. Regarding soft commodities (agricultural products), the users are usually interested in predictions on the yield rates of the next harvest as early as possible in the growing cycle. Knowing about crop shortfall in one region helps diversify and hedge early on.

Another use case is geospatial ESG.[10] It uses geospatial data to gain insight into a specific commercial asset, business, portfolio, or geographic area. It starts with pinpointing the location and defining the ownership of a commercial asset, such as a factory, mine, field, road, or retail property, known as asset data. Using various spatial approaches, it is then possible to assess the asset against observational data to gain an understanding of the initial and ongoing environmental impacts, as well as other relevant social and governance factors.

Geospatial ESG leverages geospatial AI using satellite imagery and sensor data to detect environmental or social parameter violations of companies and supply chains, such as biodiversity reduction, water source pollution, and greenhouse gas emissions. These detection and analysis models further enable investors to make more-informed decisions about a company separate from its voluntary disclosures or to monitor conformity with standards once established. There are enhanced risk assessments of ESG criteria on their investments, and access to real-time geospatial, environmental, and social data is a critical tool to enhance their evaluations.

Geospatial ESG helps validate issuer disclosures in cases where other data and information are unavailable, making ESG assessments more reliable. EO data are creating the foundation for predictability in ESG scoring/ESG performance. They help in an evolving regulatory landscape, and they are real-time, quantifiable, and measurable data for strengthening ESG analysis.

NLP and geospatial AI for sustainable finance are not only concerns of investment companies, banks, and insurance companies. Central banks around the world also are collaborating on greening the financial system and use accelerated data science, AI, and GeoAI (Papenbrock, Ashley, and Schwendner 2021) for sustainable finance.

Asset devaluation and long-term risks in ESG investing must be kept in mind. Climate risk is a critical ESG focus today. Potential infrastructure and property losses due to climate change affect organizations' long-term financial sustainability. Many investors examine a company's preparation assessment and capacity to forecast and respond to a variety of climate threats and environmental changes.

There are transition risks but also physical risks, such as extreme weather and record temperatures, that are now recognized as events that can be predicted and factored into financial planning. Droughts, floods, and wildfires are all examples of acute threats, but tropical illnesses due to rising temperatures and loss of biodiversity also fall in this

---

[9]Such as the cuSpatial library for GPU-accelerated spatial and trajectory data management and analytics: https://github.com/rapidsai/cuspatial.

[10]For more information, see https://wwf-sight.org/geospatial-esg; EUSPA (2023); European Space Agency (2022); Spatial Finance Initiative (2021); Patterson, Izquierdo, Tibaldeschi, Schmitt, Williams, Bessler, Wood, Spaeth, Fang, Shi, et al. (2022).

category. Additional risks can occur because of political instability and conflicts that climate change may generate, including supply chains and critical infrastructure that can be affected by extreme weather events.

Investors are exposed to such complex, evolving risks. Data, AI, simulation, and visualization will help investors better understand the risks and develop actions and mitigation strategies.

The adoption of such use cases will be further increased when the quality, availability, and granularity of observational climate and environmental data are enhanced. The models for predicting extreme weather events and climate change will further improve, especially becoming more granular and of a higher resolution. This outcome can be achieved by such technologies as physics-informed AI and accelerated supercomputing. An example is FourCastNet (Pathak, Subramanian, Harrington, Raja, Chattopadhyay, Mardani, Kurth, Hall, Li, Azizzadenesheli, et al. 2022). Frameworks exist for developing physics ML neural network models.[11] Visualization of simulated scenarios on a highly granular asset level is a technique that helps analysts evaluate the risks and impacts. There are platforms for building large-scale digital twin simulations of environmental processes and risks.[12]

An example workflow would involve the following components:

- (continuous, streaming) satellite imagery to model inference pipelines, such as capabilities for land/sea classification systems and GISs (geographic information systems);
- compute-powered, physics-informed neural networks and Fourier neural operators for simplification for fast predictive capability of climatic events; and
- 3D rendering and visualization to understand what is happening and see the what-if scenarios.

AI and Simulation for Diversified Portfolio Construction

There are several problems with the way modern portfolio theory (MPT) and portfolio diversification are often implemented in practice. One is backtest overfitting on the same historical data, and another is using quadratic optimization with noisy covariance estimates as inputs. In this section, I will describe approaches to mitigate these problems. The approaches are consistent with the Monte Carlo backtesting paradigm and could address the replication crisis to a certain extent. Synthetic datasets should be the preferred approach for developing tactical investment algorithms (López de Prado 2019). This approach helps investors deal with the unknown data-generating process. Using synthetic data is not new, and it is like generating realistic artificial landscapes and training industrial autonomous machines, such as robots and self-driving cars. Synthetic asset return data are a way to test AI-driven investment strategies.

Approaches to diversified portfolio construction do not always require quadratic optimization but can be solved heuristically to reduce realized risk and heavy portfolio turnover. AI can even help investors decide when to switch the approach in an interpretable way.

A lot of research has been conducted and much progress has been made on generating synthetic asset return data with typical stylized facts of asset returns using various AI-based techniques. Less focus has been placed on generating correlated returns with stylized empirical facts of asset return covariance matrices. This is important for pricing and risk management of correlation-dependent financial instruments and portfolios. Approaches using GANs (generative adversarial networks) generate realistic correlation scenarios (Marti 2020). An approach called "matrix evolutions" uses evolutionary multi-objective optimization, which can be implemented in parallel to benefit from accelerators (Papenbrock, Schwendner, Jaeger, and Krügel 2021). The idea is to address multiple stylized facts of empirical correlation matrices at the same time and join them in a multi-objective optimization problem. The user defines ranges to generate "populations" of correlation matrices that cover a variety and combination of stylized facts, on the one hand, and exhibit properties of correct correlation matrices, on the other hand. In this way, millions of realistic correlation matrices can be generated that have never been observed before. Approaches to robust investment portfolios can be tested against those populations of correlation matrix scenarios to test and analyze their behavior and robustness.

Based on these or other artificially generated asset return data, it is possible to formulate a program for ML that predicts the outperformance of a certain portfolio construction approach based on information about certain market regimes. In this way, an investment client could produce a desired portfolio of assets or asset classes, and the investment manager could respond with a recommendation for which portfolio construction method should be preferred for a certain market phase or regime to realize a very robust diversified portfolio.

The approach works as follows: Each generated market scenario is represented in terms of its stylized empirical

---

[11]For example, see the "NVIDIA Modulus" webpage: https://developer.nvidia.com/modulus.

[12]For example, see the "NVIDIA Omniverse" webpage: https://www.nvidia.com/en-us/omniverse/.

facts—across the portfolio assets and including their correlation properties. These are the input features to the ML program. The labels can be measured by the outperformance of a certain portfolio construction method in that specific market scenario. By generating millions of those scenarios, one gets millions of labeled learning datasets, which are the training material for the ML program. This can be done for several available portfolio construction methods, and in the end, the ML program can be used to recommend a more robust portfolio construction approach in a specific market phase. In addition, the machine can even produce explanations in terms such as reporting the driving properties of certain market phases leading to an outperformance of a certain portfolio construction method. This outcome is achieved with post hoc explainers such as SHAP (SHapley Additive exPlanations), which are computationally intensive and can be GPU-accelerated, and with the massively parallel exact calculation of SHAP scores for tree ensembles (Mitchell et al. 2022).[13]

The entire workflow is described in an article by Jaeger, Krügel, Marinelli, Papenbrock, and Schwendner (2021). The idea is to produce alternative portfolio construction mechanisms, such as hierarchical risk parity (HRP), that use graph theory and representation learning to construct the portfolio by cutting through the estimation noise. In many market environments and many investment universes, these approaches offer lower realized risk than can be achieved by explicit portfolio risk minimization algorithms. This sounds unreal but is achieved by the two-step approach of HRP: (1) matrix seriation and (2) recursive bisection. In this way, the natural taxonomy of assets is preserved, and the less robust matrix inversion step can be skipped.

As this procedure does not work in all market environments, an AI-driven program can identify in which constellations the new method can be used. It can also deliver some explanations using Shapley values, a method based on cooperative game theory. This explainability helps portfolio managers identify the correct approach to portfolio construction depending on investment universe and market state (Papenbrock and Schwendner 2015). Interactive dashboards allow the validation and audit of the AI models and the extraction of evidence-based, data-driven insights and narratives.

The implementation of such an approach requires several computing-intensive steps to generate market data, to train AI models, and to finally extract information about the inner decision making of the models to draw conclusions. A normal desktop PC would be able to produce reliable outcomes after several hours, whereas a small GPU cluster can produce results after a few minutes (Papenbrock 2021). The entire workflow can be extended by many steps—namely, generating synthetic multidimensional market data

in a very flexible and convenient way of matrix evolutions or producing completely new ways of constructing portfolios, as in an article by Schwendner, Papenbrock, Jaeger, and Krügel (2021). The approach and workflow can even be used to tame crypto portfolios (Papenbrock, Schwendner, and Sandner 2021).

Conclusion and Next Steps

In this chapter, I discussed some of the latest investment technologies and provided useful tools to leverage recent developments in AI infrastructure and software development.

I demonstrated how these technologies give access to new and more stable sources of alpha, advanced risk management technologies, higher levels of customization, and better meet the requirements of investment clients.

Acceleration technologies support the entire workflow and data science process—from loading large files and curating dataframe operations to conducting model building and inferencing. They can even perform the model validation and explanation steps. This support enables a more interactive and data-centric approach to AI.

The use cases on ESG investing and robust portfolio construction have demonstrated how accelerated computing platforms help leverage both alternative, unstructured data (NLP, computer vision, document intelligence) and classical time-series data, such as asset returns.

Factories for complex data processing, AI, simulation, and visualization help the industry build resilient, sustainable, and profitable investment products/services in a customized, transparent, and explainable way.

References

Alarcon, N. 2020. "Accelerating Automated and Explainable Machine Learning with RAPIDS and NVIDIA GPUs." *Technical Blog*, NVIDIA DEVELOPER (17 November). https://developer.nvidia.com/blog/accelerating-automated-and-explainable-machine-learning-with-rapids/.

Ashley, J. 2019. "NVIDIA Delivers More than 6,000× Speedup on Key Algorithm for Hedge Funds." NVIDIA (13 May). https://blogs.nvidia.com/blog/2019/05/13/accelerated-backtesting-hedge-funds/?ncid=so-twi-nrcmflssx6-84884.

Cao, Larry. 2019. "AI Pioneers in Investment Management." CFA Institute. www.cfainstitute.org/-/media/documents/survey/AI-Pioneers-in-Investment-Management.pdf.

---

[13]For a related blog on explainable ML with acceleration, see Alarcon (2020).

European Space Agency. 2022. "Space for Green Finance: Use Cases and Commercial Opportunities" (November). https://commercialisation.esa.int/2023/01/market-trend-space-for-green-finance/.

EUSPA. 2022. "EO and GNSS Market Report." www.euspa.europa.eu/sites/default/files/uploads/euspa_market_report_2022.pdf.

EUSPA. 2023. "EU Space for Green Transformation" (25 January). www.euspa.europa.eu/newsroom/news/eu-space-helps-drive-green-transformation.

Gopani, A. 2022. "How NVIDIA Trains Large Language Models." AIM (23 March). https://analyticsindiamag.com/how-nvidia-trains-large-language-models/.

Jaeger, Markus, Stephan Krügel, Dimitri Marinelli, Jochen Papenbrock, and Peter Schwendner. 2021. "Interpretable Machine Learning for Diversified Portfolio Construction." Journal of Financial Data Science 3 (3): 31–51.

López de Prado, Marcos. 2019. "Tactical Investment Algorithms" (26 September). Available at https://ssrn.com/abstract=3459866.

Marti, G. 2020. "CORRGAN: Sampling Realistic Financial Correlation Matrices Using Generative Adversarial Networks." ICASSP 2020–2020 IEEE International Conference on Acoustics, Speech and Signal Processing (ICASSP): 8459–63.

Mitchell, R., E. Frank, and G. Holmes. 2022. "GPUTreeShap: Massively Parallel Exact Calculation of SHAP Scores for Tree Ensembles." PeerJ Computer Science 8 (5 April): e880.

Papenbrock, Jochen. 2021. "Accelerating Interpretable Machine Learning for Diversified Portfolio Construction." Technical Blog, NVIDIA DEVELOPER (29 September). https://developer.nvidia.com/blog/accelerating-interpretable-machine-learning-for-diversified-portfolio-construction/.

Papenbrock, Jochen, and Peter Schwendner. 2015. "Handling Risk-On/Risk-Off Dynamics with Correlation Regimes and Correlation Networks." Financial Markets and Portfolio Management 29: 125–47.

Papenbrock, Jochen, John Ashley, and Peter Schwendner. 2021. "Accelerated Data Science, AI and GeoAI for Sustainable Finance in Central Banking and Supervision." Paper presented at International Conference on Statistics for Sustainable Finance, Paris (September). www.bis.org/ifc/publ/ifcb56_23.pdf.

Papenbrock, Jochen, Peter Schwendner, Markus Jaeger, and Stephan Krügel. 2021. "Matrix Evolutions: Synthetic Correlations and Explainable Machine Learning for Constructing Robust Investment Portfolios." Journal of Financial Data Science 3 (2): 51–69.

Papenbrock, Jochen, Peter Schwendner, and Philipp Sandner. 2021. "Can Adaptive Seriational Risk Parity Tame Crypto Portfolios?" Working paper (15 July).

Pathak, Jaideep, Shashank Subramanian, Peter Harrington, Sanjeev Raja, Ashesh Chattopadhyay, Morteza Mardani, Thorsten Kurth, David Hall, Zongyi Li, Kamyar Azizzadenesheli, et al. 2022. "FourCastNet: A Global Data-Driven High-Resolution Weather Model Using Adaptive Fourier Neural Operators." Preprint, arXiv (24 February). https://arxiv.org/pdf/2202.11214v1.pdf.

Patterson, David, Pablo Izquierdo, Paolo Tibaldeschi, Susanne Schmitt, Alicia Williams, Janey Bessler, Steven Wood, Mike Spaeth, Fei Fang, Ryan Shi, et al. 2022. "The Biodiversity Data Puzzle: Exploring Geospatial Approaches to Gain Improved 'Biodiversity' Insight for Financial Sector Applications and the Pressing Need to Catalyze Efforts." WWF-UK (December). www.wwf.org.uk/sites/default/files/2022-12/The-Biodiversity-Data-Puzzle.pdf.

Schwendner, Peter, Jochen Papenbrock, Markus Jaeger, and Stephan Krügel. 2021. "Adaptive Seriational Risk Parity and Other Extensions for Heuristic Portfolio Construction Using Machine Learning and Graph Theory." Journal of Financial Data Science 3 (4): 65–83.

Scott, L. 2018. "Finance—Parallel Processing for Derivative Pricing" (March). www.nvidia.com/en-us/on-demand/session/gtcsiliconvalley2018-s8123/.

Spatial Finance Initiative. 2021. "State and Trends of Spatial Finance 2021: Next Generation Climate and Environmental Analytics for Resilient Finance." www.cgfi.ac.uk/wp-content/uploads/2021/07/SpatialFinance_Report.pdf.

11. SYMBOLIC AI: A CASE STUDY

Huib Vaessen
Head of Research and Analytics Real Assets, APG Asset Management

The degree to which machines can help in investment decision making varies widely, depending on the investment strategy. The solution discussed in this case study is based on symbolic artificial intelligence (AI) and serves investment teams using fundamental investment strategies.

Samuel: An Automated Real Estate Portfolio Management Solution Based on Symbolic AI

Samuel is a composite AI[14] system that collaborates with humans. It acts as a digital colleague that guides the human investment team with transparent, systematized, and well-substantiated advice. Its decisions are transparently substantiated and can be tracked down to each datapoint used, allowing for efficient reconciliation with the thought process of the human team.

A composite AI system uses the AI techniques most suitable for the result. Although nonsymbolic AI, such as machine learning (ML) and its subclass neural networks, has gained much attention, many real life use cases warrant the use of symbolic AI techniques. Symbolic AI, or classical AI, is a collection of techniques that are based on human-readable and high-level representations of the problem. Examples are rule-based engines and decision trees. It was the dominant approach to AI research since its early days through the mid-1990s (Russell and Norvig 2020).

First, the use case of an automated portfolio management solution for a fundamental investor warrants typical symbolic AI techniques because the amount of available data on investments and markets has increased but is still not sufficient to allow for ML techniques in many cases. Second, given that the interaction between human and machine is crucial—because humans have to be able to understand the reasoning for high-stakes investment decisions—the transparency and interpretability of the technique is important. Third, typically there is already important human knowledge available in a fundamental investment team that one might want to leverage. Symbolic techniques allow for codifying this human knowledge as one can imagine with rule-based systems. Many systems built with symbolic AI techniques are called "expert systems." In this chapter, mainly systems built with symbolic methods are described.

Technically, the automated solution can have many forms, but in general, it constitutes the following parts as depicted in **Exhibit 1**: a knowledge base, data pipelines, knowledge pipelines, the calculation engine, and tools such as dashboards that interact with the human portfolio manager.

Exhibit 1. Example: APG Asset Management Real Estate (APG RE)

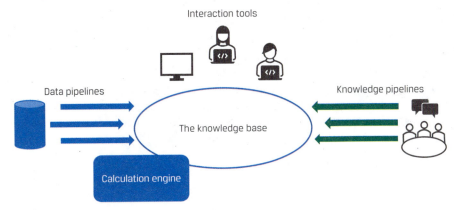

Source: APG Asset Management.

---

[14]As defined in Gartner's "Hype Cycle for Emerging Technologies, 2020," composite AI refers to a "combination of different AI techniques to achieve the best result."

Next, I will discuss each component of Samuel in more detail.

The *knowledge base* is a database that contains all data related to the decision-making process and includes all principles that need to be applied to those data in order to get the outcomes. The knowledge base is fed by data pipelines for the data and knowledge pipelines for the principles. Humans are needed to provide oversight. The knowledge base can be stored in all kinds of relational and graph databases.

The *calculation engine* applies the rules to the data and stores the outputs in the knowledge base. The calculation engine requires human oversight and needs to be configured by humans. It contains a "worker" with CPU (central processing unit) power that does the calculations and a trigger mechanism that triggers the calculations when needed.

Interaction tools enable the interaction between Samuel and humans. The output of Samuel needs to be interpreted by humans, and the input needs to be given by humans. Interaction tools can have many different forms, ranging from dashboards accessible via the web browser to search bars and forms for input. If the interaction between the humans and the digital colleague is not well organized, the hurdles to provide input will be too high and the output less valuable. Similarly, if the output cannot be found by the right people at the right time, the impact of Samuel is lost. To ensure appropriate interaction tools, constant adoption is needed to embed Samuel in the other business processes to minimize the hurdles to use the output and to provide input by humans.

The *data pipelines* are ETL (extract, transform, load)[15] flows that ingest data from various sources outside the team. Here the IDs are matched, and data are prepared for further usage. The formatting of the sources changes over time, and data pipelines might have to be adjusted for that. Additionally, new data pipelines need to be added over time and integrated with the other data. Humans are needed to build the pipelines and provide oversight. Data pipelines can be written in Python, C++, or any other coding language and triggered by an orchestration tool that decides when to run the pipeline.

The *knowledge pipelines* are an active collaboration between humans and Samuel. Knowledge is constantly evolving, and as such, the principles need to be updated regularly. Thus, it is important that whenever new knowledge is created after a group discussion, this knowledge is made explicit and codified in the form of principles. Making knowledge explicit is a time-consuming process because often implicit knowledge is incomplete or inconsistent over persons or situations. Before a team has a set of principles that adequately describes the knowledge that is consistent among persons and situations, many discussions must have been held.

Samuel: APG Real Estate Investment Team's Digital Colleague

The APG real estate investment decision-making process is top down—first an allocation across regions, then an allocation across peer groups (sectors) within regions, and lastly the selection of the opportunities within each peer group.

The real estate team introduced Samuel in the winter of 2021.

In the initial phase, a team has to map its decision-making process, state which arguments are used, and explain how these arguments are substantiated. This part of the process is a project that involves many discussions between the members of the investment team to agree on the relevance of each argument and how to substantiate it. This project takes time but is a one-off. After that, refinements of the decision-making process are an ongoing add-on so are less intense.

---

[15]*ETL* is a typical term used to indicate a process that extracts data from one source, transforms it, and loads it into another source.

Samuel collects all relevant input and updates the model when there are new data available. All this input is available for the portfolio managers' reference and forms the baseline for portfolio decisions. Whenever a human proposal is made, Samuel can also challenge that decision.

For example, Samuel updates the rental growth variable in the discounted cash flow model based on preset rules. Office rental growth is based on the quality of the building, which, in turn, is determined by the employment growth of the city, sustainability index of the building, and supply constraint in the market.

At APG Asset Management, the data that are stored in Samuel's brain are stored in a graph database as so-called triples, meaning that each fact is stored as a relation in the form of a subject–predicate–object triple, where the predicate defines the relation between the subject and the object. **Exhibit 2** shows an example of triples and the technology stack.

Exhibit 2. Examples of Triples and the Technology Stack

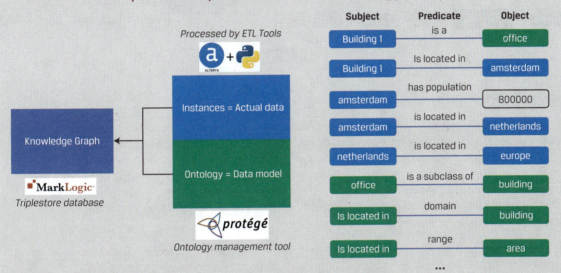

Source: APG Asset Management.

Based on the relations shown in Exhibit 2, Samuel can infer by itself additional triples, such as the number of buildings owned by a certain company in Amsterdam, the Netherlands, or Europe. **Exhibit 3** shows a more complex example.

Storing information as triples with their relations allows for advanced questions where part of the answer is reasoned by a reasoner applied on top of the graph database. The following are examples of advanced questions: What are the principles that determine the quality of an office? What is the supporting evidence that employment growth is important for the quality of an office asset? What are the supporting arguments for the attractiveness of the office building "La Défense"? The triples are stored according to W3C standards, which makes retrieving and inference possible because you can use generic tools that work on these standards.

Exhibit 3. More Complex Example of Inferred Triples

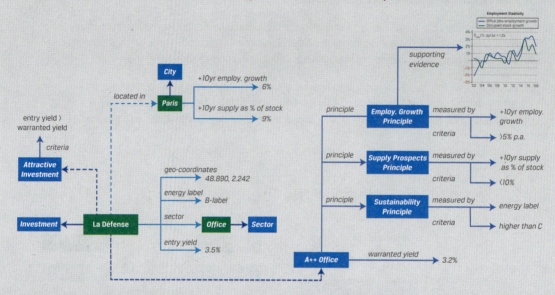

Source: APG Asset Management.

The advantages of using a graph database to store the information are that it is easy to add new types of data, one can derive new knowledge based on the existing triples, and all data and metadata are stored in the same repository (which makes data more searchable while also allowing for a rich description of the data for future interpretation) and a graph database (a database that does not consist of multiple tables that need to be joined). Both structured and unstructured data can be joined in the same database, as can be seen in Exhibit 3, where the supporting document for the employment growth principle is also stored in the same graph database.

In the example in Exhibit 3, the calculation engine is Python scripts that are run on a server. A scheduled job imports, for example, the employment growth per city via an application programming interface (API) from an external provider. The graph database identifies this update as a trigger to start inferencing whether "La Défense" still is an A++ quality building given that the employment growth outlook for Paris has changed.

In the example, the main interaction tool is the cloud-based discounted cash flow (DCF) model. This model is deeply embedded in the day-to-day workflow of the human portfolio manager. In this cloud-based DCF model, Samuel can provide its suggestions for the rental growth as a field right next to the rental growth input field. As such, whenever the portfolio manager (PM) needs to enter a growth rate assumption, Samuel's suggested value is always at hand.

Exhibit 4 provides an example of how a news email about a real estate transaction can be read with natural language processing techniques and translated into triples for the graph database. The news item reads that the company Landsec acquired a stake in a building called MediaCity. The details of the deal can be recorded as triples and serve as input—for example, the quality assessment of the portfolio of buildings of the company Landsec.

Exhibit 4. Example News Email

Kempen Daily

Landsec today announces that it has acquired a majority stake in MediaCity, a 37 acre media, digital and tech office hub in Clichy, previously owned by a 50:50 JV between Legal & General and Peel L&P. Landsec will partner with Peel L&P who will retain a 25% stake and continue to serve as asset and development manager. MediaCity has a gross asset value of £567.5m. The location hosts tenants such as BBC North and ITV to Ericsson, The Hut Group, Kellogg's and over 250 creative and tech businesses as well as schools and universities. It is home to 8,000 residents. Landsec said that the scheme was renovated 10 years ago to improve its energy efficiency label to B. It is 96% let with a WAULT of just under 10 years. It generates £31.1m of net operating income per annum (100%), reflecting a 3.15% net initial yield.

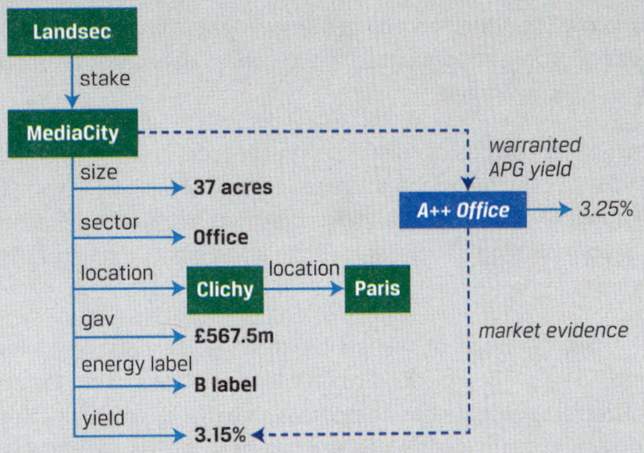

Source: APG Asset Management.

How Do PMs Interact with Samuel?

Interaction with Samuel during the investment process can be grouped into four types: evaluating the buy/hold/sell decision, preparing the proposal, portfolio monitoring, and letting Samuel learn.

The evaluation of the final decision is the moment where the human-proposed action is ranked by Samuel versus all other potential actions. If other actions are more favorable, the portfolio managers that do the proposal will have to explain why they deviate from Samuel.

In preparation of the investment proposal, the human portfolio manager can be helped by Samuel with contextualized information. For example, while making the DCF model, Samuel can provide default values. The human PM can decide whether to overwrite the assumption or stick with Samuel's assumption.

Compared to the human team, Samuel excels in portfolio monitoring. Samuel collects the characteristics to monitor from each individual investment and contains the portfolio construction principles. As an example, each investment is mapped to countries and sectors, all stored in the knowledge base, complemented by the maximum weights that are desired in a country or sector. Samuel can check every day whether the aggregated investment exposure to a country or sector exceeds the limits. This repetitive work fits Samuel well because it comes at limited cost to schedule a daily execution of the check. Variables to monitor, such as the valuations of investments, leverage, and the beta of the portfolio, can be added at a low cost. The more variables of the investment portfolio are monitored, the bigger the difference between human and Samuel's execution in terms of consistency and effort.

The last interaction discussed here is a flow of information from the human portfolio manager to Samuel. Whenever after reconciliation of the proposed action with Samuel a consistent omission in Samuel's reasoning is found, its principles need to be adjusted. Doing so requires that the omission be made explicit, and it has to be made clear what new principles need to be added. This adjustment requires a well-facilitated discussion and the embedding of the new principles and potential new data sources in Samuel. This process needs to be guided. The continuous learning aspect is critical. Samuel learns by adding new rules and new data pipelines that provide the data on which the rules are applied. In this way, the rankings become more and more sophisticated and the default values harder to ignore.

Use Case APG Real Estate (continued)

Within the real estate team at APG Asset Management, Samuel is embedded in the investment process in several ways. The global team covers an investment universe of 300 listed real estate companies and sources hundreds of private investment opportunities annually. As such, there is a high volume of investment proposals that need to be evaluated.

Each investment proposal is discussed by the team in an initial phase. A subteam of the global real estate team is tasked with interpreting the outcomes of Samuel and challenging the proposal on the basis of Samuel's input during the discussion. After this initial screening, all attractive propositions are worked out in more detail, and then they are presented to the Real Estate Investment Committee. The output of the digital colleague also is presented to the committee.

While building the proposal, the portfolio manager is helped by contextualized suggestions embedded in the workflow. The cash flow model is cloud based and transparent for all members of the investment team globally. Samuel interacts with the human portfolio manager by providing contextualized information within the model in the form of references, such as growth expectations from external research providers, or default values, such as data-generated rental growth forecasts and discount rates. In our example of rental growth, the PM sees a proposed rental growth generated by Samuel. The PM can click through via the web browser to the components. Then, each component, such as the quality rating, is further substantiated.

Another argument, besides the output of the DCF, is, for example, portfolio fit: How does this fit in the top-down vision on sector and countries, and how does this contribute to environmental, social, and governance (ESG) goals? Samuel provides an automatic assessment of these factors to be used in the proposal. Whenever there are reasons to deviate, these can be addressed in the proposal.

How Does Samuel Improve Results?

Building and maintaining an automated system such as Samuel requires attention to the investment process on a higher abstraction level than a typical portfolio manager is used to. It demands attention for when and which information is needed for which decision. It also involves skills that are not traditionally available in a fundamental investment team, such as ontology building, data engineering, and software engineering.

These skills can be embedded in the organization in various ways, ranging from being centrally located to being located within the investment team (T-shaped teams) or within each investment professional (T-shaped skills). T-shaped teams are crucial for the development and maintenance of a recommender system such as Samuel. A T-shaped team is a team that contains individuals with the traditional investment skill sets, those with the data- and technology-related skill sets, and those with a mix of these skill sets (CFA Institute 2021).

The advantages of collaborating with a digital colleague are threefold. First, it improves decision making by countering human cognitive biases. A simple rule-based model tends to outperform human judgment (Kahneman, Sibony, and Sunstein 2021) because cognitive biases cause bias in decision making. By codifying best practices and applying them consistently, Samuel improves decision quality. There is usually unwanted variation in human decision making that is not warranted by the facts. This noise can be across persons or from the same person at different times. Experts typically believe they are themselves consistent and believe that other experts would decide in a similar fashion as themselves. However, research by Kahneman et al. (2021) shows that, for example, underwriting experts who are presented the same case have material differences in their judgments. Samuel makes judgments based on agreed-on principles and guidelines and, as such, provides a consistent benchmark.

The second advantage is that it is more transparent. Transparency in decision making allows the investment team to explain clearly to clients and stakeholders how their decision was formed. For example, you can track how responsible investment considerations affect your decision making.

The third advantage is improved efficiency of the decision-making process and results. The final decision is supported by arguments, and these arguments are the result of many decisions on a lower level that are typically less complex and made more frequently, some of which can be externally sourced and provided via Samuel. Another example of a lower-level decision that can be automated to a high degree would be the building blocks for the discount rate that is used. Many of these can be automatically updated by Samuel.

Although Samuel is a valuable addition to any investment team, it is also worthwhile to discuss the edge of the human portfolio manager over Samuel and show why a collaboration is so important.

First, humans can form a vision of the future and adjust their assumptions toward that future. Samuel relies on principles that were formed in the past (by humans) and might not yet have been adjusted to a new reality, such as in March 2020 when COVID-19 was affecting the world. A human portfolio manager knows when old principles are not applicable anymore given that the circumstances have changed.

Second, Samuel likely cannot operate on its own. Although parts of arguments can be input automatically with data from external sources combined with predefined principles, there are also many assumptions for which you need a human eye. Samuel uses the human assumptions where needed and takes its own assumptions if data and principles are available. In that sense, the output of Samuel is also based on human input.

Lastly, there are likely edge cases in which the systematic way of thinking does not translate well. These cases must be recognized by humans. In the end, Samuel bases its decision on a simplified model of reality.

Conclusion

The role of machines in the decision-making process will grow. Having a digital portfolio manager on the team can improve the quality of decision making, transparency, and efficiency. To build and maintain an automated digital portfolio management solution, it is necessary to embed nontraditional investment skill sets, such as ontology building, data engineering, and software engineering, within the investment department.

References

CFA Institute. 2021. "T-Shaped Teams: Organizing to Adopt AI and Big Data at Investment Firms." www.cfainstitute.org/-/media/documents/article/industry-research/t-shaped-teams.pdf.

Kahneman, Daniel, Olivier Sibony, and Cass Sunstein. 2021. *Noise: A Flaw in Human Judgment*. New York: Little, Brown Spark.

Russell, Stuart, and Peter Norvig. 2020. *Artificial Intelligence: A Modern Approach*, 4th US ed. Hoboken, NJ: Prentice Hall.

Named Endowments

CFA Institute Research Foundation acknowledges with sincere gratitude the generous contributions of the Named Endowment participants listed below.

Gifts of at least US$100,000 qualify donors for membership in the Named Endowment category, which recognizes in perpetuity the commitment toward unbiased, practitioner-oriented, relevant research that these firms and individuals have expressed through their generous support of CFA Institute Research Foundation.

Ameritech
Anonymous
Robert D. Arnott
Theodore R. Aronson, CFA
Asahi Mutual Life Insurance Company
Batterymarch Financial Management
Boston Company
Boston Partners Asset Management, L.P.
Gary P. Brinson, CFA
Brinson Partners, Inc.
Capital Group International, Inc.
Concord Capital Management
Dai-Ichi Life Insurance Company
Daiwa Securities
Mr. and Mrs. Jeffrey Diermeier
Gifford Fong Associates
John A. Gunn, CFA
Investment Counsel Association of America, Inc.
Jacobs Levy Equity Management
Jon L. Hagler Foundation
Long-Term Credit Bank of Japan, Ltd.
Lynch, Jones & Ryan, LLC
Meiji Mutual Life Insurance Company

Miller Anderson & Sherrerd, LLP
John B. Neff, CFA
Nikko Securities Co., Ltd.
Nippon Life Insurance Company of Japan
Nomura Securities Co., Ltd.
Payden & Rygel
Provident National Bank
Frank K. Reilly, CFA
Salomon Brothers
Sassoon Holdings Pte. Ltd.
Scudder Stevens & Clark
Security Analysts Association of Japan
Shaw Data Securities, Inc.
Sit Investment Associates, Inc.
Standish, Ayer & Wood, Inc.
State Farm Insurance Company
Sumitomo Life America, Inc.
T. Rowe Price Associates, Inc.
Templeton Investment Counsel Inc.
Frank Trainer, CFA
Travelers Insurance Co.
USF&G Companies
Yamaichi Securities Co., Ltd.

Senior Research Fellows
Financial Services Analyst Association

For more on upcoming CFA Institute Research Foundation publications and webcasts, please visit www.cfainstitute.org/research/foundation.

CFA Institute Research Foundation Board of Trustees 2022–2023

Chair
Aaron Low, PhD, CFA
   LUMIQ

Vice Chair
Joanne Hill, PhD
   Cboe Vest LLC

Amra Balic
   BlackRock

Aaron Brown, CFA
   City of Calgary

Kati Eriksson, CFA
   Danske Bank

Frank Fabozzi, CFA*
   The Johns Hopkins University
   Carey Business School

Margaret Franklin, CFA
   CFA Institute

Bill Fung, PhD
   Aventura, FL

Heinz Hockmann, PhD
   Lovell Minnick Partners LLC

Punita Kumar-Sinha, CFA
   Infosys

Kingpai Koosakulnirund, CFA
   CFA Society Thailand

Lotta Moberg, PhD, CFA
   William Blair

Maureen O'Hara, PhD*
   Cornell University

Dave Uduanu, CFA
   Sigma Pensions Ltd

Kurt D. Winkelmann
   Navega Strategies, LLC

*Emeritus

Officers and Directors

Executive Director
Bud Haslett, CFA
   CFA Institute

Gary P. Brinson Director of Research
Laurence B. Siegel
   Blue Moon Communications

Research Director
Luis Garcia-Feijóo, CFA, CIPM
   Coral Gables, Florida

Secretary
Jessica Lawson
   CFA Institute

Treasurer
Kim Maynard
   CFA Institute

Research Foundation Review Board

William J. Bernstein, PhD
   Efficient Frontier Advisors

Elroy Dimson, PhD
   Cambridge Judge Business
   School

Stephen Figlewski, PhD
   New York University

William N. Goetzmann, PhD
   Yale School of Management

Elizabeth R. Hilpman
   Barlow Partners, Inc.

Paul D. Kaplan, PhD, CFA
   Morningstar, Inc.

Robert E. Kiernan III
   Advanced Portfolio Management

Andrew W. Lo, PhD
   Massachusetts Institute
   of Technology

Alan Marcus, PhD
   Boston College

Paul O'Connell, PhD
   FDO Partners

Krishna Ramaswamy, PhD
   University of Pennsylvania

Andrew Rudd, PhD
   Advisor Software, Inc.

Stephen Sexauer
   Allianz Global Investors Solutions

Lee R. Thomas, PhD
   Pacific Investment Management
   Company